SYNCHRONOUS MANAGEMENT

Profit-Based Manufacturing for the 21st Century

Volume Two

Implementation Issues and Case Studies

SYNCHRONOUS MANAGEMENT

Profit-Based Manufacturing for the 21st Century

Volume Two

Implementation Issues and Case Studies

M. Michael Umble, PhD, CFPIM, CQE
Professor of Operations Management
Baylor University
Waco, Texas

Mokshagundam L. Srikanth, PhD
President
The Spectrum Management Group, Inc.
Guilford, Connecticut

The Spectrum Publishing Company
Guilford, Connecticut

To order additional copies of this text or related texts, please contact:

The Spectrum Publishing Company
200 Concept Park
741 Boston Post Road
Guilford, CT 06437
(203) 453-2233 • Fax (203) 453-9818

For more information on the practical application of the concepts and principles contained in this text, please contact:

The Spectrum Management Group
200 Concept Park
741 Boston Post Road
Guilford, CT 06437
(203) 453-2233 • Fax (203) 453-9818

Copyright © 1997 by The Spectrum Publishing Company

The Library of Congress has catalogued Volume One as follows:

Srikanth, Mokshagundam L., 1952-
      Synchronous management: profit-based manufacturing for the 21st
century / Mokshagundam L. Srikanth, M. Michael Umble.
            p.   cm.
      Includes bibliographical references and index.
      ISBN 0–943953–06–5 (v. 1)
      1. Production management.   2. Production control.   3. Business
logistics.   4. Manufactures—Management—Case studies.   I. Umble,
M. Michael, 1947–   . II. Title.
TS155.S7556   1997
658.5—dc20   96–34929
                                                   CIP

Volume Two: ISBN 0-943953-07-3

Manufactured in the United States of America

We dedicate this book to the many men and women in pioneering organization, who continually increase the depth of our knowledge; to consultant and academic colleagues, whose keen insights motivate new ways to think about situations and new ways to apply the concepts; and to students, who are our future.

– M.M.U.

– M.L.S.

Contents

7   A Framework for Implementation   **179**
A Synchronous Management Analysis

8   Implementation Case Study   **193**

Preface

ABOUT THE BOOK

Every manufacturing organization is unique. Experience has repeatedly shown that the attributes that make each plant unique are the company culture, the performance measures, and the plant-wide policies and operating procedures—all of which have evolved over years.

But despite each plant's uniqueness, all manufacturing plants share many common attributes. This book clearly explains the dynamics that create these shared characteristics, and provides powerful insights into both the problems that plague different types of plant as well as the appropriate solutions.

This book is the second of a two-volume set that fully explains the Synchronous Management philosophy and logistical system:

Volume I: *Synchronous Management: Profit-Based Manufacturing for the 21st Century.*

Volume II: *Synchronous Management: Profit-Based Manufacturing for the 21st Century – Implementation Issues and Case Studies.*

The first volume developed the basic concepts and rationale for the Synchronous Management philosophy through discussions and illustrations. But there is a crucial difference between understanding the basic concepts of a manufacturing management philosophy and being able to successfully implement it in an organization. The problem is that the same analysis and implementation approach that works in one type of plant may fail miserably in a different type of plant. The purpose of this second volume is to enhance the reader's understanding of how to implement the Synchronous Management concepts in their own specific environment.

The main thread that runs through this second volume is that manufacturing plants can be segmented into three general categories—referred to as V-plants, A-plants, and T-plants. The behavior of real-life plants can be understood in terms of these generic plant types, since each plant closely approximates one of the categories or a combination of the categories. Each generic plant category exhibits its own set of problems when managed according to traditional management practices. And the recommended Synchronous Management approach to managing a plant varies depending on the specific plant category.

A key feature of this volume is the use of detailed case studies to illustrate systematic processes for implementing Synchronous Management and the attendant logistical system, as well as the critical implementation issues. Case studies can be very powerful, but, if not utilized properly, can be virtually useless and extremely frustrating. Case studies without the proper perspective of a systematic and repeatable process is nothing more than a random example.

Therefore, the knowledge needed to successfully perform a Synchronous Management implementation is carefully developed through the description of systematic implementation processes. We also provide a general framework for recognizing and resolving key implementation issues and obstacles.

In this volume, we present four extensive case studies. Each case study is based on an actual Synchronous Management implementation. However, before presenting a case study, we first develop the key issues and the framework for the implementation process. The case study is then utilized to illustrate the concepts and demonstrate the implementation process.

ORGANIZATION OF TEXT

The basic structure of this volume is straightforward. We first develop the foundation for the underlying structure of the three generic plant categories. Then the general characteristics, problems, and recommended implementation approach for each plant category is described in detail. Case studies are used to illustrate the implementation process for each plant type. Finally, critical implementation issues and obstacles are discussed, followed by a detailed case study that emphasizes the major implementation issues.

Chapter 1 makes the case for the need to change from a cost-based to a throughput-based manufacturing system. The key concepts from Volume I are also summarized in this chapter.

Chapter 2 introduces the concept of the product (process) flow diagram and how it can be constructed for each plant type. A case-by-case analysis of the various types of resource-product interactions that characterize manufacturing operations is presented. The process flow diagram can be used to represent the basic nature of the resource/product interactions that dominate a specific manufacturing plant. The discussion focuses on resource overactivation and the resulting problems of misallocation of resources and misallocation of material.

Chapter 3 presents the V-A-T system of plant classification and a discussion of each category of plant, as well as combination plants. A full explanation of V-plant, A-plant, and T-plant behavior based on resource and material misallocation is provided in this chapter. For each plant type, the dominant product flow patterns and general characteristics are described. Then an explanation of the business issues and problems faced by each plant type is provided. Finally, we present a brief overview of the general Synchronous Management approach to managing and controlling each category of plant.

Subsequently, the application of Synchronous Management is discussed in detail for V-plants (Chapter 4), A-plants (Chapter 5), and T-plants (Chapter 6). For each plant category, we formulate the typical business issues that need to be addressed, describe the process of constraint identification, and discuss how the drum-buffer-rope system should be set up. We also discuss appropriate constraint-based performance measures at the plant level. Finally, each chapter ends with a case study that illustrates the concepts described in the chapter.

Chapters 7 and 8 provide a detailed case study of a real-life Synchronous Management implementation. Chapter 7 presents the general framework for implementation, and Chapter 8 discusses the application in a specific company. The steps involved and the various phases of implementation are presented, highlighting. the critical implementation issues and the results achieved.

THE TRANSITION TOWARD SYNCHRONOUS MANAGEMENT

A wise man is one who sees the storm coming before the clouds appear.
– Elbert Hubbard, 1923

THE INEVITABILITY AND NECESSITY OF CHANGE

"Survival of the fittest." This oversimplification of the Theory of Evolution implies much about the dynamics of systems and the inherent process of change. One certainty in any system is that the only constant is change. Over time, all systems evolve. And individual entities within the system must continually adapt in order to survive and prosper.

In this two-volume series we are primarily concerned with manufacturing organizations. In the first volume, we presented the basic principles and concepts of Synchronous Management—a philosophy that organizations can adopt to achieve peak performance in today's highly competitive manufacturing environment. In this volume, our focus is on the implementation process, and we emphasize the critical implementation issues and obstacles to change.

Generally speaking, manufacturing businesses must continually improve in order to survive. A business that does not improve is a business that is losing ground to competitors. While not every change is an improvement, every improvement requires a change. And, as we will demonstrate, significant improvements often require significant changes in the basic mindset of how the business is managed.

In order to maintain a competitive edge in the manufacturing environment, necessary changes may require a major paradigm shift. That is, managers must perceive reality with a totally different mindset. To understand the magnitude of the changes required, it is helpful to refer to a simpler, but very different, analogous environment. By using a simple analogy, we can focus on the big picture and more easily appreciate the key issues involved. By making the analogy different from normal activities, it can be looked at objectively, free from preconceptions and other emotional baggage.

The Evolution of Football: A Fictional Analogy

Although many good analogies are possible, we have chosen the sport (and business) of football as an analogy to the competitive business of manufacturing. We have selected football because it is a highly developed team sport that requires a competitive edge to be successful.

Our analogy is meant to be an entertaining "fictionalized account" of the evolution of the game of football. Although generally correct, we have taken some significant liberties with historical accuracy in order to make key points. Furthermore, our fictionalized characters are not meant to portray any specific individuals.

In the early days, football was a basic game that demanded very little preparation. Meticulously prepared game plans, intensive video analysis, careful player selection, and rigorous training for special skills were absent. Although quite simple and crude by today's standards, games were normally exciting because they were competitive. Despite being a team sport, the outcome of most games was usually determined by the spectacular abilities of a few individual players. Generally, the team with the best star players won the game.

This soon changed. One team had a particularly innovative coach by the name of Henry F. Opposing coaches soon began to notice that Henry's team was playing the game differently (and better) than before. At first, opposing teams were bewildered. How could *that* team beat us like that? Those individual players are no better than ours! At first, the success of Henry's team was probably attributed to luck. However, it soon became clear that his team was doing something different that provided a clear competitive advantage.

This major innovation of coach Henry was the planned play—the diagrammed X's of today's football terminology. Before the snap of the ball, Henry would signal a play. The entire offense would then execute the play that was called. The former freewheeling offense had been replaced by the disciplined execution of a few pre-planned and well practiced plays. For the first time, the entire offense operated as a synchronized unit. The probability of successfully executing a play was greatly enhanced, particularly since the other team's defense was not similarly prepared. The precise execution of well practiced plays provided Henry's team with such an overwhelming advantage that it sometimes appeared as if it could score at will. Henry's team generally won its games by simply outscoring the opposition. One interesting result of this success was that offense came to be recognized as the prime requirement for success and the role of playing defense was downplayed.

Since the planned play provided Henry's team with such an overwhelming advantage, the team had no reason to develop and master complex plays. His team simply concentrated on executing basic running plays, over and over again. It was not that the rules of football did not permit the pass plays, reverses, and other variations we see today. It was just that the precise execution of basic running plays was proving so successful that the pass and other plays with higher risk were avoided. Besides, for the relatively unskilled players of those early days, learning how to run a variety of intricately designed plays would not have been easy.

As with all successful innovations, the use of the planned play was soon copied by a few early adopters, and eventually by the masses. It became accepted football wisdom that success was based on the proper planning and execution of conservative running plays.

Once the reason for success became widely understood, the basic strategy spread like wildfire—design some good running plays, practice execution of these plays, and win the game by scoring more than the opponent. Within a few years, general competitive parity had been restored as other teams developed the ability to plan and execute the basic running plays.

The response to this offensive innovation came fairly quickly. Alfred S., a rival coach, started introducing the concept of defensive play calling. Developed to counter the basic offensive running plays, each member of the defense would have a specific assignment and would try to disrupt the offense in a well-rehearsed manner. Defensive play calling—the diagrammed O's of today's football terminology—became the new weapon in the football arsenal. This new innovation—the ability to disrupt the other team's offense—propelled Alfred's team to several championships. His team often won by preventing the other teams from scoring.

This new emphasis on defensive play again changed the nature of the game. Teams that were slow to adopt this new defensive strategy found themselves losing more and more games. Ultimately, the widespread improvement in the level of defensive play led to intense physical confrontations between the offense trying to execute its basic plays and the defense trying to disrupt them.

With the new offensive and defensive parity, whichever team could best execute its offensive and defensive strategies usually won. Many coaches quickly realized that in these physical confrontations, the team with the stronger players would usually prevail. Thus, player strength became the key ingredient for success.

The game of football had reached its next plateau in terms of quality and competitiveness. Games were, once again, very competitive. And the game was again characterized by a new mindset: football was a game of strength. Once this mindset took hold, the future evolution of the game and its management proceeded along predictable lines:

- Systems were developed to measure and catalog player strength.
- Players were ranked by strength.
- Player compensation (in the professional ranks) was often based on strength ranking.
- Player experience and knowledge were not highly valued. A player was replaced as soon as a stronger player was available.
- Post-game analysis would focus on identifying the weaker players.
- Training programs geared towards improving player strength became very popular.
- The running play became the de facto play in football. In a circuitous way, the preoccupation with strength aided this development.
- Game plans and post-game analysis were often based on the success of a team's running game compared to that of the opponents. A primary example is the fact that time of possession was viewed as a key indicator of success.

More innovative coaches came along—W. Edwards D., Taiichi O., and Eliyahu G. They exposed the inherent fallacies of the mindset characterized by these concepts and performance measures. These innovative coaches elevated the passing game to new heights. They developed sophisticated defenses to counter the evolving high-powered offenses. They elevated special teams' play to an important component of the overall game strategy. The stream of innovations has been virtually nonstop in an attempt to gain a competitive advantage. On offense, high-profile innovations have included multiple sets, motion offenses, option offenses, three and four wide receivers, the run-and-shoot, and the West Coast passing offense. On defense, to counter the latest prevailing offensive strategies, we have seen the flex defense, blitz packages, 3-4 defenses, nickel backs, and even as many as seven or eight defensive backs on the field.

As a result, the game of football has evolved considerably from that of earlier times. For example, today, a "big-play" passing game is almost considered a prerequisite to winning a championship. Teams can no longer depend solely on a strong running game. Almost any good defense can stop such a one-dimensional attack.

As a result of the flood of innovations, a complete re-evaluation of what it takes to win was required. The mindset that characterizes football today can be described as:

- Football is a team sport that requires sophisticated game plans executed by well coached, highly disciplined, and highly skilled players.

This change in mindset means significant changes in how coaches coach and how players are evaluated. For example:

- Strength is no longer the only measure of a player's value to the team.
- Important player skills include game intelligence, speed, agility, and strength.
- Game plans are complex and are designed to leverage the team's strengths and exploit the opposition's weaknesses.
- Player knowledge and experience are key assets.
- Post-game analysis evaluates details about the game plan as well as its execution—first by the team as a whole and then by individual members.
- Players need to understand both the overall game plan and their specific roles.
- Players must play within the requirements of the offensive or defensive system.

We now show how difficult it can be to change a previously successful paradigm or mindset. And the longer a once-successful paradigm has been in place, the harder it is to eliminate. Note that the long-standing measure known as "time of possession" is still routinely reported in all game statistics as a key measure of team performance and impact on the game. When some very successful offenses were sometimes referred to as "three yards and a cloud of dust," time of possession was indeed a key measure of a team's ability to control the game.

However, time of possession inherently favors running plays more than passing plays. Thus, time of possession now has little relevance for most teams since today's football is a game of "big plays" on offense, defense, and special teams. For analysts who still like to keep track of a team's ability to control the ball, a game statistic such as the number of offensive plays might have more relevance.

Except in blowout games, it is no longer true that the team that wins the "time of possession" battle generally wins the game. (In fact, as this chapter was being drafted, six college bowl games between fairly comparable teams were played on January 1, 1997. In those games, Texas, Northwestern, Arizona State, Michigan, West Virginia, and Brigham Young all had the edge in time of possession. However, of these six teams, only Brigham Young won its game.)

Every newspaper dutifully includes time of possession in its summary of game statistics. Game announcers still talk about it. Time of possession has been a performance measure of the game for so long, it has become virtually "entrenched." Sometimes, old habits die slowly!

The Cost-Based Manufacturing Paradigm Dies Slowly

Similar to the football analogy described above, it is safe to say that the development of U.S. manufacturing has undergone a series of evolutionary changes. Through several stages, U.S. industry evolved from one based primarily on cottage industries to one that now includes globally competitive conglomerates. Companies that couldn't successfully make the transition from one paradigm to the next did not survive. However, until recently, most manufacturers managed to make the jump from one paradigm to the next.

For a lengthy period after World War II, American manufacturers had a stunning run of success using the mass production approach to manufacturing. Post-World War II plants were managed according to cost-based principles that encouraged what can be described as "high-inventory" systems. Unfortunately, the very success enjoyed by U.S. manufacturers created a significant amount of reluctance to abandon old "tried and true" approaches. After all, it is difficult to displace a system of manufacturing management that has been so deeply entrenched and so successful for several decades.

In the first volume of *Synchronous Management: Profit-Based Manufacturing for the 21st Century*, we focus on the critical area of overall system strategy where the new and old manufacturing paradigms are diametrically opposed. Currently, there is a major misalignment between the old operating paradigms still used by most manufacturing companies and new marketplace requirements. The manufacturing paradigm shift must be completed in order to align the capabilities of manufacturers with current marketplace demands. To make this shift, manufacturers need a new game plan for managing the entire team. In this volume, we describe in detail how to develop and implement that new game plan.

We have used the term "Synchronous Management" to describe a successful manufacturing management approach for today's environment. Some have coined the term "lean production system" to describe a key paradigm in today's manufacturing environment. Lean production is a low-inventory mode of production. The major competitive elements by which manufacturing companies compete with one another are product features, quality, delivery, service, and price. In Figure 1.2 in *Volume I*, we summarized the major advantages of the lean production system (or synchronized flow environment) over the high-inventory environment that is characteristic of the old manufacturing paradigm. For your convenience, this summary is presented again in Figure 1.1 below.

The high-inventory, traditional mass production approach is clearly unsuited for today's competitive marketplace. This much is well understood by most

FIGURE 1.1

Comparison Between Synchronized and Nonsynchronized Operations with Respect to Several Competitive Elements

Competitive Element	Nonsynchronized or High-Inventory Operation	Synchronized or Lean-Production Operation
Service Responsiveness	Production pipeline clogged, making quick response impossible.	Short manufacturing lead times and "clean" pipelines permit quick deliveries.
Delivery Reliability (On-Time Shipments)	Chaotic shop environment. Constant expediting required to be close to promise on at least some production orders.	Smooth, coordinated flow ensures reliable delivery of product.
Price	Quality problems, poor resource utilization, shop chaos, and expediting contribute to high product cost.	Smooth flow leads to improved "utilization" of resources. This and better quality significantly reduce cost.
Quality	Causes are buried in high inventories, expediting and "firefighting." Leaves no time for fixing the process.	Causes can be quickly and easily identified. Encourages and enables fixing the problem.

manufacturing managers. However, the transition from the traditional high-inventory environment to the Synchronous Management low-inventory environment has not been easy. There are two factors that contribute to the persistence of the high-inventory environment.

First, the cost-based accounting systems still used in most manufacturing companies to support decision making and evaluate performance encourages high-inventory environments. This is due to:

1. The measurement systems derived from the accounting system and used at all levels of management encourages "activation," or "keep busy" policies. As demonstrated in *Volume I*, higher than necessary activation always creates high inventories.

2. The measurement system treats inventory as an asset. Reducing inventory will result in an operating loss during the period in which the reduction occurs. This often discourages aggressive inventory reduction programs from being implemented.

The second factor contributing to the high-inventory production environment is that systematic techniques for successfully managing material flow in a low-inventory environment were not fully developed until the 1980s. Traditional planning and control systems are high-inventory systems because:

1. They fail to recognize the high level of interdependencies in a manufacturing operation. Everything from batch sizing rules to product cost calculations assumes that decisions can be made locally, and in isolation, for each product and each resource.

2. All resources are treated in a similar manner. Specifically, the key concepts of bottlenecks and constraints are given only superficial recognition.

3. Planning systems, resource capabilities, and operating rules are designed to promote high local efficiencies.

THE SYNCHRONOUS MANAGEMENT GAME PLAN

The game plan for success based on Synchronous Management principles enables manufacturing companies to be responsive and lean. Synchronous Management provides the guidelines to manage all resources in such a way as to achieve overall team (business) success.

The principles and methods developed in *Volume I* are valid for any manufacturing organization. The detailed operating rules that emerge from applying these universal principles to a specific plant vary—depending on the nature of the interactions between the plant's resources and the products.

While each manufacturing plant is unique in many ways, plants can be systematically classified. In this book, we present a classification system that enables us to tailor the application of Synchronous Management principles to specific plant types. Plants that belong to the same classification generally exhibit common problems and require similar Synchronous Management solutions. Plants in the same category also share similar techniques for identifying constraints and for establishing the drum-buffer-rope logistical system. The processes for developing and implementing a solution can also be more specifically defined for plants of a given category.

We believe that the classification system and the discussion of the application to each plant type provide the critical bridge needed to apply the general principles of Synchronous Management to the unique case of each individual plant. *(Note that here we refer to "plants" and "plant types" since we are talking about manufacturing companies. However, the principles and concepts discussed actually refer to the "process flow" or "process flow types." Thus, the classification system and attendant solutions that will be presented are equally applicable in an office/service environment as they are in a manufacturing environment.)*

Before proceeding further, we first present a summary of some of the key concepts of Synchronous Management developed in *Volume I*.

SUMMARY OF KEY CONCEPTS FROM *VOLUME I*

The first volume of this two-volume series was devoted to developing a system of manufacturing management that would be free of the shortcomings of the cost-based manufacturing management systems, and that would optimize total system (business) performance. A new set of operational measures—Throughput

(T), Inventory (I), and Operating Expense (OE)—were introduced. These measures overcome the distortions and the dysfunctional decisions associated with the standard cost-based systems. These measurements are defined as follows:

Throughput
Money generated through sales, not through production.

Inventory
Amount of money tied up in materials the company intends to sell.

Operating Expense
Money spent by the company to convert Inventory (I) into Throughput (T).

These definitions have two important characteristics. They evaluate performance as it relates to the entire system, not just local areas. And they are intrinsic to manufacturing and are easy for everyone to understand. In traditional cost-based systems, the business goal of making money has often been oversimplified to a quest for reducing costs. In Synchronous Management, the objective of making money translates to increasing Throughput, reducing Inventory, and reducing Operating Expense, ideally, all at the same time. Management decisions (from batch sizing decisions to capital expenditure decisions to sourcing decisions) are made by analyzing the predicted impact of those decisions on Throughput, Inventory, and Operating Expense.

In addition, three key terms—bottleneck resource, non-bottleneck resource, and constraint were defined as follows:

Bottleneck Resource
Any resource whose capacity is less than or equal to the market demand placed on it.

Non-Bottleneck Resource
Any resource whose capacity is greater than the market demand placed on it.

Constraint
Any element that limits the organization from achieving higher levels of performance, where performance is measured in terms of the organization's goal.

The organization's constraints determine the upper limit on overall business performance. Failure to properly identify and manage constraints cause the actual performance of the organization to be lower than the limit set by the constraints. Constraints are classified into three major categories—physical, market, and policy.

Analyzing the effect of interactions between the resources and the product flow in manufacturing operations lead to several principles that highlight key Synchronous Management concepts. These principles are summarized in Figure 1.2.

Based on a solid understanding of proper organizational goals and Synchronous Management principles, the manufacturing planning and control system described as drum-buffer-rope (DBR) was developed. The DBR logistical system establishes a product flow that is manageable and can compensate for disruptions inherent in every manufacturing process. DBR is designed to maximize system throughput and organizational competitiveness while minimizing inventory and operating expenses.

The *drum* is the detailed master production schedule that sets the pace for the entire plant. The drum must reconcile customer requirements with the system's constraints. If system constraints are capacity constraints, the master production schedule is based on the processing capabilities of and the requirements on the capacity constraint resources (CCRs). This drum then determines the pace and production sequence for the entire plant. We define a capacity constraint resource (CCR) as any resource whose available capacity limits the organization's ability to meet the product volume, product mix, or demand fluctuation required by the marketplace.

The *buffer* refers to time buffers or stock buffers (at minimal inventory cost) used at a few critical points in the process to protect the system throughput. The nature, location, and size of the buffers depend on the detailed nature of the product flow diagram and actual customer requirements. The key is to have minimal buffers, but design them for maximum protection. Analysis of the buffers can be used to identify both policy changes and process improvements that enable the reduction of buffers and improve system performance.

The *rope* is the last link in the DBR system. The purpose of the rope is to provide effective communication throughout the organization of those actions that are required to support the master production schedule. Every aspect of the operation must be synchronized to the requirements of the drum so the planned product flow may be executed.

FIGURE 1.2

Synchronous Management Principles

Synchronous Management Principle 1
Do not focus on balancing capacities, focus on synchronizing the flow.

Synchronous Management Principle 1a
Focus on the flow of work and not on the efficiency of individual tasks.

Synchronous Management Principle 2
The marginal value of time at a bottleneck resource is equal to the throughput rate of the products processed by the bottleneck.

Synchronous Management Principle 2a
The marginal value of a unit of constrained material is equal to the purchase price of the constrained material plus the throughput value of the finished products requiring this material.

Synchronous Management Principle 2b
The marginal value of a sales order in a constrained market is equal to the throughput value of that order.

Synchronous Management Principle 3
The marginal value of time at a non-bottleneck resource is negligible.

Synchronous Management Principle 3a
The marginal value of a unit of non-constrained material is its purchase price.

Synchronous Management Principle 3b
The marginal value of a sales order in a non-constrained market is minimal.

Synchronous Management Principle 4
The level of utilization of a non-bottleneck resource is controlled by the constraints of the system.

Synchronous Management Principle 4a
The level of utilization of a non-constrained material is determined by the constraints of the system.

Synchronous Management Principle 5
Resources must be utilized, not simply activated.

Synchronous Management Principle 5a
Material must be utilized, not simply consumed.

Synchronous Management Principle 6
The transfer batch need not, and many times should not, be equal to the process batch.

Synchronous Management Principle 7
A process batch may be variable both along its route and over time.

Operational Measures Principle
Throughput should be going up, Inventory should be going down, and Operating Expense should be going down, ideally, all at the same time. However, it is possible and may even be desirable to have one of the measures go in the wrong direction in order to improve another one.

Finally, we presented a constraint-based improvement process designed to drive continuous improvement in business performance. This Constraint Management Process can be described as follows:

Step 1:   ***Identify and choose the system constraint(s).***
Step 2:   ***Design operating rules to optimize system performance, given the limitations of the chosen constraint(s).***
Step 3:   ***Improve system performance by focusing on the system constraint(s).***
Step 4:   ***Repeat the cycle.***

The operational measures of T, I, and OE, the basic principles of Synchronous Management, the drum-buffer-rope logistical system, and the Constraint Management Process provide the foundation for managing a complex manufacturing business in today's highly competitive environment.

Chapter 2

MISALLOCATION PROBLEMS IN MANUFACTURING PROCESSES

Luck is what happens when preparation meets opportunity.
– Darrell Royal, 1976

Darrell Royal, the legendary football coach at the University of Texas, had it exactly right. His quote applies to manufacturing organizations as well as to football teams. Appropriately, this two-volume series on Synchronous Management is all about preparing managers to take full advantage of available opportunities.

However, in this chapter, we emphasize the significance of the exact opposite. That is, when the opportunity to mismanage the production process is coupled with ill-advised, misdirected encouragement, the inevitable result is disaster. We illustrate how out-dated management policies, operating rules, and performance measures, based on traditional cost-based systems, lead to overactivation, and to misallocation of resources and materials in production processes. Through a series of cases, we describe various key scenarios of overactivation and misallocation, as well as the manufacturing and business problems they create. The implementation of Synchronous Management principles in specific plants is based on the implications derived from these cases.

UNDERSTANDING PERFORMANCE SHORTFALLS

There are numerous ways to get into trouble managing a manufacturing organization. Improper management of the product flow—the way the mix of products moves through plant resources—is at the top of the list in most companies. This fact has been increasingly recognized by manufacturing managers. The resulting attempts at resolving the problem have generally focused in two areas; improving the way each product moves through the various resources and reducing the number and diversity of products that flow through a particular resource. Specific techniques that promote improved product flow include focused factories, work cells, and improved factory layouts.

Because of management philosophies such as Just-in-Time (JIT), Total Quality Management (TQM), and lean production, the value of more effectively managing product flow through the process has not gone unnoticed. Most managers clearly understand that what needs to be managed in their operations is product flow (or more generally, the value stream)—the movement of material from suppliers through the factory resources to customers. They also understand the competitive advantage to be gained from shortened lead times, increased reliability of delivery promises, and improved flexibility, as well as improved quality and reduced production costs.

Most of these management philosophies have encouraged beneficial change. Unfortunately, major problems still exist in most plants, and overall performance has generally fallen far short of expectations and potential. We believe that the continuing shortfall in performance can be largely traced to managerial oversights in two critical areas:

1. Constraints and non-constraints exist in every plant, and they require totally different approaches in managerial control.

2. Managing product flow is more complex than managing individual resources, since multiple products and multiple resources must be considered. Most current management policies, operating rules, and performance measures are not designed to maximize overall product flow (or system performance).

The existence of constraints and non-constraints is universal to all organizations, especially manufacturing operations. Fortunately, most manufacturing managers now acknowledge the existence of constraints and non-constraints (or at least bottlenecks and non-bottlenecks). In many cases, this basic recognition and level of understanding has led managers to modify existing production control systems—usually with excellent results.

However, this only scratches the surface of what is possible. What we are after is a quantum leap in performance. In order to achieve it, we investigate the validity of the following important concepts, which will be thoroughly developed throughout this book:

- *Specific product flow building blocks result in specific types of problems.*

- *Most complex manufacturing systems contain a variety of building block elements. However, some of these building blocks dominate the system, causing very specific and predictable behaviors.*

- *Manufacturing systems that share the same dominant building blocks exhibit similar characteristics, behaviors, and problems.*

- *The appropriate Synchronous Management strategy must be aligned with the specific characteristics, behaviors, and problems that define a given plant.*

THE PRODUCT FLOW DIAGRAM

Our in-depth analysis of manufacturing operations begins with the introduction of a format that allows an accurate representation of the product flow. The traditional way of thinking about a manufacturing plant reflects a resource focus or resource orientation. This can be seen by how companies organize and by how managers and operators describe themselves. Operators describe themselves in terms of the work centers they typically run—Press Operator, Furnace Operator, etc. Managers describe themselves in terms of the resources they control, or "own"—Press Department, Heat Treat Department, etc. The measurement system also reflects this resource bias by tracking resource activities. The primary measure of managerial performance is effective resource management—keeping resources busy processing parts and producing products.

When asked to describe or map material flow, most will draw a diagram that shows the resources as the primary focus, and product flow as secondary. Typically, resources are drawn as boxes (one box per resource type) and lines represent the path of product from one resource to the next. Such a diagram is called a *resource flow diagram*. Figure 2.1 shows the routing of two products produced in a plant. The corresponding resource flow diagram is shown in Figure 2.2. Note that resource R3 performs both operations 30 and 50 for product B, represented by the looping back of the path of product B (dashed line in Figure 2.2).

FIGURE 2.1

Simplified Routing for Two Products Manufactured Using Shared Resources

Product A   **Input material: Raw material A**

Operation	Resource
010	R1
020	R2
030	R3
040	R4

Product B   **Input material: Raw material B**

Operation	Resource
010	R1
020	R2
030	R3
040	R4
050	R3

Note: For the purpose of mapping the flow, the process times are not needed and are not included in the table above.

A key theme of Synchronous Management is to shift from a resource focus to a product-flow focus. To facilitate this viewpoint in Synchronous Management, the map of the product flow is constructed from the perspective of the product or material. It is a time-oriented description of the manufacturing process. The resulting map is called the *product flow diagram*. We begin by describing the basic elements of a product flow diagram and illustrating it with a simple example.

FIGURE 2.2

**Resource Flow Diagram
for Products A & B Described in Figure 2.1**

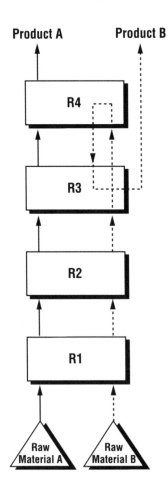

——— Product A
----- Product B

The Basic Elements of a Product Flow Diagram

The most basic element of manufacturing is the operation (or processing of material), performed on a part by a resource. But the same operation can be performed on two different part numbers (e.g., when the only difference is the length of the material). Therefore, we use a new term, referred to as a *station*, to emphasize a key point.

Station

A basic element in a manufacturing flow that defines a specific operation performed on a specific part at a specific resource.

The general information required to define a station includes part identification, the operation identification, and the specific resource (work center) identification. To facilitate ease of understanding, in a product flow diagram the basic information that defines a specific station is generally presented in the format indicated in Figure 2.3.

For example, consider the routing for the manufacture of a product identified by the part number H2786, as shown in Figure 2.4. Each operation in the routing is represented by a station. For example, operation 030 for part number H2786 is characterized by the following elements:

- Part identification: H2786
- Specific operation identification: Operation number 030
- Specific resource identification: Drill press with the shop identification number 03-201

FIGURE 2.3

The Format Used to Present Station Information

Part Identification – Operation Identification
Resource Identification

FIGURE 2.4

Engineering Routing for Part H2786

Part H2786

Operation	Resource	Run Time per unit (minutes)	Setup Time (hours)
010	02-176	2.76	0.00
020	04-110	9.60	0.42
030	03-201	6.30	0.75
040	03-201	11.74	0.50
050	06-413	4.16	0.00
060	02-100	29.22	0.25
999	99-000	0.00	0.00

Note: The first station in this routing is defined as operation 010 on part H2786 at resource 02-176.

Each station identifies a specific stage in the production of a uniquely identified part. Manufactured products typically move through several resources during processing. Thus, the transformation of each product from raw material to a completed product can be represented by a unique sequence of stations connected by *arrows*.

Arrows are used in the product flow diagram to designate the sequence of the product flow. An incoming arrow at any station indicates the existence of an earlier activity in the routing that must be completed before the work defined by the current station can be performed. Similarly, an outgoing arrow from a station indicates additional steps are required before the product can be shipped.

The manufacture of part H2786, as defined in the routing of Figure 2.4, can be represented by the sequence of stations shown in Figure 2.5. The product flow diagram for part H2786 represents the transformation of the raw material into a finished product, with each transformational step represented by a station.

Similarly, the product flow diagram for the plant described in Figure 2.1 is shown in Figure 2.6. Note that two separate paths are used to represent the flow of the two distinct products A and B.

A station may have either zero, one, or more than one incoming arrow. Stations

FIGURE 2.5

Product Flow Diagram for Part H2786

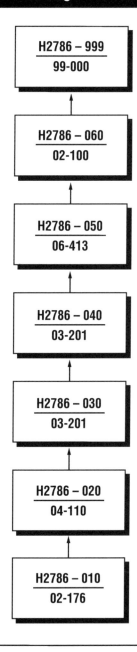

with no incoming arrows represent gateway operations and indicate the entry of material into the production process. No preceding processing activity exists for these stations. All other stations have at least one preceding station connected by one or more incoming arrows.

An assembly station, for example, requires two or more input materials (components) for the activity to occur. Thus, a station representing an assembly operation has multiple incoming arrows, one from each station identifying the last processing step for each required component. Figure 2.7(a) illustrates a station representing an assembly operation requiring two component parts. Any station that has more than one input arrow signifying the convergence of material flows is called a *convergence point* in the product flow diagram.

A station may also have either zero, one, or more than one outgoing arrows. A station that has no outgoing arrows clearly signifies the end of the manufacturing process and the last step before shipment or sale. All other stations must have at least one outgoing arrow leading to the next station(s) in the production process.

Figure 2.7(b) shows a case of more than one outgoing arrow. When this situation occurs, each outgoing arrow represents a possible next activity for this same product. This commonly occurs in two situations. The first is in industries that process the same basic material into a variety of unique end products. The same material at one step (yarn, for example, in the textile industry) can be used to produce two or more products at the next step (dyed into a multitude of different colors). The second situation is where a manufactured component is used as a common part for several different assemblies. Any station that has more than one outgoing arrow signifying that a common material has alternate applications, is called a *divergence point* in the product flow diagram.

In our product flow diagrams, we also use a triangle to represent the entry of materials into the process. When this device is used prior to a gateway operation, an arrow is typically used to connect the triangle with the gateway operation. Moreover, a triangle must be used to indicate the introduction of additional materials or parts at a non-gateway station.

The manufacturing process for any product or group of products can be represented by a network of stations (and triangles). The resulting product flow diagram indicates the required raw materials, all of the different processing and fabricating activities performed on all component parts, and all subassembly and assembly activities. Clearly, the product flow diagram for some manufacturing operations may be quite complex, involving a large number of stations.

The utility of the product flow diagram is that it enables one to understand process characteristics, business problems, and even potential solutions. To see how product flow diagrams enable this, it is necessary to understand the result of

FIGURE 2.6

Product Flow Diagrams
for Products A & B Described in Figure 2.1

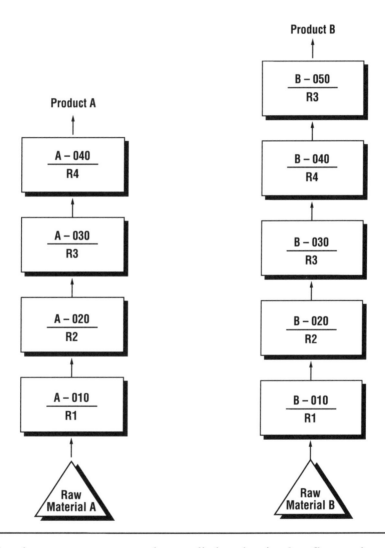

traditional management approaches applied to the simplest flows—the so-called building blocks of product flow diagrams. Once one understands how the simple building block flows behave, it is possible to understand how complex product flows behave—by breaking down and analyzing the complex diagram into the building block elements of which it is composed.

FIGURE 2.7

Stations with Multiple Incoming and Outgoing Arrows

(a) Assembly Point with Multiple Incoming Arrows – Part A1000

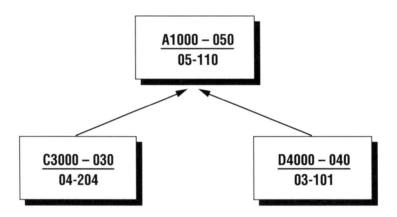

(b) Divergence Point with Multiple Outgoing Arrows – Part B2000

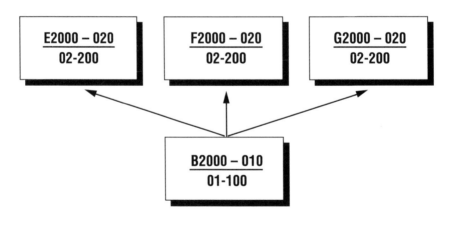

THE BUILDING BLOCKS OF PRODUCT FLOW

Managing product flow is complicated by the fact that multiple products and multiple resources must be considered. Product flows are also influenced by the presence of constraints. In this section we consider the performance that results by managing the simplest cases (basic building blocks) under traditional management rules. We begin with the simple case involving just one product.

Cases With Multiple Resources and Only One Product

The most basic manufacturing flows involve situations where each resource works on a single product. There are five basic cases involving the use of bottleneck and non-bottleneck resources in the production of one product. We refer to these five cases as the five basic building blocks of product flow. In Chapter 5 of *Synchronous Management: Profit-Based Manufacturing for the 21st Century – Volume I*, we referred to these five building blocks as the five basic resource interactions. More precisely, they are the five basic resource-product interactions involving only one product. A description of the resulting resource-product interactions and the major implications of each case was described in detail in Chapter 5 of *Volume I*. The five cases are shown in Figure 2.8. For continuity and ease of reference, each case and its major conclusions are summarized.

Case 1 – Product Flows from Bottleneck to Non-Bottleneck
When material flows from a bottleneck to a non-bottleneck resource the supply of material available at the non-bottleneck is restricted to a quantity less than the capacity of the non-bottleneck. Therefore, the bottleneck can be fully utilized. However, the non-bottleneck cannot be overactivated, and its capacity cannot be fully utilized. This gives rise to:

> ### *Synchronous Management Principle 4*
> *The level of utilization of a non-bottleneck resource is controlled by the constraints of the system.*

A key concept in this case is that non-bottlenecks cannot raise the throughput of the plant beyond the level established by the bottleneck. However, poor performance at the non-bottleneck (for example, lost units due to scrap) can lower overall plant performance. Therefore, non-bottleneck performance should not be evaluated in isolation, but in terms of how it supports overall plant performance.

FIGURE 2.8

The Five Basic Product Flow Building Blocks
(Cases With One Product)

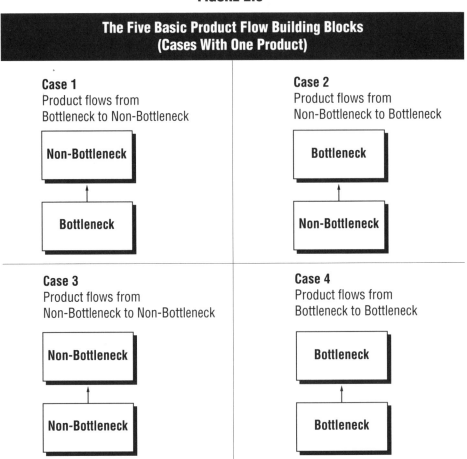

Case 1
Product flows from
Bottleneck to Non-Bottleneck

> Non-Bottleneck
>
> ↑
>
> Bottleneck

Case 2
Product flows from
Non-Bottleneck to Bottleneck

> Bottleneck
>
> ↑
>
> Non-Bottleneck

Case 3
Product flows from
Non-Bottleneck to Non-Bottleneck

> Non-Bottleneck
>
> ↑
>
> Non-Bottleneck

Case 4
Product flows from
Bottleneck to Bottleneck

> Bottleneck
>
> ↑
>
> Bottleneck

Case 5
Convergence point is supplied
by both Bottleneck & Non-Bottleneck

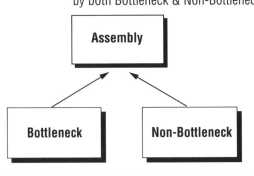

> Assembly
>
> ↑ ↑
>
> Bottleneck   Non-Bottleneck

Case 2 – Product Flows from Non-Bottleneck to Bottleneck

In this case, the non-bottleneck processes material before it is moved to the bottleneck. The non-bottleneck can process more units than the bottleneck has capacity to process. In traditionally managed plants, where high efficiency and traditional resource utilization numbers translate into high performance, this is a very real danger. However, Synchronous Management Principle 4 is still valid. Moreover, this case leads to:

Synchronous Management Principle 5
Resources must be utilized, not simply activated.

Recall the key Synchronous Management definitions of utilization and activation from *Volume I:*

Activation
The employment of a resource to process materials or products.

Utilization
The employment of a resource to process materials or products that contribute positively to company performance—throughput.

The non-bottleneck is being utilized only when its production is matched to that of the slower bottleneck. Any additional production at the non-bottleneck beyond this level is overactivation. Clearly, such *overactivation* results in excess work-in-process inventory, increased manufacturing lead time, and higher operating expenses.

Case 3 – Product Flows from Non-Bottleneck to Non-Bottleneck

In this case, material is processed by two non-bottleneck resources. By definition, the capacity of each resource exceeds that required to support the current level of market demand. Therefore, each resource can only be utilized to the extent that output matches the quantity required by the marketplace. In this case, the limited market demand is the system constraint, which limits resource utilization.

Overactivation at one or both of the two non-bottleneck resources only creates excess inventory somewhere in the system, either work in process or finished goods. Such overactivation does not enhance throughput, and detracts from overall system performance.

Case 4 – Product Flows from Bottleneck to Bottleneck

The existence of two bottlenecks in a process means that neither resource has the capacity to satisfy available market demand. In this case, two major scenarios must be considered.

If the first bottleneck has more capacity than the second bottleneck, the first bottleneck assumes the characteristics of a non-bottleneck and the second bottleneck becomes the true constraining resource. All of the interactions and the impact on system performance as described in Case 2 (Product Flows from Non-Bottleneck to Bottleneck) apply. For example, the first bottleneck is overactivated if it is allowed to process more material than the second bottleneck can handle.

If the second bottleneck has more capacity than the first bottleneck, then the first bottleneck is the constraining resource and the second bottleneck assumes the role of a non-bottleneck resource. The second bottleneck has capacity above and beyond the first bottleneck and cannot be overactivated. The scenario is essentially the same as Case 1 (Product Flows from Bottleneck to Non-Bottleneck) together with its implications.

In short, the operating rules and policies for a bottleneck resource should be a function of how it affects the product flow. Each bottleneck resource must be managed differently, depending on its potential to contribute to, or detract from, overall system performance.

Case 5 – Convergence Point is Supplied by Both Bottleneck and Non-Bottleneck

The focus in this case is on the situation where a non-bottleneck operation (assembly operation) assembles two parts. One part is processed by a bottleneck and the other part is processed by a non-bottleneck. The bottleneck's available capacity is less than needed to satisfy market demand. Thus, the bottleneck's available capacity must be fully utilized. Each of the non-bottlenecks can produce at a rate faster than required by the market, and definitely at a faster rate than the bottleneck. Since assembly can process materials only as fast as parts are provided by the bottleneck, it is not possible to overactivate the assembly operation. However, the non-bottleneck feeding operation can be overactivated. This occurs if this operation processes material at a rate faster than the bottleneck. If this non-bottleneck is overactivated, the result is accumulation of excess work-in-process inventory in front of the assembly operation.

This case again shows that system throughput and the utilization potential of non-bottlenecks are controlled by system constraints. Moreover, interactions can exist even between resources that are not directly connected.

Cases With Multiple Resources and Two Products

Material flow in real-life manufacturing environments is much more complex than the cases of the five basic building blocks. For the remainder of this chapter, we utilize a commonly accepted notation for classifying various resources. We identify bottleneck resources by BN and non-bottleneck resources by NBN. In the case of multiple bottleneck or non-bottleneck resources, we use "BN_1", "BN_2", "NBN_1", "NBN_2", etc.

Two Products and Dedicated Resources   Actual manufacturing product flows are complex because routings for a given product usually involve more than two resources. However, as long as each resource processes only one product, the resource-product interactions are limited. This gives rise to Case 6, which is a straightforward combination of Cases 1, 2, and 3.

Case 6 – Two Products Are Manufactured, But Each Resource Works On Only a Single Product

A production process that involves multiple resources and two products (A and B) is shown in Figure 2.9. This is a fairly special case because each resource processes only one product. The analysis of operating such a facility according to traditional guidelines is straightforward, as this situation is a combination of cases 1, 2, and 3.

If there is a bottleneck resource (BN), as represented in Figure 2.9(a), the process can be separated into two regions—the region up to and including the bottleneck and the region from the bottleneck to the end of the process. In the region prior to the bottleneck, NBN_1 feeds NBN_2 and this in turn feeds BN. This is simply a combination of Cases 3 and 2. Since NBN_1 and NBN_2 are both capable of producing faster than the bottleneck, the result of overactivation is a build up of inventory in front of BN. Depending on the relative production capacities of the non-bottleneck resources, work-in-process queues may also build up between the work centers. At all of these work centers, it is possible to achieve high local activation.

In the region after the bottleneck, BN feeds NBN_3 which feeds NBN_4. This is a combination of Cases 1 and 3. There is no opportunity to overactivate NBN_3 and NBN_4. Hence, local measures of activation will be poor, but there will be no buildup of inventory.

Now, consider the case where there is no bottleneck resource, as shown in Figure 2.9(b). This is a straightforward extension of Case 3—multiple non-bottlenecks feeding each other. The result of trying to maximize the activation level of each resource will be excess finished-goods and work-in-process inventory. The relative size and locations of the in-process queues will depend on the relative production rates of the various resources.

Two Products with Non-Dedicated Resources   Case 6 describes dedicated manufacturing lines where each line produces only a single product. Clearly, this is not the usual situation. Thus, the remaining cases describe the more common manufacturing environments where multiple resources exist and any given resource may be used to process a variety of products. To understand the interactions and consequences when each resource processes multiple products, it is necessary to first understand the simplest case—the processing of two products at a given resource.

FIGURE 2.9

Case 6: Two Products Are Manufactured Using No Shared Resources

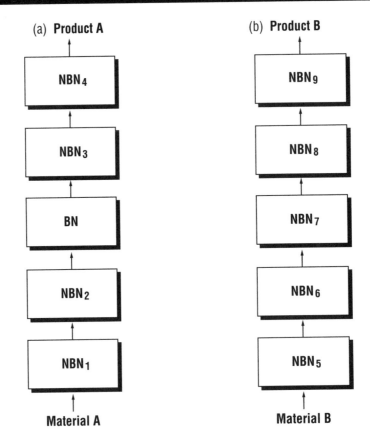

The resulting high level of complexity creates an enormous increase in the interactions between resources and products. *Volume I* described how disruptions can be transferred between resources and products in a relatively simple process. As the manufacturing process becomes more complex, the resource-product interactions become more numerous and the potential for spreading disruptions throughout the system increases exponentially. Thus, the potential for mismanagement increases.

As we analyze the remaining cases, we describe the expected consequences if management adheres to traditional cost-based operating practices that focus on efficiency and local optimization. Each of the Cases 1, 2, and 3 (of the five basic building blocks) generates two distinct scenarios when two products are involved. The first scenario occurs when products A and B are first processed by a given resource. Product A is then further processed by a second resource and product B is further processed by a third resource. The second scenario occurs when one product processed by a given resource can be further processed into two distinct products at the next operation. (An example of the second scenario is where the first operation is a metal cutting operation, and the second operation is a stamping operation. Large sheets of metal of a given thickness are cut to a specific size and then sent to the stamping presses, where they can be formed into a number of different shapes, each defining a different product.) These two scenarios for each of Cases 1, 2, and 3 give rise to Cases 7 through 12.

As previously discussed, Case 4 can be described as a special case of either Case 1 or Case 2. Therefore, we will not develop extensions of Case 4 for two products.

Case 5 describes the implications of mismanaging the operation when assembly operations are involved. Cases 13 and 14 provide an extension of the assembly environment to two products.

Figure 2.10 shows how Cases 1, 2, 3, and 5 have been extended for two products, giving rise to Cases 7 through 14.

Case 7 – Bottleneck Feeds Two Different Materials to Non-Bottlenecks, Making Two Different Products

This case is represented in Figure 2.11 and is an extension of Case 1. Two different products, A and B, are each processed by bottleneck resource BN. Product A is then further processed by non-bottleneck resource NBN_1. Product B is then further processed by non-bottleneck resource NBN_2. We generalize this case by assuming that NBN_1 and NBN_2 are different resources. However, the implications from this case are the same even if NBN_1 and NBN_2 are the same resource.

FIGURE 2.10

Extensions of the Basic Building Blocks from One Product to Two Products

Basic Building Blocks (with One Product)	Extensions to Two Products
Case 1 - Product flows from bottleneck to non-bottleneck	**Case 7 -** Bottleneck feeds two different materials to non-bottlenecks, making two different products

Case 8 - Bottleneck feeds the same material to non-bottlenecks that make two different products |
| **Case 2 -** Product flows from non-bottleneck to bottleneck | **Case 9 -** Non-bottleneck feeds material A to a bottleneck and material B to a non-bottleneck

Case 10 - Non-bottleneck feeds the same material A: (1) to a bottleneck to make product B, and (2) to a non-bottleneck to make product C |
| **Case 3 -** Product flows from non-bottleneck to non-bottleneck | **Case 11 -** Non-bottleneck feeds two different materials to non-bottlenecks, making two different products

Case 12 - Non-bottleneck feeds the same material to non-bottlenecks that make two different products |
| **Case 5 -** Convergence point is supplied by both bottleneck and non-bottleneck | **Case 13 -** Two different products are assembled from unique materials, and some of the materials are processed by a common resource

Case 14 - Two different products are assembled and share a common material |

Note that Figure 2.11(a) shows the product flow diagram with all the details displayed in each station (i.e., part identification, operation identification, and resource identification). However, for the purpose of our discussions of Cases 7 through 14 here, we will use the simplified representation as shown in Figure 2.11(b). This will help emphasize the major points being discussed.

The key point in this case is that the bottleneck can be overactivated! (Remember that in the one-product situation of Case 1, this was not possible.) The bottleneck can be overactivated because it is required to produce more than one product. For example, if the bottleneck produces more of product A than required to fill current customer orders, two things happen. Of primary importance is that while BN is being overactivated on product A, capacity that should have been utilized to produce product B has been misallocated. This causes some orders for product B to go unfilled, which causes a loss of throughput from product B. According to the definitions of utilization and activation, this is clearly overactivation of the bottleneck resource. As with all cases of overactivation, this results in excess inventory. Thus, a secondary result is that the excess units of product A cannot immediately be converted into throughput, and exist as excess inventory until sold.

In summary, overactivation of BN automatically results in two problems:

1. A loss of throughput.
2. An increase in inventory.

It is also possible for the overactivation of BN to cause late shipments (which may also cause a loss of throughput). Suppose that BN can process product B faster than NBN_2. (It is still true that BN is the bottleneck, when production of both products are considered.) If we overactivate BN on product A, this delays switching BN over to the production of product B. This delay causes NBN_2 to fall behind schedule. If the slippage is severe enough, this causes product B to be shipped late.

As a side note, resource NBN_2 appears to be a temporary bottleneck at this stage, since the delay in shipping product B appears to be NBN_2. However, the real problem is not NBN_2, but the overactivation of BN on product A.

Thus, in this case, poor management of the bottleneck may result in the following erroneous conclusions by management:

1. The management, and actual performance, of the bottleneck resource is acceptable.
2. The capacity at one or more non-bottleneck resources is inadequate.

FIGURE 2.11

Case 7: Bottleneck Feeds Two Different Materials to Non-Bottlenecks, Making Two Different Products

(a) *Product Flow Diagram with All Details*

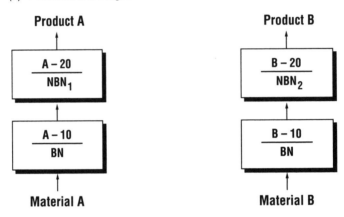

(b) *Product Flow Diagram – Simplified Representation*

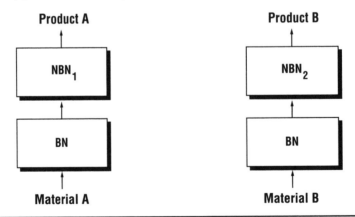

However, the actual results are:

1. The creation of temporary bottlenecks, and a consequent slip in delivery performance.
2. Excess inventory.
3. A delay in, or loss of, throughput.

This case highlights the misallocation of a bottleneck resource that feeds two products to non-bottleneck resources. The bottleneck is assigned to work on products with no immediate sales orders at the expense of products that have pending sales orders. This is usually a direct result of focusing on the local efficiencies of the individual resource. But the misallocation can cause excess inventory, temporary bottlenecks, poor delivery performance, and loss of throughput.

Case 8 – *Bottleneck Feeds the Same Material to Non-Bottlenecks That Make Two Different Products.*

This case is represented in Figure 2.12 and is also an extension of Case 1. A single type of material (A) is first processed by BN, then by NBN_1 to make product B or NBN_2 to make product C. We generalize this case by assuming that NBN_1 and NBN_2 are different resources. However, we also describe the slightly different implications if NBN_1 and NBN_2 are the same resource.

In this case, it is not possible to overactivate the BN resource because all of the bottleneck capacity is used only for material A. However, NBN_1 or NBN_2 can be overactivated. For example, NBN_1 is overactivated if it is allowed to produce an excess of product B. As a result, not enough of material A is left to satisfy the demand for product C. Overactivation of either non-bottleneck resource will simultaneously create:

FIGURE 2.12

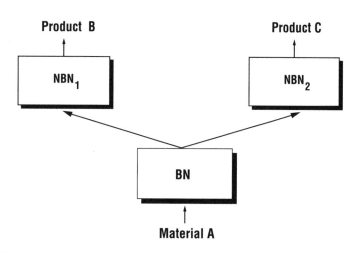

Case 8: Bottleneck Feeds the Same Material to Non-Bottlenecks That Make Two Different Products

1. Excess inventory of one product; and
2. Shortage of the other product.

A key point is that resource overactivation in this case implies a *material misallocation*. Materials are used to produce products that have no immediate sales demand at the expense of those that do. A very serious feature of this misallocation is that the bottleneck resource is required to process more of material A. In fact, when there is a material misallocation, all resources preceding this point may be required to process the material that was misallocated, or "stolen." Material misallocation is more serious than resource misallocation, since more products and resources are affected. Moreover, material misallocation also means that resource(s) have been misallocated.

Overactivation of either NBN_1 or NBN_2 can be accomplished only at the expense of the other. That is, if NBN_1 is overactivated, NBN_2 cannot be fully utilized. Of course, this may also affect the local performance measures of each non-bottleneck resource. In an environment where resource performance is measured based on activation levels, the system encourages overactivation. The likelihood of such overactivation, resource misallocation, and material misallocation is greatly increased.

Now consider the slight variation where NBN_1 and NBN_2 are the same resource. In this case, non-bottleneck resources are less likely to steal from themselves and cause material misallocation. However, overactivation and the subsequent material misallocation can still occur, and can even be encouraged by a poorly controlled system. Consider, for example, what happens when excessively large process batches are run at the NBN resource. Once again, the resulting effect is material misallocation, which generates excess inventories of one product while creating shortages of the other product.

Case 9 – Non-Bottleneck Feeds Material A to a Bottleneck and Material B to a Non-Bottleneck

This case is represented in Figure 2.13, and is an extension of Case 2. Non-bottleneck NBN_1 processes materials for products A and B. Product A material is next processed at a bottleneck resource (BN), while product B material proceeds to non-bottleneck NBN_2. What are the expected effects of overactivation in this case?

In this case, the primary overactivation occurs at resource NBN_1, and it can be overactivated by processing too much of either material A or B. However, the severity of the damage differs, depending on which product is overproduced by NBN_1.

FIGURE 2.13

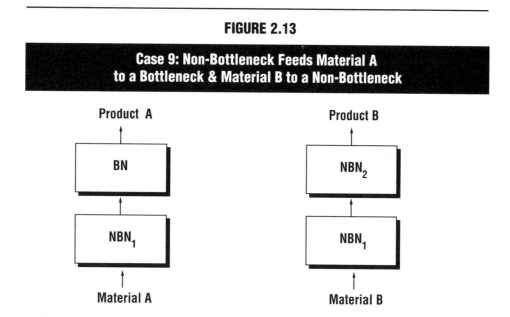

**Case 9: Non-Bottleneck Feeds Material A
to a Bottleneck & Material B to a Non-Bottleneck**

When NBN_1 is overactivated to produce an excess of product A, excess work-in-process inventory piles up ahead of resource BN. However, a bigger problem is that NBN_1 is also required to produce product B. Depending on the amount of time NBN_1 wastes in overproducing product A, one or both of the non-bottlenecks NBN_1 and NBN_2 may become temporary bottlenecks. This can happen if the start of production of product B is sufficiently delayed so one or both resources do not have enough time left to completely process product B by the required shipping date. Thus, overactivating NBN_1 on product A causes excess work-in-process inventory, and may also create temporary bottlenecks.

When NBN_1 is overactivated and produces an excess of product B, the consequences are more serious. This creates excess inventory of product B, either as work in process or finished goods. This also allows NBN_2 to be overactivated. But the major harm of NBN_1 overactivation on product B is that the processing of product A may be delayed sufficiently to cause the bottleneck to run out of material, forcing it to shut down. While turning non-bottlenecks into temporary bottlenecks may cause a delay in completion of an order, starvation of a true bottleneck means a loss of production and throughput that cannot be recovered.

*Case 10 – Non-Bottleneck Feeds the Same Material A To a Bottleneck to
Make Product B and a Non-Bottleneck to Make Product C*

This case is represented in Figure 2.14 and is also an extension of Case 2.
Resource NBN_1 first processes material A. This material is then processed at the next
stage by either resource BN to create product B or by resource NBN_2 to create product
C. In this case, either of the two non-bottleneck resources may be overactivated.

Resource NBN_1 is overactivated if units of material A are produced in excess of
what is needed to support the demand for products B and C. This results in either
excess work in process at BN or NBN_2, or in excess finished goods of product C.

By definition, the capacity at the bottleneck BN is less than the demand for
product B. Therefore, BN should work 100 percent of the time. Thus, even though BN
shares a common material with non-bottleneck NBN_2, BN cannot be overactivated.

The biggest potential for damage in this case occurs if resource NBN_2 is
overactivated, causing a misallocation of material A. The automatic result is an
accumulation of excess finished-goods inventory of product C. However, the major
problem occurs if NBN_2 consumes material scheduled for BN, resulting in starvation
at the bottleneck. This, in turn, causes a shortfall in output of product B. Loss of
production at the bottleneck resource causes a shortfall in output of product B and a

FIGURE 2.14

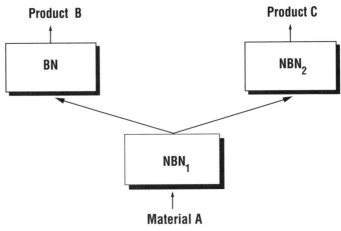

**Case 10: Non-Bottleneck Feeds Material A
to a Bottleneck to Make Product B and
to a Non-Bottleneck to Make Product C**

loss of system throughput. Resource NBN_1 has to process additional amounts of material A to replace the misallocated material. If NBN_1 has any problems obtaining and processing the required replacement material, this can turn resource NBN_1 into a temporary bottleneck and further aggravate the starvation problem at BN. The overall impact is an additional loss of system throughput.

Case 11 – Non-Bottleneck Feeds Two Different Materials to Non-Bottlenecks, Making Two Different Products

This case is represented in Figure 2.15, and is an extension of Case 3. Non-bottleneck NBN_1 processes materials for products A and B. Product A material is next processed at non-bottleneck resource NBN_2, while product B material proceeds to non-bottleneck NBN_3. We generalize this case by assuming that NBN_2 and NBN_3 are different resources. However, we also describe the slightly different implications if NBN_2 and NBN_3 are the same resource.

Resource NBN_1 can be overactivated to produce excess units of material for either product A or product B. Resources NBN_2 and NBN_3 can be overactivated only if extra material is available. That is, NBN_2 and NBN_3 can only be overactivated if NBN_1 is first overactivated.

If resource NBN_1 is overactivated on material for product A, inventory of product A material accumulates, either in front of NBN_2, or beyond NBN_2 depending on the relative rates of NBN_1 and NBN_2 production.

If NBN_1 is overactivated on product A material, the delay in switching over to the production of product B may cause additional problems. Resource NBN_1, although activated, is working on the wrong material. Meanwhile NBN_3 is starved for material while falling further behind schedule. As a result, NBN_1 and/or NBN_3 may become temporary bottlenecks in the timely production of product. This may affect the plant's ability to ship product B on time.

If resource NBN_1 is overactivated on material for product B, the same situation prevails with the only differences being the obvious ones. There will be a build up of inventory of material for product B, and there may be difficulty in shipping product A on time due to temporary bottlenecks.

Now consider the special case where NBN_2 and NBN_3 are the same resource. Problems arise if NBN_1 is much faster than the NBN_2/NBN_3 resource. In that case, NBN_1 has the capability to keep materials for both product A and product B readily available at the NBN_2/NBN_3 resource. This then allows the NBN_2/NBN_3 resource the opportunity to overactivate by producing too much of one product at the expense of the other. Once again, the NBN_2/NBN_3 resource cannot be overactivated unless NBN_1 has first been overactivated by supplying more material than needed to meet scheduled shipments.

FIGURE 2.15

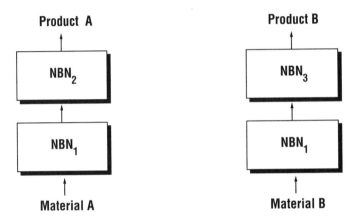

Case 11: Non-Bottleneck Feeds Two Different Materials to Non-Bottlenecks, Making Two Different Products

Case 12 – Non-Bottleneck Feeds the Same Material to Non-Bottlenecks That Make Two Different Products

This case is represented in Figure 2.16, and is also an extension of Case 3. A single type of material (A) is first processed at the non-bottleneck resource, NBN_1, then processed by NBN_2 to make product B or NBN_3 to make product C. We generalize this case by assuming that NBN_2 and NBN_3 are different resources. However, we also describe the slightly different implications if NBN_2 and NBN_3 are the same resource.

All of the resources can be overactivated. However, in this case, either NBN_2 or NBN_3 can be overactivated without the overactivation of NBN_1.

Let's first consider the possibilities if NBN_1 is overactivated. Overactivation of NBN_1 alone results in accumulation of inventory of material A. If either NBN_2 or NBN_3 are also overactivated, this extra material at least partially exists as excess product B and/or product C. Note that the availability of extra A material also allows for higher levels of overactivation by NBN_2 or NBN_3 than would otherwise be possible. In this scenario, it is possible for all resources to have very high activation levels without good overall system performance.

Any overactivation of either NBN_2 or NBN_3 results in excess inventory of

FIGURE 2.16

Case 12: Non-Bottleneck Feeds the Same Material to Non-Bottlenecks That Make Two Different Products

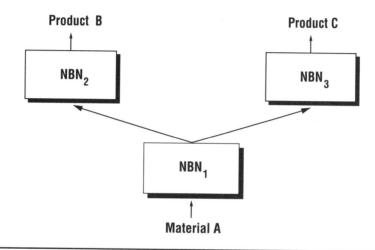

product B or C. Importantly, such overactivation of NBN_2 or NBN_3 may involve material misallocation. For example, let's suppose that NBN_2 is overactivated. If NBN_1 has not been overactivated, NBN_3 will not have sufficient material to meet its scheduled production of product C. It also causes an additional load on resource NBN_1 to supply material for NBN_3. This may cause NBN_1 and/or NBN_3 to become temporary bottlenecks, reducing the plant's ability to ship product C on time.

What if NBN_2 and NBN_3 are the same resource? As described in Case 8, overactivation and subsequent material misallocation can be encouraged by a poorly controlled system. For example, when excessively large process batches are run at the NBN_2/NBN_3 resource, this generates excess inventories of one product while creating shortages of the other product.

Two products, Non-Dedicated Resources, and an Assembly Operation

In considering the extensions to Case 5 with two products involved, it is important to note that it is the assembly operation that makes this case different from Cases 1, 2 and 3. As the discussion in the previous section demonstrates, the distinction between resource misallocation and material misallocation is critical. Cases 13 and 14 are designed to illustrate these two categories of misallocation.

Case 13 – Two Different Products are Assembled from Unique Materials, and Some of the Materials are Processed by a Common Resource

Consider the case represented in Figure 2.17. Material A is processed by resource NBN_1, materials B and C are processed by resource NBN_2, and material D is processed by NBN_3. Materials A and B are then used by assembly resource Z to make product E, while materials C and D are used by the same assembly resource Z to make product F. This case is generally representative of assembly operations where a variety of unique parts are required to assemble distinctly different end items.

Suppose NBN_2 is overactivated, producing material B to the extent that resource misallocation occurs. That is, material C, which is also processed by NBN_2 may not be available as needed at assembly. Of course, if even a single material is not available as needed at assembly, the scheduled assembly operation cannot be performed. This means assembly schedules slip and shipping deadlines are missed.

Misallocation can also occur at the assembly operation itself. Suppose resource NBN_1 and NBN_2 are overactivated and more units of materials A and B are available at assembly than needed to satisfy customer demand. If the assembly operation is allowed to overactivate, the assembly department continues

FIGURE 2.17

Case 13: Two Different Products are Assembled From Unique Materials Using a Shared Resource

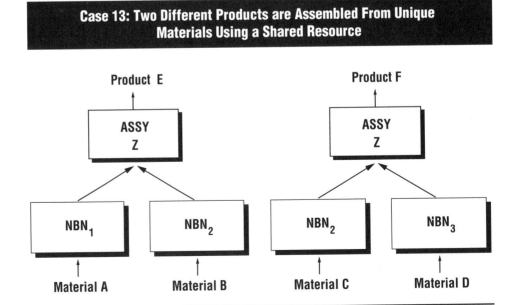

producing product E until materials A and B are depleted. Meanwhile, product F, which is needed to fill immediate customer orders, is not being assembled.

As in previous cases, when overactivation also leads to resource misallocation, excess inventory of one material or product is created at the expense of a shortage of another. This is particularly damaging in an assembly environment where many parts are needed to build a single product. Even a temporary shortage of a single part can lead to a late shipment.

Case 14 – Two Different Products are Assembled and Share a Common Material

In the case represented in Figure 2.18, materials A and B are required to produce product D at assembly operation Z; and materials B and C are required to produce product E at assembly operation Z. The key characteristic is that material B is a common part, used to produce both product D and product E.

Suppose assembly is scheduled to produce 100 units of product D and then 100 units of E. Further suppose that 200 units of material A and 200 units of material B are available, but material C is currently not available at assembly. Assembly has all the materials necessary to produce 200 units of product D, but cannot produce product E because material C is unavailable. If the assembly operation is allowed to make all 200 units of product D, material misallocation has occurred.

FIGURE 2.18

Case 14: Two Different Products are Assembled and Share a Common Material

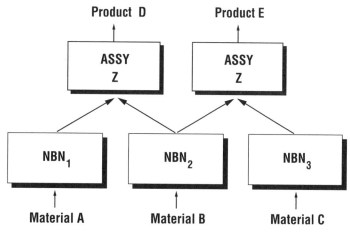

What is the result of the material misallocation? First, 100 units of product D wind up as excess finished goods. Second, and more damaging, when the 100 units of material C do show up, there is no material B available to assemble product E. In fact, material B will have to be replaced before product E can be assembled. Thus, the impact on the timely delivery of product E is not just the time the assembly resource is working on product D; it also includes the time to replace the misallocated material. As with previous cases of material misallocation, there is excess inventory of one product and production of the other is seriously affected.

RESOURCE & MATERIAL MISALLOCATION IN PLANT ENVIRONMENTS

Cases 6 through 14 analyze the implications of managing manufacturing operations that produce two products according to traditional guidelines of cost, efficiency, and activation. However, very few plants produce only two products. Fortunately, the logical extension of the analysis to cases that involve multiple products and multiple resources is a straightforward task. The complex product flows can simply be viewed as a combination of the cases. The consequences of overactivation can then be constructed from the known consequences for each of the individual cases. Since most manufacturing organizations still primarily use traditional performance measures of cost, activation, and efficiency, the results of traditional management practices can be predicted from a knowledge of the product flow diagram for that plant.

These cases demonstrate that managing manufacturing plants according to traditional guidelines often cause three major problems:

1.   Overactivation of resources;
2.   Resource misallocation; and
3.   Material misallocation.

It is possible to overactivate a resource without misallocating that resource away from the production of scheduled products. For example, if a resource has excess capacity, it can process all orders to meet required throughput levels and still be able to process additional excess materials. Of course, such overactivation of a resource always creates excess inventory somewhere in the system. This additional inventory may exist as either work in process or finished goods.

Resource misallocation implies that the resource is overactivated and therefore leads to excess inventory. But resource misallocation also implies that the overactivation of a resource on one product is performed at the expense of other products. This occurs when an excessive amount of one material or product is processed while other materials needed to maintain the required throughput are left waiting in queues. Resource misallocation can cause resources to become temporary bottlenecks, resulting in production delays that lead to missed due dates. Further, if the misallocation results in starvation of a true bottleneck, the system will lose throughput.

Material may be misallocated when a resource has the option of transforming a given piece of material into two or more different materials that are not interchangeable. The misallocation actually occurs when a resource is overactivated and processes material into a form that cannot be converted into immediate throughput.

Even though resource misallocation is harmful, material misallocation normally has even more severe consequences, because material misallocation requires a misallocation of the resource performing the task. Also, since the misallocated material must be replaced, an additional load is placed on all resources that have processed the material up to the point of misallocation. Therefore, in managing material flow through a plant, particular emphasis must be given to reducing the possibility of misallocating material.

The product flow diagram for a complex manufacturing operation is likely to contain most of the building blocks described in this chapter. However, some of the basic building blocks dominate the system, and thus determine the primary behaviors of the entire plant. This means that in some plants, the major problem is resource misallocation, while in other plants, material misallocation is the key problem.

In either case, there is a key point that must be re-emphasized. In every type of plant, there are enormous opportunities for overactivation, which leads to resource or material misallocation. However, opportunity by itself is not a problem. To cause significant damage, the opportunity to overactivate must be coupled with the encouragement to overactivate. Unfortunately, as these cases show, standard operating procedures and performance measurement systems based in the traditional cost-based system generate plenty of encouragement. Ultimately, resolving the problems means addressing the source of the encouragement.

Understanding the dominant resource-product interactions that characterize different manufacturing systems makes it possible to classify manufacturing systems into three basic categories. These categories are fully defined in Chapter 3 as V-plants, A-plants, and T-plants. This classification system provides a strong foundation for our discussion throughout the rest of the book. It also facilitates the further development of Synchronous Management control systems that can be systematically applied to all plants that exhibit similar characteristics and problems.

Chapter 3

V-A-T CLASSIFICATION
AND ANALYSIS

The value of a principle is the number of things it will explain.
– Ralph Waldo Emerson, 1883

"We're different!" Managers are quick to suggest that their plant is not like any other facility. The statement is both true and false. On one hand, every manufacturing organization has unique characteristics. But these characteristics are typically a function of company culture, management style, and established operating policies. On the other hand, despite each plant's uniqueness, every plant shares significant similarities with many others.

These similarities are derived from the resource-product interactions that characterize specific types of plants. As suggested in Chapter 2, all plants that have the same type of dominant building blocks and resource-product interactions have similar characteristics and problems. The dominant resource-product interactions that characterize different manufacturing environments provide the basis for classifying manufacturing plants into three major categories: V-plants, A-plants, and T-plants. Plants that exhibit significant characteristics of more than one of the three categories are referred to as combination plants.

In this chapter, we describe the basic characteristics of the three plant types, the consequences of traditional management practices of them, and give a brief overview of how the basic Synchronous Management strategies can be employed. As this chapter unfolds, it is important to realize that manufacturing plants evolve over time as a Synchronous Management environment develops, and that the particular set of problems facing management changes over time as the plant becomes increasingly synchronized. As a given set of problems is resolved, a new set of problems appears. But the plant will be operating at a higher level of performance.

In a given plant category, specific management actions implemented determine the nature of the new problems and opportunities that arise. As a result, it is not possible to identify all possible problems. Likewise, it is not possible to identify the particular Synchronous Management actions that could be implemented as a particular category of plant evolves toward synchronous operation. Therefore, this chapter assumes that plants are operating in a relatively traditional management mode and have not yet evolved significantly toward Synchronous Management practices.

V-PLANTS

V-plants consist of those plants that convert basic raw materials or partially processed items into a variety of end items, sold either as consumer goods or as materials or component parts for other manufacturers, including assembly plants.

Dominant Product Flow Characteristics of V-Plants

V-plants are dominated by resource-product interactions where a single product at one stage of processing can be transformed into several distinct products at the next stage. Such a point in the product flow is referred to as a divergence point, since at this stage the flow of material diverges in several directions. The product flow diagram for a plant exhibiting this basic divergence characteristic throughout the process is shown in Figure 3.1. Notice that the product flow diagram resembles the letter V, hence the name V-plant. [In addition, the different products share common resources at most stages of the process.]

A good example of a divergent process is found in a steel rolling mill, where sheets of steel are rolled, hardened, and cut to exact specifications. The first step in the process is annealing, where sheets of steel are softened in preparation for rolling. At the rolling operation, a given piece of steel may be rolled into any of a large number of different thicknesses. Rolling represents the first divergence point in the product flow diagram. At each additional divergence point, the number of distinctly different products continues to increase. For example, after leaving rolling, the steel goes through heat treat, where the material is tempered to any of a large number of combinations of desired strength and hardness characteristics. Finally, after heat treat, the steel is cut into the desired widths or strips at the slitting operation.

Figure 3.2 represents the product flow diagram for a typical steel rolling mill. The various steps involved in the process are identified on the left-hand side of the figure.

FIGURE 3.1

Typical Product Flow in a V-Plant

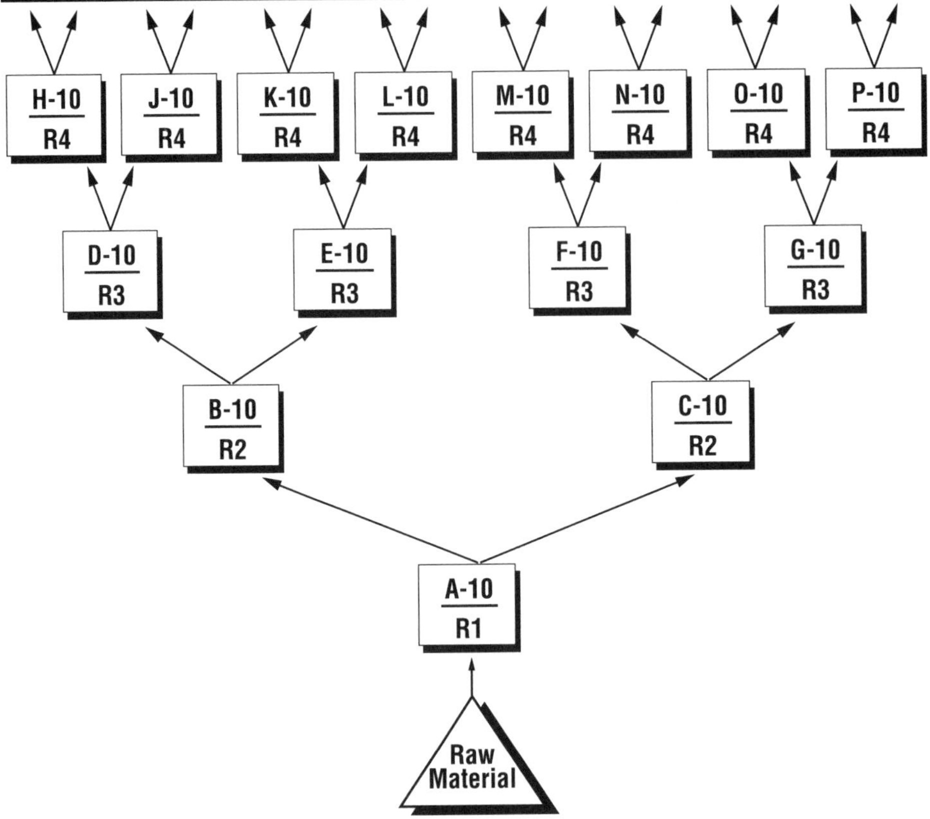

The number of different products that can be identified at each stage of the process is indicated on the right-hand side. Significantly, the same diagram that describes the product flow of a steel rolling mill could also describe the product flow for a textile plant. (See the V-plant case study in Chapter 4.)

Since the product flow diagram identifies the key characteristics of a manufacturing environment, it follows that two plants with similar product flow diagrams should exhibit similar business characteristics. Textile mills and steel mills, for example, share many characteristics and problems associated with the existence of divergence points.

FIGURE 3.2

Divergence of Products in a V-Plant (Steel Rolling Mill) as the Material Moves Through the Process

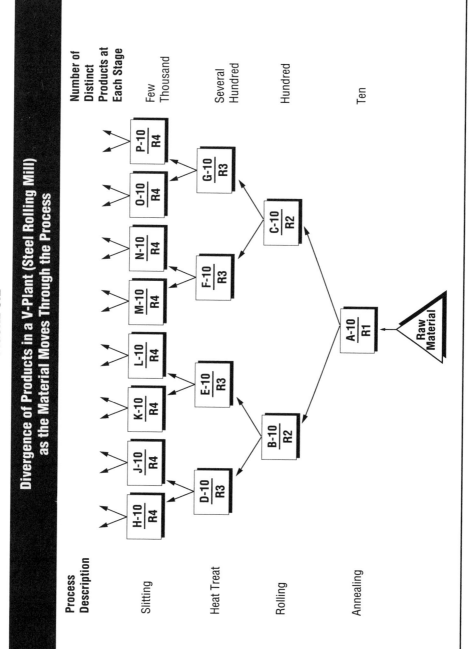

General Characteristics of V-Plants

The existence of divergence points gives rise to three primary characteristics found in V-plants, regardless of industry:

1. *The number of end items is large compared to the number of raw materials.* Because divergence points may exist at any stage of production, by the time several stages have been completed, the number of different products being processed can be very large.

2. *All end items sold by the plant are produced in essentially the same way.* All products are processed through the same basic operations and in the same sequence. For example, in steel rolling mills, every piece of finished product goes through the same sequence of annealing, rolling, heat treat, and slitting.

3. *The equipment is generally capital intensive and highly specialized.* Evolution into capital intensive production is not difficult to understand. Since every product goes through the same sequence of operations, there are relatively few basic operations performed repeatedly. Because the focus of improvement under traditional cost-based systems is to reduce the product's direct-labor content, the "solution" chosen is specialized, high-volume, capital equipment. Direct labor content is effectively reduced. But the unfortunate side effect is a loss of production flexibility.

Consequences of Traditional Management Practices in V-Plants

In plants dominated by divergence points, each individual divergence point represents an opportunity for material misallocation. When there is a sequence of divergence points, the potential for misallocation increases arithmetically. Any resulting material misallocation results in excess inventory of some products and a shortage of others. In most cases, the excess inventory simply inflates finished-goods stocks, but sometimes it exists as high levels of work in process. Meanwhile, the material shortage creates stockouts and a constant scramble throughout the system to expedite materials necessary to fill customer orders.

Identifying the Problems   The types of problems encountered in a V-plant depend on whether the system has a bottleneck resource. If there is no bottleneck, the entire plant has extra capacity. The mere existence of extra capacity, coupled with the numerous opportunities to misallocate material, is sufficient to cause significant overactivation and excessively large inventories (of the wrong products). If the plant is also managed according to traditional cost-based performance measures, there are built-in incentives to overactivate the resources, and the magnitude of the problems is greatly increased.

If there is a bottleneck (or CCR) in the system, the following occurs:

1. Material misallocation and overproduction ahead of the bottleneck creates a large inventory in front of the bottleneck. But because of the misallocation, this inventory is likely not to be the material necessary to meet customer demand. To meet its utilization criteria, the bottleneck is forced to process the wrong products. As a result, throughput is lost and shipping schedules are jeopardized. The bottleneck also becomes subject to additional disruptions from expediters as the plant scrambles to meet shipping schedules.

2. Misallocation beyond the bottleneck has two major consequences. The first is finished-goods inventory of the wrong products. Second is an increased load on the bottleneck because the bottleneck has to make up for the misallocated material that it has already processed. Again, throughput is lost and delivery performance is poor since a bottleneck's capacity is less than or equal to the market demand placed upon it.

Managers of V-plants are often puzzled when, despite holding large finished-goods inventory, they have to scramble to meet market requirements. They invariably blame the constantly changing demand pattern. While demand changes do occur, most of the problems are self-inflicted. The inability to respond to the market is not in spite of the inventory, but because of the inventory. Since excess inventory is created by misallocation, the available inventory should not be expected to match customer orders. In addition, every misallocation causes increased work loads at all upstream work centers and further constrains the system's ability to produce the required product mix in a timely manner.

Management should understand that this misallocation is not committed in a covert and undisciplined fashion. The misallocation is generally the result of carefully planned managerial actions that are intended to enhance efficiency and reduce cost. Typical examples of these actions include accelerating the release of material to increase levels of utilization to "acceptable levels" and using excessively large batch sizes.

A major factor in the overactivation and misallocation that occurs in V-plants is the lengthy setup time often required by V-plant resources. The long set-up times are a typical by-product of the normal evolution of V-plants into capital-intensive operations. The lengthy setups encourage production supervisors to increase batch sizes, to minimize setups by combining batches whenever possible, and to produce families of products together. These actions are consistent with traditional performance measures, but often cause production priorities to be ignored and production lead times to become unpredictable. In addition, the large production batches cause manufacturing lead times to increase. Thus, managing according to traditional practices results in large and unpredictable lead times, which ultimately leads to missed due dates.

To sum up, some of the major concerns facing managers of V-plants are:

1. Finished-goods inventory is too large.
2. Customer service is poor.
3. Manufacturing managers are uncomfortable with the apparent constant change in demand.
4. Marketing managers complain about the lack of responsiveness from manufacturing.
5. Interdepartmental conflicts are common within the manufacturing area.

Conventional Strategies for Improving Performance   In most V-plants, management's approach to improving performance focuses on improving customer service and reducing production costs. The conventional approach to improving customer service normally includes increasing the level of finished-goods inventory and improving forecasting ability. The conventional approach to reducing production costs includes reducing the amount of direct labor in the product, reducing scrap, and improving yields.

Faced with large and unpredictable lead times, managers rationalize that the only way to maintain a reasonable level of customer service is to carry finished-goods inventory. Thus, the excessive finished-goods inventory occurs not only because of material misallocation, but also because it is planned. However, given the large number of final products typically produced by V-plants, the actual finished-goods inventory usually matches poorly with market demand. This becomes a rationale for even higher levels of finished goods.

The painful realization that carrying finished-goods inventory has not helped improve customer service has caused managers a great deal of frustration. The traditional attempt to solve this problem has been to try to improve the company's forecasting ability. But in a competitive market, the ability to accurately forecast demand is severely limited. The producer would like to have firm orders as far out in time as possible, to enable better planning. But the customer prefers a short lead time for placing orders to keep its options open as long as possible. In a competitive market, the balance definitely tilts in the customer's favor. The resulting forecast accuracy in competitive markets can be described by the curves shown in Figure 3.3.

The fact that total sales can be predicted with some degree of accuracy is of no help to manufacturing managers. They must manufacture specific products. Even producing according to forecasted demand for product family is of no value. Manufacturing managers must work with the forecast for specific products, or stockkeeping units (SKUs). The accuracy of this type of forecast is extremely poor, and the longer the required production lead time, the less useful the forecast becomes.

FIGURE 3.3

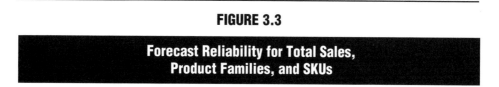

Forecast Reliability for Total Sales, Product Families, and SKUs

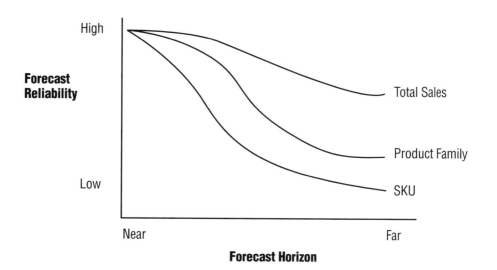

Because of the inefficiencies typically found in V-plants, in a highly competitive market management often exerts great pressure to reduce production costs. One traditional approach is to reduce the product's direct labor content. This takes the plant further in the direction of capital-intensive operations and specialized equipment. The result is reduced labor content, but usually at the expense of reduced flexibility. This is too high a price to pay in today's competitive market.

Another conventional approach to reducing product cost is to reduce the cost of poor quality, including increased cost in scrapped material, additional labor for rework, and warranty cost. This requires that the problem areas be identified and engineering solutions found. Efforts to improve quality should be applauded. But unless the improvement efforts are consistent with the principles of Synchronous Management, the system-wide impact is likely to be disappointing.

Synchronous Management Applied to V-Plants: An Overview

The recommended Synchronous Management strategy to improve performance of a V-plant is very different from the traditional approach. This strategy requires that the key competitive elements be viewed in terms of the operational measures of throughput, inventory, and operating expense.

As shown in Volume I, the best way to improve customer service is to reduce manufacturing lead time. Reducing production lead time is equivalent to reducing work-in-process inventory in the system. Thus, improving service translates into reducing overall work-in-process inventory. This strategy is exactly the opposite of the traditional approach of trying to meet customer demand by increasing the amount of inventory carried.

In order to understand how to reduce product cost, it is necessary to consider how each decision and action will affect throughput (T), inventory (I), and operating expense (OE). The desired approach is to pursue those activities that increase T but reduce I and OE, ideally all at the same time.

An increase in throughput requires that the company not only produce more, but sell more. To increase sales, the company's competitive position must be improved. For example, it may be necessary to improve the service level, which requires a reduction in the manufacturing lead time. To actually make more products with the same resources requires the proper identification and management of the system's constraints. The principles of Synchronous Management provide the necessary guidance.

A reduction in overall inventory levels will immediately affect the company's operating expense by decreasing inventory carrying cost. But a reduction in work-in-process inventory also positively affects the company's competitive elements and increases system throughput.

Reducing operating expense involves taking actions that eliminate some wasteful elements of production, such as quality problems. In the conventional approach to improving a manufacturing operation, management actions focus on reductions in operating expense as guided by the standard cost system. In Synchronous Management, the focus is not on calculated cost reductions, but on the global measures of T, I, and OE. Engineering and manufacturing activities are given priority based on the expected impact on these global measures.

The exact procedures for applying Synchronous Management concepts to a specific V-plant vary greatly from one plant to the next, and general procedures are described in detail in the next chapter. However, the general application for V-plants is as follows.

The systematic procedure begins with identification of the physical constraints (capacity and material) that limit system performance. In the case of a V-plant, there is usually only one CCR. The location of that CCR in the product flow is critical. The extent that management can influence which of the several resources will be a CCR becomes an important strategic decision.

Once the CCR has been identified, buffer requirements for the system should be determined. This involves deciding on the size and placement of both stock and time buffers. Remember that stock buffers are used to help service customer demand and should be located according to specific needs, while time buffers are designed to protect the system throughput from the normal disruptions that occur in manufacturing. In a V-plant, time buffers should be placed in front of CCRs and before shipping. (Chapter 9 of Volume I has a more detailed discussion of stock buffers and time buffers).

The derived master schedule for the plant must be consistent with the capabilities of the previously identified constraints. Once the master schedule has been developed, the next step is to ensure that all resources are managed to support the planned product flow. The schedule control points in a V-plant occur at material release, divergence points, and CCRs. Given the nature of the V-plant, it is likely that many work centers in this type of environment will be schedule control points.

A-PLANTS

In its simplest terms, a plant that builds relatively few distinct products, such as large generators, composed of mostly different components, is an A-plant.

Dominant Product Flow Characteristics of A-Plants

A-plants are dominated by resource-product interactions where two or more component parts are assembled together to yield only one parent item. Such points in the product flow are commonly known as assembly points. These points are also referred to as convergence points, since the flow of material converges from several different sources to form a single item. A typical product flow diagram for a plant exhibiting this basic convergence characteristic throughout the process is shown in Figure 3.4. In this type of plant, the number of purchased materials greatly exceeds the number of end items. Several levels of subassemblies may be required prior to the final assembly operation. Since the overall product flow for the plant is convergent rather than divergent, the product flow diagram resembles an inverted V, thus the name A-plant.

The manufacture of a jet engine is an excellent example of an assembly operation with a large number of components. To build a jet engine, many of the various components are first combined into subassemblies. In fact, most of the major component parts are subassemblies composed of several hundred parts each. The product flow diagram contains a very large number of purchased materials, and manufactured components, all of which converge to a single product. The product flow diagram for a jet engine assembly plant has a very wide base and a very narrow top.

General Characteristics of A-Plants

A-plants are dominated by the existence of convergent assembly points, and share four common characteristics.

1. *Assembly of a large number of manufactured parts into a relatively small number of end items.* Each assembly point represents a decrease in the number of distinct part numbers (two or more parts are combined to create one new part). After only a few assembly operations, the number of distinct items decreases dramatically.

2. *The component parts are unique to specific end items.* This is a key feature that distinguishes A-plants from T-plants. For example, consider the component parts of a jet engine. Each component part, such as a compressor blade, is unique to a specific type of jet engine. Although every jet engine has a compressor blade, the blades are not interchangeable from one engine type to another.

FIGURE 3.4

Typical Product Flow Diagram for a Single Product in an A-Plant

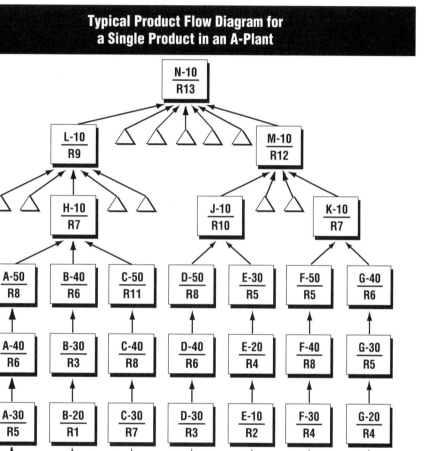

△ = Raw Material or Purchased Components

3. *The production routings for the component parts are highly dissimilar.* It is not at all uncommon that one manufactured part involves 50 operations while another part, required for the same assembly, involves very few operations and at totally different resources.

4. *The machines and tools used in the manufacturing process tend to be general purpose.* In an A-plant, the same machine is often used to process a large number of different parts. In fact, a given part may be processed at the same machine several times in the course of its routing. Thus, much of the machinery is usually quite flexible, in contrast to the highly specialized equipment found in V-plants.

Consequences of Traditional Management Practices in A-Plants

A-plants are dominated by the resource-product interactions that occur at convergent assembly points. As a result, there is usually very little opportunity for material misallocation because the parts being processed are mostly unique to specific end items. Instead, A-plants are characterized by the problems that result from resource misallocation. In A-plants, resource misallocation is usually caused by products that are processed and/or transferred in excessively large batches. Large batch sizes are often the result of attempts to cut production costs by reducing the number of setups.

Identifying the Problems   Processing products in excessively large batches causes a wave-like flow of material. And the use of large batches at one work center causes downstream work centers to receive material in a very erratic fashion. This erratic material flow creates two problems that appear to be contradictory, but are both typical of A-plants. The first problem is unsatisfactory resource utilization. Because of the erratic material flow, work centers often have to wait for material to process. This waiting causes a low level of resource usage. The second problem is the frequent use of overtime to meet promised delivery dates. The overtime is required because the work centers are idle for long periods of time due to a lack of material. Then, when the material finally arrives, it is too late to complete the remaining operations on time, and management must resort to the use of overtime to try to meet due dates.

Just as with material misallocation in V-plants, resource misallocation in A-plants is the result of well-intentioned actions that are inappropriately focused on cost and efficiency, not of malevolent employees or managers, or a lack of discipline on the shop floor. Misallocations are the result of planned managerial actions such as excessively large batch sizing (to reduce costs) and accelerated release of material (to maintain labor efficiencies).

The same feast-or-famine situation commonly experienced by non-assembly work centers also exists at the assembly operation. However, unlike other work centers, assembly normally requires that all parts be available before processing can begin. The arrival of a large batch of a single part is not sufficient to allow assembly to begin. The wave-like material flow throughout the plant makes it unlikely that all of the component parts will be available when needed, so assembly is constantly short of one or more parts required to assemble the product. These missing parts must be tracked down and expedited to assembly. Because of the wave-like material flow, the piles of inventory constantly change location. This can give the false appearance of bottlenecks that seem to "wander" about the plant. As a result, shortages occur frequently, causing constant expediting. In fact, in many A-plants, it is not stretching the truth to say that expediting is "a way of life."

Managers of A-plants typically have trouble comprehending the apparent inconsistencies that plague their operation. Despite the existence of large work-in-process and component-part inventory, there is a severe shortage of parts. Ironically, the resource misallocation that creates excessive inventory also causes shortages and the need to expedite.

The unsatisfactory level of resource utilization and the use of overtime cause the operation to be less productive than expected. This also means that production costs are higher than expected. The apparent contradictions between low utilization levels and the use of overtime, and between high inventory levels and constant expediting, are difficult for managers to understand. These contradictions also create the impression that the operation is out of control. Managers often conclude that the manufacturing process is out of control because the information and control systems are inadequate.

In summary, the major concerns facing managers of A-plants are:

1. Assembly is continually complaining of shortages.
2. Unplanned overtime is excessive.
3. Resource utilization (not activation) is unsatisfactory.
4. Production bottlenecks seem to wander about the plant.
5. The entire operation appears to be out of control.

Conventional Strategies for Improving Performance   The traditional approach to improving performance of an A-plant usually emphasizes reducing unit cost of the product and improving control of the operation. In an attempt to reduce product cost, management typically stresses the following:

1. *Improve the efficiency of the operation.*   This effort is specifically directed at improving the efficiency of the direct labor involved in production. The low utilization seems to suggest the existence of too many production workers. Hence, in A-plants, there is often pressure to reduce the size of the labor force.

2. *Control the use of overtime.*   Because of the low utilization rates, the use of overtime is rigorously scrutinized and grudgingly approved. As a result, approval of overtime requests is often delayed. This tends to aggravate the problem, making it even more difficult to meet schedules.

3. *Focus engineering efforts on reducing the unit cost of production.*   This often means replacing manual processes with automated processes. If this results in a loss of flexibility or longer set-up times, the result of automation may be to further aggravate the problem of erratic material flow.

The problem of lack of control is often addressed by attempting to implement the latest computerized information and control system. In large organizations, this is a mammoth task. Suffice it to say, a new computer information system is not the answer to the problems if all that is done is to automate mistakes.

The problem of designating and successfully implementing a single integrated system is made more difficult by the fact that different functional areas of the organization have different criteria for defining good information and control. Each functional unit lobbies for a system designed to assist in achieving its local goals. Since local goals often conflict with the global goal, suboptimization is the natural result. For example, the marketing/sales function is always looking for new ways to differentiate the company's product from the competition. This often leads to design or engineering changes. But engineering changes can cause major problems in manufacturing and are often accompanied by a loss of efficiency (at least temporarily). Thus, the local goals of marketing and manufacturing conflict. Thoughtful deliberation is needed to develop appropriate goals and guidelines for both functional areas that maximize overall organizational goals.

Synchronous Management Applied to A-Plants: An Overview

In most A-plants, the key competitive issues are a function of the major problems (poor resource utilization, excessive overtime, part shortages, and wandering bottlenecks) identified earlier. While it is likely that these problems will lead to poor customer service, the critical issue in most A-plants is that product costs are excessively high. In order for A-plants to reduce product costs, it is necessary to develop and implement a strategy that eliminates the root problems.

The Synchronous Management strategy to improve performance of an A-plant is very different from the traditional approach. The primary cause of the feast or famine syndrome in A-plants is the wave-like flow of material. Thus, measures must be taken to eliminate or drastically reduce this phenomenon. The solution is obvious. The wave-like material flow must be replaced by a more uniform and synchronized flow. To reduce inventory levels and establish a more uniform material flow, the process and transfer batch sizes should be as small as possible. A uniform flow enables the workload on the various assembly and non-assembly work centers to be leveled. This will largely solve the problem of low utilization and the excessive use of overtime to compensate for this lost capacity.

The drum-buffer-rope logistical system can be used to help establish the necessary synchronized material flow. The general procedures that exist for implementing the Synchronous Management concepts in an A-plant are described in Chapter 5. But here is the general approach.

First, the constraints that limit plant performance must be identified. A-plants, unlike V-plants, are often characterized by more than one CCR. And the procedures used to identify CCRs in an A-plant are vastly different from the procedures developed for V-plants.

After the constraints have been identified, the time and stock buffers must be determined. Stock buffers can be used to great advantage in an A-plant, but in a much different way than in V-plants. Given the nature of the A-plant process, it is of little advantage to hold stocks of some component parts as work in process in anticipation of customer demand. But stock buffers can be used to simplify the problem of controlling a large number of the minor component parts required for assembly, especially those that may be common to several different end products. The time buffers in an A-plant serve the purpose of protecting the throughput from the numerous disruptions that exist in this type of manufacturing environment. In an A-plant, time buffers should be placed before CCRs, before assembly, and before shipping.

The various system constraints must be considered when deriving the master production schedule. Once the MPS is determined, all resources in an A-plant must be managed so as to fully support the planned product flow established by the MPS. The product flow for the entire plant can be successfully managed by controlling a relatively few schedule control points. The schedule control points in an A-plant are at material release, assembly operations, and CCRs. Clearly, given the large number of different resources that exist in a typical A-plant, the number of resources will normally greatly exceed the number of schedule control points.

T-PLANTS

The critical feature of T-plants is that final products are assembled using a number of component parts, most of which are common to many different final products. This situation usually occurs in companies that produce product families that have a variety of options or offer a number of different packaging variations. In addition, most manufacturers of household and small appliances are T-plants.

Dominant Product Flow Characteristics of T-Plants

In T-plants, a relatively small number of component parts may be combined to form a large number of different assemblies. As a result, the number of end items can greatly exceed the number of component parts. The product flow diagram thus expands at the top, resembling the letter T. Hence, the name T-plant.

T-plants are typically found in assemble-to-order environments, where the required customer lead times are relatively short, component procurement and processing time is relatively long, and demand for the individual products is difficult to forecast. As a result, the components necessary to produce the various products are master scheduled and stocked prior to final assembly. The resulting interactions between the available components, required products, and limited resources dominate the T-plant environment.

The final assembly region of the T-plant product flow diagram is referred to as the top of the structure, while the region containing all the processes prior to final assembly is referred to as the base of the structure. The top of the T-plant diagram always has the same basic structure: a set of mostly common component parts exploding into a much larger number of end items. The pure T-plant case is shown in Figure 3.5, where a number of final products (some of which are identified as E through L) are generated from a pool of common component parts (some of which are identified as A through D). Notice that the base of the T-plant structure in Figure 3.5 contains no divergence or assembly points. A pure T-plant is defined here as one where the base structure is essentially an "I" shape. That is, purchased components are neither subassembled nor processed through divergence points. In this environment, the number of purchased components is essentially equal to the number of components used in final assembly.

A relatively simple example of a T-plant is a factory that manufactures household door locks. In order to qualify as a pure T-plant, the lock components are purchased as mostly finished parts. Any remaining processing on the component parts at the plant does not involve divergence points or subassembly. The major components of a cylindrical door lock are the inner rose, inner knob, lock body, striker plate, outer rose, and outer knob. Each of these component parts may come in a number of variations. Moreover, each variation of every component is common to many similar locks. For example, the same lock body can be used with the same style knob, but with different finishes, different style knobs for each finish, and so on. In addition, any one of the knobs used with a given lock body can be assembled with several different lock bodies. The result of this high degree of commonality is that from a finite number of knobs, lock bodies, striker plates, and roses, an almost endless variety of complete locks can be assembled. This creates the sudden explosion of the product flow diagram to create the T shape.

The following numerical example demonstrates the very large number of different end items that are theoretically possible from a limited number of interchangeable component parts. Suppose that any of the 6 component parts of the cylindrical door lock can be combined in any fashion with the other 5 components parts. If there are just four variations of each component part, then the number of possible end products is $4 \times 4 \times 4 \times 4 \times 4 \times 4 = 4,096$. That is, from only 24 distinctly different component parts, 4,096 end products are possible. If there were 10 variations of each component part, then there would be 60 distinct component parts, but 1 million different end items.

General Characteristics of T-Plants

At first glance, A-plants and T-plants are very similar. It is true that they are both dominated by the interactions that occur at assembly operations, and many plants that have the distinctive T-plant characteristics at final assembly have an A-plant type of base structure. But the product flow diagram illustrates that these two types of plants have major differences, especially that the nature of the assembly points are exactly opposite. In A-plants the assembly points represent an area of convergence in the product flow, while in T-plants the assembly points represent an area of divergence in the product flow. Thus, A-plants are characterized by what we refer to as "convergent assembly points," while T-plants

FIGURE 3.5

Partial Product Flow Diagram for a Pure T-Plant

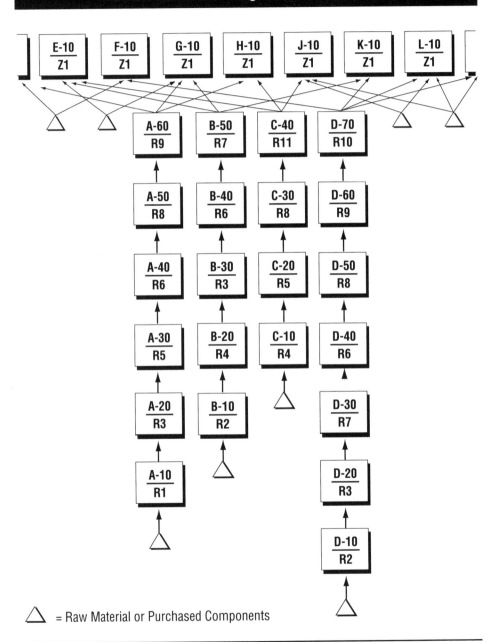

△ = Raw Material or Purchased Components

are characterized by "divergent assembly points." Additionally, the component parts used in final assembly in T-plants are common to many end items, while in A-plants the component parts are generally unique to a specific end item.

T-plants and V-plants share the common characteristic of divergence. However, in T-plants, the divergence points are concentrated in one section (assembly) of the production process. In V-plants, the material flow is dominated by non-assembly divergence points throughout the process.

To summarize, these are the four distinguishing characteristics of T-plants:

1. *A number of common manufactured and/or purchased component parts are assembled together to produce the final product.*
2. *The component parts are common to many different end items.*
3. *The production routings for the component parts do not include divergent or assembly processes.*
4. *The production routings for those component parts that require processing are usually quite dissimilar.*

To be sure, our definition of a classic T-plant is somewhat restrictive. Some individuals may prefer to allow the base structure of a T-plant to include processes that are dominated by either divergence or assembly points. However, we have elected to categorize these types of plants as combination plants, which will be discussed later in this chapter.

Consequences of Traditional Management Practices in T-Plants

In T-plants, the dominant interactions occur at divergent assembly points, featuring common component parts. Because of this, T-plants are dominated by the effects of material misallocation at the assembly operation.

Identifying the Problems   In order to demonstrate the effects of material misallocation in a T-plant, consider the case shown in Figure 3.6. This simple case shows the assembly-level structure of the product flow diagram, which involves component parts A, B, C and D, and assembled products E, F, G and H. The arrows between the component parts and the assemblies define how each product is made. The figure also indicates the available inventory (stock) of each component part. Now suppose that an order for 100 units of product E is due to be assembled and shipped. The assembly of product E, which requires 100 units of part A and 100 units of part B, is next on the assembly schedule. As seen in Figure 3.6, although there are 100 units of part B in stock, part A is not currently

FIGURE 3.6

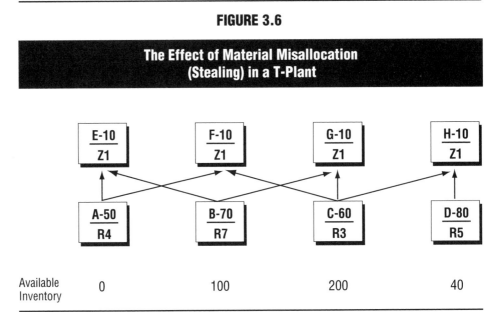

The Effect of Material Misallocation (Stealing) in a T-Plant

available. An expediter will have to be dispatched to accelerate the arrival of part A to the assembly operation. (With luck, the needed material will be somewhere in the plant.) In the meantime, the assembly operation is idle. Although product E cannot be made, there is an adequate supply of material to produce 100 units of product G, which requires parts B and C. If the decision is made to activate the assembly operation and assemble product G, even though it is not currently scheduled, then part B and part C will have been misallocated.

The misallocation of part B to produce units of G (for which there is no current demand) leads to the inescapable effect of all material misallocation, namely inventory. Finished-goods inventory of product G will have been created. But the harm of this particular misallocation is more severe than the creation of inventory. When component A is finally expedited to the assembly area, it is no longer possible to assemble product E. This is because the part B component required to assemble product E has been consumed in the production of product G. Part B, of which there was sufficient stock in the beginning, will now have to be expedited in order to process the order for product E. Meanwhile, the sales order for product E remains unfilled.

Misallocation of part B has created inventory and at least a temporary loss of throughput. Furthermore, while part B is being expedited, the newly acquired stock of part A can be assembled with part C to produce units of product F. Such further activation of the assembly operation and material misallocation creates additional excess inventory and starts the vicious cycle of component part shortages all over again.

A term often used to describe this specific situation in T-plants is "stealing." (Manufacturing people in most T-plants understand this concept all too well.) As a result of stealing, finished-goods inventory is unduly high in most T-plants. Also, because of stealing, the plant's due date performance for customer orders is unsatisfactory. In T-plants where stealing is rampant, it is common to find that the number of orders completed early is roughly equal to the number of orders completed late. In fact, in many T-plants about 30 to 40 percent of the orders are completed early, while about 30 to 40 percent are completed late. In general, the severity of the problem is directly related to the degree of commonality of the components and the number of components required for a typical assembly.

The component manufacturing areas (which may be separate plants) must deal with the inefficiency of constant expediting. It appears to them that the managers of the assembly department have little ability to assess their component part needs. Because of the assembly department's perceived inability to adequately forecast its requirements, managers of the component part manufacturing areas often try to compensate. In an attempt to make sure that the necessary parts are available when requested, the manufacturing managers inflate their forecasts. The result is that component parts production is based on an overly generous estimate of actual usage. The overestimates, coupled with the desire to reduce the number of setups, result in batch sizes that are much too large.

The large batch sizes cause lengthy production lead times. The long production lead times, combined with the difficulty of predicting the demand for specific products, results in T-plants having problems similar to V-plants—a large finished-goods inventory (even larger than the generous one planned) and a poor match between what is in stock and actual demand. It is not uncommon for T-plants to have very low inventory turns (often less than six turns per year).

The large batch sizes for component parts may cause the same wave-like material flow as in A-plants. If this occurs, all of the problems associated with the wave-like flow will be present in T-plants, including low resource utilization, frequent overtime at underutilized resources, and continuous shortages of parts at assembly (further aggravated by stealing).

The effect of material misallocation eventually filters back to the purchasing department. Just as the component part production schedule is disrupted by undisciplined assembly activities, the purchase of materials and components is also adversely affected by changing production requirements. The result is that the purchasing department has little faith in material forecasts based on scheduled usage. Instead, purchasing may rely on experience to plan material purchases. Since the actual usage figures are often greater than forecasted, purchasing inflates orders. As a result, raw material stocks are too large. Thus, at all stages of the operation, from raw material stocks to finished goods, inventory is likely to be excessive.

The discussion has focused on some of the major concerns facing T-plant managers, such as:

1. Large finished-goods and component part inventories.
2. Poor due date performance (30-40 percent early and 30-40 percent late).
3. Excessive fabrication lead times.
4. Unsatisfactory resource utilization in fabrication.
5. Fabrication and assembly act as separate, unsynchronized plants.

Conventional Strategies for Improving Performance   The primary concern in most T-plants is the generally poor level of customer service. In this context, customer service may be viewed as either the proficiency in meeting promised shipping dates or the ability to ship off the shelf. A typical secondary concern is high product costs. These two problems are closely related.

A high level of customer service is difficult to achieve because of the chaos caused by stealing at assembly. And as a result, it is unlikely that the products actually produced will match scheduled production. Therefore, many customer orders are shipped late. Satisfying demand off the shelf is also difficult because having the required mix of products in inventory is highly unlikely.

Carrying higher levels of inventory is a conventional approach to address these problems. Higher levels of work in process are used to decouple manufacturing operations, while increased levels of finished goods are designed to improve deliveries off the shelf. But this approach has proved unsuccessful. In fact, because of the adverse effects on manufacturing lead time and operating expenses, an increased level of inventory is actually detrimental to overall company performance.

Many T-plants are found in the consumer products sector, where the product price is often perceived to be a major (sometimes, the primary) competitive element. Thus, in addition to trying to improve customer service, management typically makes every effort to reduce the cost and price of the product. As a result, the conventional approach to improving performance in a T-plant generally includes the following two strategies:

1. Improve deliveries off the shelf by developing better product forecasting techniques and improving inventory planning and control. In T-plants, extensive analysis of forecasting models and available and planned inventories are frequently undertaken. However, in highly competitive environments, it is usually difficult to develop accurate forecasts for specific products. In addition, due to the chaos caused by stealing component parts, any widespread effort to plan inventories in anticipation of forecasted future demand is doomed to fail.

2. Reduce product cost by improving operational efficiency. This effort consists of attempting to improve the operation by focusing attention on wasteful elements such as frequent setups and overtime. But consider, for example, what happens if managers try to economize on setups. As the number of setups in the system is reduced, the batch sizes are increased, and the wave-like material flow becomes worse. This merely aggravates the problems of production lead times, inventories, and the need for overtime. The true efficiency of the plant deteriorates.

The improvement effort may also be directed at reducing product cost through product design. If product design concentrates primarily on the calculated unit cost, the result may be a proliferation of products. This happens as each component is "optimally" designed to meet the requirements of the end product at the least cost. The impact this has on inventory and delivery performance is devastating. The total cost for the plant is likely to actually increase due to the dramatic increase in inventory and the required number of setups.

Another avenue for supposed improvement is to emphasize the use of new technologies to replace manual processes with automated processes. However, this will be beneficial only if throughput can be increased or if labor costs can be reduced sufficiently to pay for the new equipment. In addition, there must be no significant loss of flexibility due to increased set-up times. Because of the forecasting issue, the penalty for lost flexibility is more severe in a T-plant than in an A-plant.

Synchronous Management Applied to T-Plants: An Overview

The Synchronous Management approach to improving business performance in a T-plant is very different from the conventional approach. The primary problem faced by most T-plants is poor delivery performance. Secondary problems include excessive inventory and the inability to respond quickly to a dynamic market. Two basic conditions are essential for improving customer service and reducing inventory.

First, the material flow must be totally synchronized. Material release, component fabrication, and assembly must be in step with demand. A critical prerequisite for achieving a synchronized flow is elimination of material misallocation at assembly. This also significantly reduces overtime and inventory required to support the desired service level.

Second, engineering efforts must be focused on improving the operating efficiency of those elements that are most critical to the smooth flow of material to the assembly operation. This results in a system that is more responsive to the market. Such an effort involves looking at the entire product mix rather than each product individually and developing marketing, engineering, manufacturing, and inventory strategies that work in unison to improve overall performance.

In order to implement the drum-buffer-rope logistical system in a T-plant, the first order of business is identifying constraints. In many T-plants, there are no true bottlenecks, because bottlenecks in a T-plant would cause major problems in production of a large number of different end items. This usually causes management to take whatever action is necessary to increase the capacity to the level where bottlenecks are eliminated. As a result of overreacting to the threat of bottlenecks, some T-plants do not even have a true CCR. The problems experienced in meeting delivery requirements are not related to capacity availability, but rather to capacity management.

After identifying the constraints that limit system performance, the buffers should be determined. The logical place to establish stock buffers in a T-plant is at the component-stock level in front of final assembly, which is also the major divergence point in the flow. Many of the required minor component parts can be controlled with very little effort through use of stock buffers. Time buffers in a T-plant should be placed before any CCR, at the component-stock level, before assembly, and before shipping. Placing time buffers at these locations will protect system throughput from the normal disruptions that occur in a T-plant.

T-plants can be best managed as two separate plants–an assembly plant that produces the end items, and a fabrication plant that supplies component stores with the component parts. The assembly part of the operation should be run as an assemble-to-order operation, with special procedures to guard against stealing components from one order to build ahead for future orders. The non-assembly part of the plant should be run as a make-to-stock operation with the component stores functioning as its only customer. The MPS must be established to satisfy the needs of both parts of the plant. The schedule control points in a T-plant occur at material release, CCRs, and assembly.

COMBINATION PLANTS

Many plants fall neatly into one of the three major classifications. When a plant is clearly either a V-plant, A-plant, or T-plant, identifying the problems is a relatively straightforward task. This also makes it easier to formulate an appropriate strategy to improve plant operations. But there are many plants that have key characteristics of more than one category. Such plants are called combination plants.

Plant Structures

The three pure categories of plants—V, A, and T—represent manufacturing environments where a particular type of resource-product interaction dominates the behavior of the entire plant. V-plants do not have assembly operations, and are dominated by the existence of divergence points throughout the production process. A-plants have no divergence points and are dominated by the existence of convergent assembly operations. T-plants, like A-plants, exhibit no divergences in the production of component parts, but assembly is a major divergence point that dominates the plant.

Combination plants typically occur in manufacturing facilities that have a high degree of vertical integration. In some highly vertically integrated plants, the distinctive characteristics of V-plants, A-plants, and T-plants may all be found in one facility. However, it is most common for combination plants to exhibit significant characteristics of only two of the three pure plant types.

There are many possible variations of combination plants. Any attempt to identify all possible combinations would likely prove futile. However, there are a few basic combinations that are sufficiently common to warrant a brief discussion. Figure 3.7 illustrates the basic structure of five different combination plants. These variations are (1) a V-base with a T-top, (2) an A-base with a T-top, (3) a V-base with an A-top, (4) a V-base with an A-middle and a T-top, and (5) an A and a V side by side, topped off by a T. We briefly discuss each of these five variations.

1. V-Base With a T-Top

The base structure has the characteristics of a V-plant, except that the customer is another part of the plant. Typically, a few basic materials are purchased and processed through a series of divergence points to form a larger number of components or products. These items are then used at final assembly to produce a much larger number of end items. The T-plant at the end of the process is the dominant structure. The primary problems found in this type of plant are caused by the interactions at final assembly. An example of this

FIGURE 3.7

The Basic Structure of Five Different Combination Plants

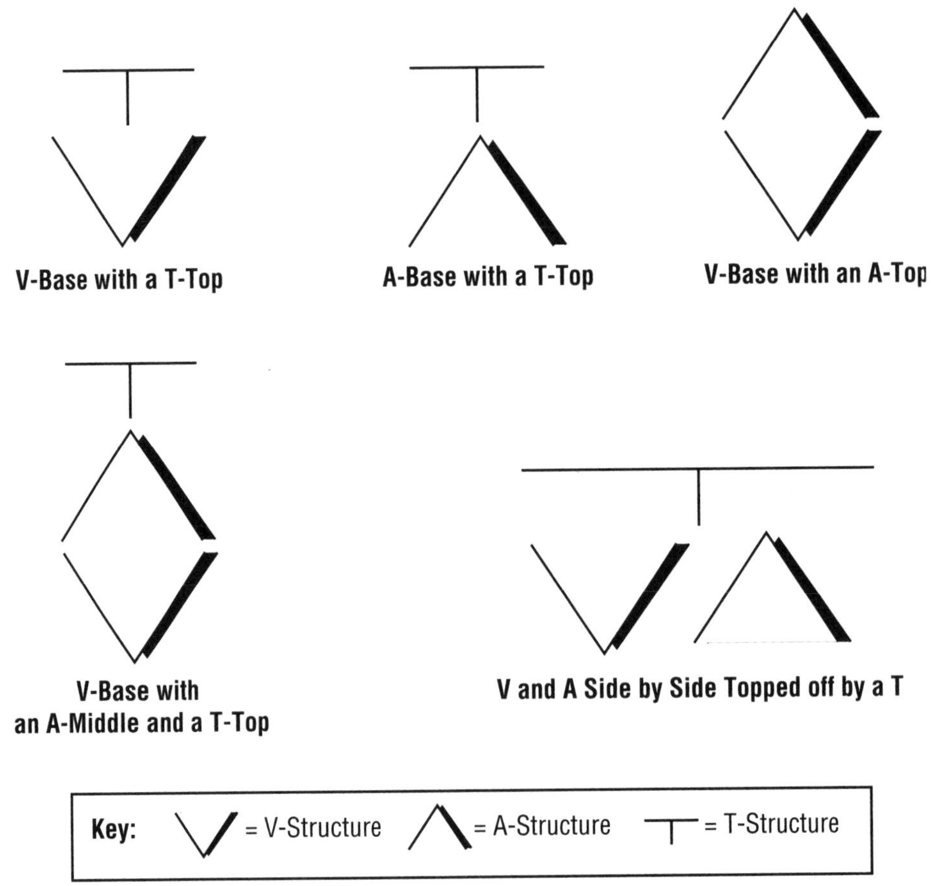

V-Base with a T-Top   A-Base with a T-Top   V-Base with an A-Top

V-Base with
an A-Middle and a T-Top   V and A Side by Side Topped off by a T

Key: ∨ = V-Structure   ∧ = A-Structure   ⊤ = T-Structure

type of plant is a vertically integrated paper mill, where pulp is processed into a number of different paper products. The various paper products are usually master scheduled and subject to a large number of packaging variations before being shipped to customers.

2. A-Base With a T-Top   The base structure has all of the characteristics of an A-plant, except that the products at the completion of the A-process are not end items to be shipped. In this type of plant, it is typical that a large number of materials and component parts are purchased, fabricated, and subassembled to form a relatively few major subassemblies that are stocked at a staging area for final assembly. These component subassemblies are then combined into a large number of distinctly different end items at final assembly. Just as in the V/T combination, this plant is also dominated by the interactions originating at the final assembly point. The plant cannot be adequately controlled until the T-plant type problems are successfully addressed. An example of this type of plant is an assemble-to-order manufacturer of computer hardware products.

3. V-Base With an A-Top   The base structure has the characteristics of a V-plant, except that the items produced become the basic component inputs for the A part of the process. These components are then assembled (and perhaps fabricated) to form end items for the plant. Only a few materials are used as inputs, and there are a relatively few end items. But between the beginning and end of the process, there are a large number of different component parts. An example of this type of plant is a manufacturer of wooden chairs and tables.

4. V-Base With an A-Middle and a T-Top   This type of plant is essentially a combination of two earlier cases, the V/A combination in sequence with the A/T combination. The discussion for each of these two combination plants may be applied to this case. A typical plant of this structure is a manufacturer of upholstered furniture. In the previous V/A example, the manufacturer produces wooden chairs and tables. Now suppose the manufacturer specializes in upholstered chairs and sofas. The V/A part of the process now yields the frame for the various chairs and sofas. The T part is the addition of the stuffing and any of a large number of patterns and materials to the frames to produce the highly differentiated final products.

5. A and V Side by Side, Topped off by a T   In some cases, different processes exist side by side with neither process feeding the other. In this particular case, an A and a V exist side by side and their outputs become the input for a T-plant structure at final assembly. An example of this is a plant that produces magnetic tape in cassettes. The production of the magnetic tape is a V process, while production of the cassette container has an A structure. The tape and the containers are combined at final assembly. This part of the process has a T structure since relatively few component parts can be combined to produce a much larger number of distinctly different end items.

Synchronous Management Applied to Combination Plants

The greater the degree of vertical integration in a plant, the more complex the problems become and the more difficult the plant is to manage and control. However, the problems found in pure V-plants, A-plants, and T-plants will also be found in those parts of the combination plants that resemble the pure counterpart. The basic analysis for the pure V-plants, A-plants, and T-plants therefore extend to, and are valid for, the various combination plants. One approach that may simplify the management process is to use a focused factory approach to plan and control each different structural part of the plant as a separate process and as a pure case of a V-plant, A-plant, or T-plant.

A GENERALIZED SYNCHRONOUS MANAGEMENT IMPLEMENTATION PROCESS

As the previous discussion clearly illustrates, each type of plant has a fairly unique set of characteristics. In addition, when each of these plant types is managed according to traditional guidelines, a predictable set of problems is created. However, regardless of the specific plant category, there is a generalized Synchronous Management drum-buffer-rope implementation process that can be used to provide guidance for managers. The generalized process consists of five sequential steps:

1. Identifying and choosing the constraints.
2. Setting the buffers.
3. Establishing the master schedule.
4. Tying the ropes – establishing the schedule control points.
5. Monitoring performance and progress.

The implementation of any Synchronous Management system should always begin by identifying plant constraints. Material constraints are those materials that, by their limited availability, reduce the plant's ability to service customers. Capacity constraints are those resources that limit the plant's ability to service customers.

In many plants, the location of the capacity constraint resource has a significant impact on overall plant performance. Fortunately, managers often have a choice of whether to let a given constraint remain a constraint. (For a review of this important concept, see Chapter 11 in Volume I.) Managers should be aware that determining whether a specific resource should be a constraint is a key strategic decision. Just because a particular resource is currently a capacity constraint does not automatically imply that it should remain a constraint.

Once the location of the capacity constraint has been determined, the next step is establishing buffers. This includes determining the types of buffers needed, where they are required, and how large they should be to achieve overall plant goals. Decisions on both stock buffers and time buffers are required. Stock buffers should be provided whenever customers require orders to be filled in less than the current production lead time. Stock buffers may exist as either finished goods or partially processed parts. Time buffers are used to protect plant throughput from the normal disruptions inherent in any manufacturing process. While a plant may or may not require stock buffers, every manufacturing plant generally needs at least one time buffer.

Once the constraints have been identified and the stock and time buffers set, the master production schedule must be determined. The master schedule should be established so as to satisfy all customer orders subject to the limitations of the material and capacity constraints. Of course, the stock and time buffers will also partially determine the level and timing of production established by the master schedule.

The next step is to ensure that all resources produce only what is needed, when it is needed, in order to support the master schedule. A key feature of the drum-buffer-rope system is that communication of the requirements and control of production are simplified—by limiting the need for micro management to few schedule control points. The general location of schedule control points, where a detailed schedule specifying quantity and sequence/timing are necessary, were identified and discussed earlier in this chapter for each plant category.

As the Synchronous Management logistical system is being implemented, it is necessary to monitor the performance and progress being made. Bottom line financial measures take too long to collect and are too general to be of specific value. The operational measures of throughput, inventory, and operating expense have their place and will help managers make decisions that move the company in the right direction. However, for two reasons, a number of more detailed measures should be specifically developed for each plant. One obvious reason is to better monitor the specific critical details of the progress being made as the implementation proceeds. A second, and probably more important reason, is that having appropriate performance measures in place actively encourages the desired team-oriented actions by both managers and workers. As we will see later, the nature of the recommended performance measures will vary according to plant category.

In the next three chapters, we describe the implementation of Synchronous Management systems for V-plants, A-plants, and T-plants in greater detail. The basic structure for our discussion is the generalized five-step Synchronous Management implementation process described in this section.

Chapter 4

IMPLEMENTING SYNCHRONOUS MANAGEMENT IN V-PLANTS

The man with a new idea is a Crank, until the idea succeeds.
– Mark Twain, 1897

OVERVIEW OF V-PLANT ISSUES

As discussed in Chapter 3, a V-plant is a manufacturing plant whose behavior is dominated by the presence of divergence points. The main characteristics of V-plants, which are generally found in processing and semi-processing industries, are:

1. The number of end items is large compared to the number of raw materials.
2. All end items are produced in basically the same way—the same operations are performed in the same sequence using the same type of equipment.
3. The equipment tends to be capital intensive and highly specialized.

The two main business issues affecting overall plant performance are generally:

1. Improving customer service levels; and
2. Reducing production costs.

Conventional approaches intended to address these problems generally emphasize a two-pronged attack–increasing inventory levels to resolve customer-service deficiencies, and increasing batch sizes to keep equipment fully activated in an effort to reduce unit costs. Of course, this approach is not only ineffective, but actually aggravates the problems.

In Synchronous Management, we address these two business issues quite differently:

1. *Improving customer service levels.* Reducing manufacturing lead times and improving on-time delivery performance is accomplished by lowering work-in-process inventory and establishing appropriate time and stock buffers.

2. *Reducing production costs.* Per-unit production cost is lowered by reducing overall inventory levels, and by emphasizing improvements in the key competitive elements that lead to higher sales and production volumes. This enables overhead expenses to be spread out over a larger number of units.

THE DRUM-BUFFER-ROPE IMPLEMENTATION PROCESS

Identifying Constraints

The objective of a Synchronous Management control system in a V-plant is to simultaneously increase throughput and reduce inventory. The Synchronous Management DBR implementation process begins with the identification of the physical constraints—both capacity and material—that must be considered when setting up the material control system.

Material Constraints   A material constraint is any material that, because of limited availability, reduces the plant's ability to service customers. Whenever a material constraint exists, some or all of the products that require this material will be in short supply.

Knowledge of those products that are unavailable or late should provide a good indication of which materials are constraints. However, there are two reasons why this is not always true for V-plants. First, material misallocation is a potential problem in V-plants. Second, there is always the possibility of a wide variety of production problems. The existence of either material misallocation or major production problems can significantly cloud the issue. Therefore, to confirm the existence of a true material constraint, two alternative possibilities must be ruled out:

1. Product shortages must not be the result of material misallocation. This can be easily checked because material misallocation not only causes product shortages, it also causes overproduction of other products. Therefore, if the analysis reveals a shortage of some products but an excess of other products requiring the same material, material is not a constraint.

2. Product shortages must not be caused by production-related problems. Since any number of production problems could cause a temporary shortage of one of more products, a single snapshot of product shortages may be misleading. It is necessary to identify the products that are consistently late or in short supply.

Once material misallocation and production problems have been ruled out as causes of product shortages, the process of identifying material constraints is easy. From the list of consistently short products, the common material can be identified. This common material is the material constraint.

Capacity Constraints   A capacity constraint is any resource that limits the plant's ability to service customers. In many plants, products that are processed by a capacity constraint resource (CCR) are in short supply. Hence an analysis of delivery performance by product appears to contain the clues to identifying capacity constraints.

Unfortunately, in V-plants, this procedure is not generally valid, because most products in V-plants are processed by the same resources. Thus, determining the products that are in short supply normally yields little or no useful information. If there is a CCR, it will likely affect most of the plant's products.

Another alternative sometimes used by analysts to identify capacity constraints is information from the capacity planning system. To identify the most loaded resource, one merely has to determine the available capacity of each resource and compare it to the required load. The most heavily loaded resource is the CCR. Despite its logical appeal, this approach has two drawbacks, one that is common to all plants and one specific to V-plants.

The general drawback is that the capacity and load calculations are based on information contained in the manufacturing database. But in most cases, the integrity of that database is far from acceptable. The resulting inaccuracies introduced into the calculations make the conclusions highly questionable.

The drawback specific to V-plants is that the capacity required to set up and process a batch of material is highly dependent on the sequence in which the products are processed. Very few capacity planning systems have the sophistication to recognize all the factors that influence the hours required to set up and process a specific batch. The net result is that the capacity requirement as calculated by the system and the true capacity actually required can be significantly different.

Hence, a totally different constraint identification procedure for V-Plants is needed, one that does not require database accuracy or sophistication.

Using Inventory Profiles to Identify Capacity Constraints   The key to identifying capacity constraints in a V-plant is the distribution of inventory in the system. In V-plants, two factors play a critical role in determining inventory distribution:

1. The linear flow of material and the linear arrangement of equipment that characterizes V-plants.
2. The tendency of traditional management practices to overactivate resources.

Understanding the implications of these two factors provides the clue to the location of capacity constraints.

Consider, for example, the V-plant shown in Figure 4.1 (next page). Each product goes through four processing steps. Assume further that the capacity constraint resource is the one performing the third processing step. This R3 resource is indicated by the notation "CCR." Resource one (R1), resource two (R2), and resource four (R4) all have more capacity than the third resource and, in fact, more capacity than required to fill customer orders.

In V-plants, any non-CCRs prior to the CCR are definitely subject to overactivation because they have extra capacity and often have access to material. In traditionally managed companies, local efficiency and equipment utilization measures usually cause overactivation and create excess inventory. In Figure 4.1, this means that resources R1 and R2 will likely be overactivated. Since the CCR, R3, cannot keep pace with the overactivated R1 and R2 resources, the bulk of this excess inventory will end up in front of R3.

Resources that follow constraint resource R3 do not have the same degree of opportunity for overactivation. In fact, all resources involved in the processes that follow the CCR have more than sufficient capacity to process everything provided by the constraint. Their activation is limited by the material made available from the constraint. Thus, the processes following the constraint will be periodically starved for work and rapidly process any material made available. As a result, very little work-in-process inventory will be found after the CCR. The typical distribution of work-in-process inventory found in traditionally managed V-plants is illustrated in Figure 4.2.

Moreover, because of the characteristic linear organization of equipment in V-plants, one can predict the physical location of the excess inventory. All one needs to do is to trace the route followed by the material from the gateway operation to the shipping dock. In that area of the plant up to and including the CCR, the shop floor is likely to be clogged with inventory. But that area of the plant after the

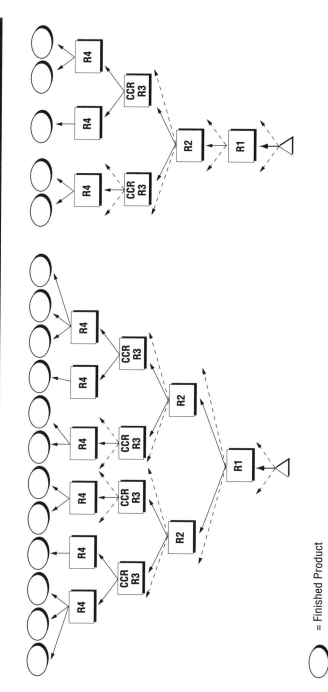

FIGURE 4.1

Representative Product Flow Diagram
for a V-Plant with Four Resources

◯ = Finished Product

Note: Dotted line arrows are used to indicate that additional products exist but are not represented in the diagram.

FIGURE 4.2

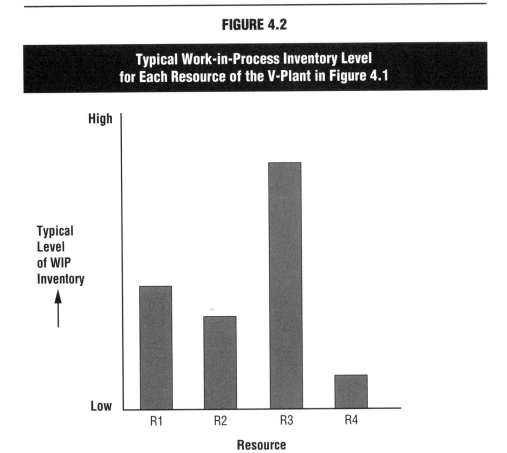

Typical Work-in-Process Inventory Level
for Each Resource of the V-Plant in Figure 4.1

constraint is likely to be relatively free of inventory.

The standard pattern of inventory distribution can be used to identify the location of the constraint. The capacity constraint is the resource that separates the region of high inventory from the region of low inventory!

The Impact of Setups on the Inventory Profile   One factor that has a significant impact on the distribution of inventory is the complexity of the setups involved at the different processing steps. Figure 4.3 illustrates the impact of setups on the distribution of inventory in V-plants.

In Case A, there is no significant setup at any resource, including the constraint. The work-in-process inventory profile is similar to that shown in Figure 4.2. Inventory levels for finished goods are relatively low, since orders can be processed fairly quickly when necessary to meet customer demand.

Case B shows the distribution of inventory when the setups at all resources are significant but depend on the same parameters. Due to the set-up times, the tendency is to produce in batches that are larger than the order quantities. This supposedly utilizes the equipment more efficiently, reduces set-up costs, and reduces unit product cost. But any production in excess of immediate market demand ends up as finished-goods inventory. The result of producing these large batches in today's competitive marketplace is poor customer service despite high levels of inventory.

Case C shows the distribution of inventory when each of the processing stages has a long and complex setup. The term "complex setup" is used to indicate that the set-up time involved is controlled by a number of factors, including the previous material processed. This means that the set-up time for a given material will vary greatly. Additionally, in Case C, it is assumed that the product parameters that make for a quick setup vary from one resource to another. For example, consider a textile plant where two of the major processes include yarn dyeing and weaving. The set-up requirements at yarn dyeing depend on the color sequence. The set-up requirements at weaving are determined by the pattern and have little to do with color. Compared to Case B, the set-up characteristics of this case create even larger amounts of in-process inventory. In addition to the fact that batch sizes exceed order quantities, extra WIP is required to permit the manager of each resource to choose the optimal production sequence. Finished-goods inventory is also much larger than in Case B, primarily because the production sequence is more variable, causing production lead times to be more uncertain. Higher levels of finished goods are used to try to improve delivery performance.

Validating the Identity of the Constraint   While the inventory profile is an excellent tool to identify capacity constraint resources, there are situations that make the technique susceptible to error. For example, sometimes the product cannot be stored just prior to the constraint resource due to a lack of floor space. Alternately, if material has a limited shelf life, this will likely affect the work-in-process inventory level. To make sure the CCR has been properly identified, additional validations should be performed, such as:

1. Determining the amount of overtime worked at various resources. If a resource is a constraint, it should be the resource with the most difficulty maintaining the production pace needed to satisfy customer orders. Therefore, overtime at a constraint resource should regularly exceed overtime at other resources.

FIGURE 4.3

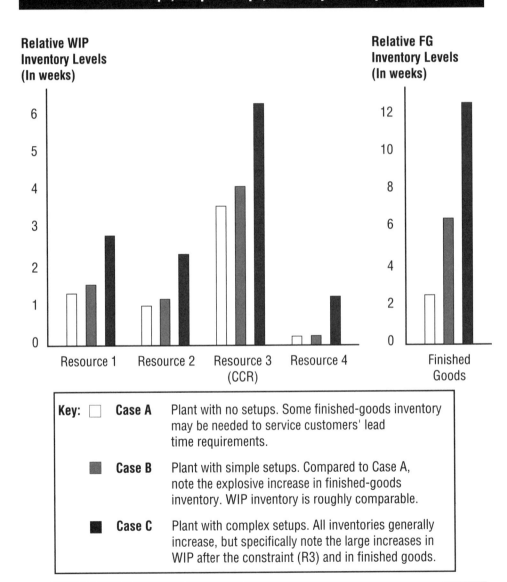

**Work-in-Process and Finished Goods
Inventory Profiles for Three Cases:
No Setups, Simple Setups, and Complex Setups**

**Relative WIP
Inventory Levels
(In weeks)**

**Relative FG
Inventory Levels
(In weeks)**

Resource 1   Resource 2   Resource 3
(CCR)   Resource 4   Finished
Goods

Key:	Case A	Plant with no setups. Some finished-goods inventory may be needed to service customers' lead time requirements.
	Case B	Plant with simple setups. Compared to Case A, note the explosive increase in finished-goods inventory. WIP inventory is roughly comparable.
	Case C	Plant with complex setups. All inventories generally increase, but specifically note the large increases in WIP after the constraint (R3) and in finished goods.

2. Checking set-up and run times at the various resources. Since most V-plants involve a small number of processing steps, this is a relatively easy task. The objective is not to perform an independent load verification, but to spot inconsistencies. For example, the alleged CCR will be suspect if it has a faster run time and a shorter set-up time than another resource that has the same number of machines.

One goal of the validation process is to either confirm or invalidate that the alleged capacity constraint, tentatively identified through the use of inventory profiles, is actually a constraint. Another goal is to reveal inconsistencies. An inconsistency occurs when a resource identified as a capacity constraint is then shown not to be so. Other inconsistencies occur when expected V-plant characteristics or problems do not apply to the plant in question. Whenever an inconsistency is uncovered, the contradictory evidence will have to be carefully considered.

The importance of the validation process must be emphasized. There are clear expectations of V-plants operating under traditional management guidelines. However, every plant is different. The validation process helps reveal many of the critical features that make the specific plant different from the generic plant. These critical features can then be used to modify the generic solution to each individual case. It is for the purpose of highlighting these critical distinguishing features that the identification and resolution of inconsistencies are imperative.

Choosing the Location of the Constraint   The procedures outlined above help identify the CCR in the plant as it is currently managed. However, this does not automatically imply that the current CCR should be the CCR. Since management generally has the ability to increase or decrease resource capacities, management can actively determine which resource is the CCR. The actual location of the CCR has a major influence on plant performance. We illustrate this point by considering two extreme cases for a V-plant, as shown in Figure 4.4. This figure highlights several key differences in plant performance, depending on whether the CCR is located at the beginning of the product flow or at the end. The generalizations of Figure 4.4 can be used to determine the expected results of locating the constraint at different points in the production process.

For each plant, management should carefully analyze the specific environment, competitive market conditions, and the impact of alternative CCR locations on expected plant performance. Based on this critical analysis, management should determine the optimum location for the capacity constraint resource. One of the most important strategic decisions that can be made in a V-plant is constraint location

FIGURE 4.4

Key Differences in Plant Performance Between a CCR Located at the Beginning or at the End of the Product Flow in a V-Plant		
	CCR is at the first operation	**CCR is at the last operation**
Complexity of managing flow	Simple–fewer products can be processed at constraint, natural input control	Complex–large number of products can be processed prior to constraint; Managerial controls a must
On-time Deliveries	Variability at any step of process can impact deliveries	More robust due to availability of protective material and capacity
Responsiveness	Response lead times are longer, but can be more responsive in this time with same inventory	Response lead times are shorter, but due to material dedication at this late stage, less responsive for same inventory
Throughput	Can be erratic due to process variations at any step in process–likely to be lower as a result	Subject only to CCR variations– likely to be higher
Buffer Inventories	Stock Buffers tend to be smaller and more flexible	Stock Buffers tend to be larger and less flexible

Setting the Buffers

Once the CCR location is set, the next step is to establish the buffers. Designing an appropriate buffer policy for a plant involves several critical decisions–the types of buffers needed, the optimum locations, and the appropriate sizes.

Stock Buffers   Stock buffers are necessary whenever customer orders must be filled in less than the normal manufacturing lead time. For products that are required "off the shelf," *finished-goods stock buffers* are required. For products needed in less than normal manufacturing lead time, but not "off the shelf," *material stock buffers* composed of partially processed materials are usually sufficient. Material stock buffers simply reduce the manufacturing response time. Specific market requirements and plant capabilities largely determine the eventual product/material composition, locations, and sizes of the stock buffers.

Stock buffers must be designed in accordance with customer-service needs. A market analysis should be performed to determine the actual customer delivery requirements for each product or product family produced by the plant. This should be the basis for determining whether a finished-goods stock buffer for a given product is required. Compared to finished-goods stock buffers, material stock buffers composed of partially processed materials are much more flexible for filling future customer orders. For products that do not require immediate delivery, material stock buffers are usually preferable to finished-goods stock buffers. This is in clear contrast to the common practice of trying to keep most products in finished-goods inventory.

Once the need for a material stock buffer has been established, the next step is to choose an appropriate location, considering the following factors.

1. The forecast for materials at earlier stages of the product flow is more accurate than for materials at later stages. This is because there are fewer distinct items at earlier stages. (Remember that in V-plants the number of distinct products increases as material moves through the process.) As a result, forecasting errors for individual products are more likely to average out at earlier stages in the process.

2. There is greater flexibility in using the material for different end products if it is in the early stages of production. At each successive divergence point in the product flow, flexibility is diminished. The greater the number of divergence points the product has been processed through, the fewer the number of different items the material can be used to produce.

3. The production lead time to respond to customer demand increases when the inventory is at the early processing steps. This is simply because more operations have to be performed before the required products can be completed.

Thus, the fewer divergence points the material has gone through, the smaller and more flexible the required material stock buffer. However, the lead time required to fill customer orders from this material stock buffer will be longer. *We therefore conclude that material stock buffers should generally be established at the earliest production step from which it is possible to respond to customer demand in a timely fashion.*

To illustrate the process of designing stock buffers, consider the following market and production characteristics for Plant XYZ:

*   To meet customer expectations, the company has a "quick ship" policy for all standard products. Standard products account for 20% of all products but over 80% of all dollar sales volume. These products are to be shipped the same day the order is received.
*   Customers expect delivery for all other products in three weeks.
*   The current production lead time for all products is four weeks.
*   Resource R3 is the capacity constraint resource.

In Plant XYZ, there is a clear need for a finished-goods stock buffer for the "quick ship" products. However, only the standard products (20% of all products) are included in this stock buffer. Demand for the non-standard products can be satisfied with stock buffers of partially processed material. To meet customer delivery requirements, the material stock buffers must be placed in the product flow at a stage where the remaining processing time is three weeks or less. Figure 4.5 shows the location and composition of the required stock buffers. Suppose that after resource R1 processes material, the remaining production lead time is three weeks. An appropriate decision would be to locate the material stock buffer after R1, prior to R2. This provides maximum material flexibility while satisfying the three-week processing time requirement.

Once the stock buffer locations are determined, the sizes can be established. The guidelines are straightforward. The stock buffer must be large enough to achieve a satisfactory level of service during the time it takes to replenish the buffer. Replenishment time is the production lead time from the feeding stock buffer. In our example, the size of the finished goods stock buffer for quick-ship products should be sufficient to satisfy three weeks' worth of demand. This three-week time is based on the replenishment lead time from the material stock buffer, not the full four-week production lead time. All material stock buffers should be large enough to provide one week's worth of demand for the material in the buffer. This one-week figure is based on the one-week lead time to get materials through the R1 resource.

Considering the function stock buffers perform, the primary responsibility for establishing these buffers should be assigned to the marketing/sales department. Marketing/sales should determine the product composition of the finished-goods and material stock buffers based on customer requirements. The location and size of the material stock buffers should be determined in conjunction with the production department. Once determined, the production department's responsibility is to stock and replenish these buffers in the manner requested by marketing/sales. It is marketing's responsibility to analyze the stock buffers continuously and to adjust them as needed to be consistent with marketplace dynamics. Meanwhile, appropriately targeted improvement programs should be eliminating the reasons for having these inventory buffers.

Time Buffers   Time buffers are needed in virtually every manufacturing operation. They are required to accommodate the disruptions inherent in all manufacturing processes, such as equipment breakdowns, absenteeism, temporary work overloads, and yield problems.

In V-plants, time buffers are generally needed at three points:

1. *At the capacity constraint resource.* Time buffers are always needed in front of CCRs to prevent starvation of the constraint, to maintain schedule integrity, and to monitor system performance.

2. *At each stock buffer.* It is important to maintain adequate levels of inventory in stock buffers in order to meet customer requirements. Therefore, stock buffers should be treated like an "internal customer." Material movement to stock buffers should be monitored and protected with time buffers.

3. *For those products without a finished-goods stock buffer, a time buffer (referred to as a shipping buffer) is needed at the end of the process.* Time buffers are always needed at the end of the process in order to protect delivery performance and to monitor system performance.

Figure 4.5 shows the location of time buffers for Plant XYZ, as well as the location of stock buffers.

FIGURE 4.5

Composition and Location of Stock Buffers and Time Buffers for Plant XYZ

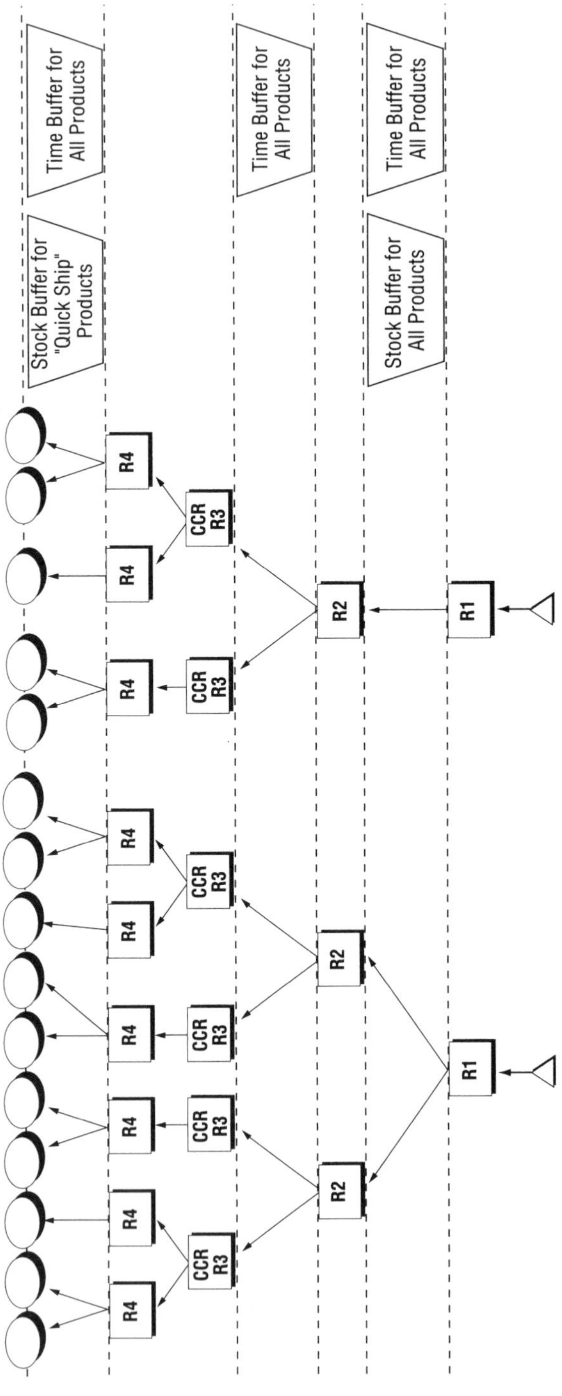

The size of a time buffer is unrelated to factors such as usage or desired service level, which determine the size of stock buffers. Time buffer size is determined by the likely impact of disruptions on the planned production flow. In principle, the appropriate size of a time buffer can be established by extensively analyzing the nature of the disruptions. Every situation is unique, but experience indicates that often a good starting point is about one quarter of the current production lead time.

Establishing the Master Schedule

The master production schedule has to be established consistent with marketplace demands, and within the limitations of any material and capacity constraints.

Material Constraint Considerations   The inclusion of material constraints into the master scheduling process is straightforward. The total amount of products sold and scheduled in any given time frame cannot exceed the availability of the known material constraint. A material constraint is not generally defined by the timing of the available material, but rather according to the quantity of material available. Most problems of timing can be accommodated through the use of appropriate time or stock buffers in the raw-material stage.

Whenever a material constraint exists, particular attention should be paid to usage of this material. This is particularly true in V-plants, since material can be misallocated at many resources. To avoid material misallocation, process batch size on those products that require a constraint material must be closely matched with actual customer orders. If this causes excessive set-up time at a resource, it is best to try to recover set-up time on products that do not require a constrained material.

Capacity Constraint Considerations   The critical decisions when establishing the master production schedule involve the determination of the production priority sequence and the process batch sizes. We will consider two cases. The simple case occurs when the CCR does not require set-ups. The much more typical case is when set-ups are required at the CCR.

Constraints That Do Not Require Setups   Effectively managing capacity constraints is generally a matter of properly managing setups. However, if the capacity constraint resource does not require setups, the CCR should work in priority sequence and only in the exact quantities required to fill actual customer orders. The only two additional questions that need to be addressed are:

1. Is there enough capacity to meet demand?

   If there is not enough capacity, the number of past-due orders will increase and so will their lateness. In this case, the various alternatives for increasing capacity discussed in Chapter 6 of Volume 1 should be considered.

2. Is the production lead time needed to complete the post-constraint processing steps excessive for some products?

   If the answer is yes, some re-sequencing of orders may be appropriate. However, a better solution is to try to reduce the production lead times through smaller transfer batches and expedited material handling.

Constraints That Require Setups   The objective of a plant, and the ultimate reason for generating a master production schedule, is to maximize profitability. This generally translates directly into maximizing throughput. If a plant has a bottleneck-category CCR that requires setups, any capacity wasted on unnecessary setups reduces throughput. The problem clearly becomes one of determining the process batch sizes and the production priority sequence that generates maximum plant throughput.

The nature of the V-plant puts a unique slant on this batch-sizing decision. Because many products are produced from a single common material, when a CCR processes material, that material will be used to satisfy demand for a number of different products. In a V-plant, the selected process batch size for a given material should be large enough to satisfy the projected demand for all products requiring that material over a specified time period. This time period is sometimes set equal to the order horizon. In that case, the length of the order horizon determines the process batch size at the capacity constraint. These product-demand estimates covering the "order horizon" often include a combination of firm orders and forecasted demand.

Determining an appropriate process batch size is not easy. There are valid arguments to be made for both smaller and larger process batches.

The argument for larger process batches is straightforward. Larger process batches reduce the total number of setups required at the CCR, which reduces the total time required for setups at the CCR. This directly increases available processing capacity, which may be converted into additional throughput.

But the disadvantages of larger process batch sizes are equally significant. Larger process batches for one material mean other materials must wait for longer periods before being processed. This may cause some products requiring a different material to not be produced in a timely manner and buffers to not be replenished in a timely manner. That is, larger process batches increase production lead times, can distort the production priority sequence, and often cause buffers to be larger than otherwise necessary.

In addition, larger process batches increase the relevant order horizon. And the longer the order horizon, the more the projected product demand must rely on forecasts instead of reflecting actual customer orders. The demand inaccuracies introduced by forecasts automatically cause excess finished-goods inventory of some items and shortages of others.

When one has to depend on forecasts that degrade with time, yield to market pressures and accept rush orders, the use of larger process batches (and hence long lead times) can be detrimental. Even if one begins with a plan that has a small number of setups, many unplanned setups are needed to satisfy market needs. The number of actual setups, not the number of planned setups, determines plant performance. As increasingly larger process batches are used in planning, more unplanned setups are required.

Thus, smaller process batches have some appeal. When smaller process batches are used in planning, fewer expedites and unplanned setups are necessary. Also, smaller process batches have a greater likelihood of being primarily composed of actual firm orders for products that require the specified material. If they closely reflect actual product needs, excess finished-goods inventory will be minimal.

Figure 4.6 illustrates the point, that there is a general relationship between process batch sizes at a CCR and plant performance as measured by throughput and customer service. Over some range, as process batch sizes increase, throughput increases. In this range, the extra processing capacity generated from saving setups is more significant than any problems caused by inaccuracies of product forecasts or distortions of production priority sequence. However, beyond some point, the problems caused by grouping product requirements eventually outweigh any benefits derived from saving additional setups. Specifically, if customer service deteriorates, customers may cancel orders and cause a loss of current throughput. Of course, poor customer service affects future orders and future throughput.

Note from the shape of the curve in Figure 4.6 that actual plant performance can be identical when one errs on the side of larger or smaller process batches. In Synchronous Management, it is better to err on the side of lower inventory, i.e., on the side of smaller process batches.

Obviously, an "optimum" process batch size exists only in theory. In fact, the appropriate process batch size is variable and dynamic. It varies according to the

FIGURE 4.6

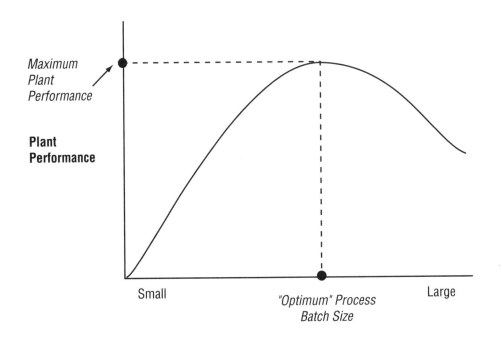

The Relationship Between Process Batch Size at CCR and Plant Performance as Measured by Throughput and Customer Service

material to be processed and changes over time for each material depending on the pattern of orders. Realistically, the goal should be to constantly determine process batch sizes that "minimizes" total setup time at the constraint without creating significant production and inventory distortions.

Once process batch sizes have been established, additional savings in set-up time, if required, sometimes can be achieved by grouping together "like" materials. If the setup time is significantly lowered by processing families of similar materials in sequence, additional processing capacity is generated. Once again, the trade-off from changing the processing sequence is apparent. Additional processing time is made available at the constraint resource, but true priorities are distorted. This distortion of priorities means that the lead times are unpredictable as products wait for the right grouping of materials at the constraint. This adversely affects the ability to respond to customer demands and may increase required stock buffer quantities. Clearly, grouping similar materials together should only be done when the additional capacity generated is absolutely essential.

Tying the Ropes - Establishing the Schedule Control Points

Schedule control points in a V-plant are material release, divergence points, and capacity constraints. In many plants, the number of schedule control points is a small fraction of the total number of resources. However, in a typical V-plant, most resources represent divergence points in the product flow, and are thus schedule control points. It must be remembered that failure to adequately control production at divergence points leads to material misallocation, which in turn creates inventory and causes a misallocation of resource capacity. The latter has the potential to create capacity constraints.

Production control must start at the material release points. Only scheduled material should be released to the gateway resource–nothing less, and certainly nothing more. If material entering the process is not controlled, the whole plant will be out of control.

Every resource that represents a divergence point must be carefully controlled, a far from trivial exercise in V-plants. Since material misallocation is always possible at divergence points, detailed attention is required when developing schedules for these resources. In addition to developing a schedule, divergence point resources should be continuously and closely monitored.

Of course, CCRs must always be carefully controlled and monitored since they determine plant throughput and establish the schedule for the rest of the plant. While it is important to monitor CCR output, timely flow of input materials required at the CCR must also be monitored to ensure that the integrity of the CCR schedule is maintained.

In addition to these three schedule control points, the flow of material into every time buffer should be monitored. Remember that in addition to time buffers at CCRs, time buffers also exist at stock buffer locations and at the end of the process. The deviations between planned material flow and actual flow into these time buffers provides critical information used to determine if and when material should be expedited, to analyze system performance, and to make process and procedural improvements.

As an aside, the need for scheduling and control should not be confused with optimizing production at local work centers. In fact, the opposite is true. Due to the nature of V-plant resources, the tendency under traditional management guidelines is to run large batches at all resources. To the degree that this results in material misallocation, the resulting impact on overall plant performance is very serious. This is why detailed schedules must be provided and carefully followed at all schedule control points.

Monitoring Performance and Progress

Implementing a drum-buffer-rope (DBR) system and steadily moving toward a more synchronized environment usually requires that fundamental changes be made in the current performance measurement system. For two reasons, an appropriate set of detailed operational measures must be developed. One is to monitor progress being made so managers know when problems occur and when adjustments are necessary. The second is that detailed operational measures, correctly tied to the performance evaluation system, encourage appropriate actions.

Detailed operational measures should be able to identify changes in critical variables directly and immediately—even before the impact registers on the bottom line. They also should be measurable on an on-going basis. Some examples of appropriate detailed operational measures in V-plants are:

1. **Throughput at the CCR**   Since CCRs control the total amount of product the plant can produce, a key objective of Synchronous Management is to increase throughput at these resources. This is basically accomplished through improved scheduling of constraint resources, effective utilization of available constraint capacity, focusing improvement projects at the constraint, and ensuring that other resources operate in such a way as to support the smooth operation of the constraint. Throughput at the capacity constraint, and for the entire plant, should show rapid improvement as the DBR system is implemented.

2. **Scrap/Yield at Work Centers After The CCR**   Work centers that process material already processed by the constraint must be carefully monitored. If a unit of material is scrapped or otherwise lost at a post-constraint operation, this is equivalent to losing capacity at the constraint, which results in a loss of throughput. Scrap at work centers that process material before it reaches the constraint is not as critical; the financial impact of material lost at this stage is generally limited to the purchase cost of the material.

3. **Scrap/Yield of Constraint Material**   If there is a constraint material, this cannot be replaced when scrapped or otherwise lost, and any loss translates directly into a loss of throughput for the entire plant. Thus, all constraint materials should be closely monitored. Constraint material losses should decrease through greater care in processing and through process improvements designed to improve yields or reduce scrap.

4. **Finished-Goods Inventory**   A key objective of Synchronous Management is to reduce the disparity, both in quantity and time, between what is produced and what is sold. As the system becomes increasingly synchronized, a greater percentage of production should be applicable to near-term customer orders. This means less finished-goods inventory is needed to satisfy customer orders. It also should reduce obsolete inventory.

5. **Cycle Time**   As the plant becomes more synchronized, material flow becomes more streamlined and the cycle time—manufacturing lead time—rapidly shrinks. Cycle times for various products can be measured by how long it takes materials to move all the way through the production process. Moreover, since cycle time is related to work-in-process inventory levels, this inventory experiences a significant reduction as cycle time is reduced.

A number of other detailed operational measures are possible. The relative importance of these and other measures varies according to the particular business. While they do not replace the overall financial measures, they do provide an immediate and intuitive set of measures that provides continuous and easily measurable feedback about the progress of the Synchronous Management implementation.

V-PLANT CASE STUDY: AN OVERVIEW OF THE A&B TEXTILE MILL

Background Information

The A&B Textile Company, headquartered in South Carolina, was founded in the early 1900s. It grew from a single plant to several dozen plants located in both the U.S. and foreign countries. Following the general pattern of most American manufacturing companies, A&B Textile is organized into operating divisions that serve specific markets. Each division is responsible for production as well as sales (or merchandising, as it is referred to in the textile trade). This case study deals with one plant in one division.

The mill's basic products include drapery and upholstery fabrics, and can be categorized as either yarn-dyed fabrics or piece-dyed fabrics. Goods are sold and distributed through several channels, including converting houses that convert finished fabric into finished products such as draperies; retail fabric-based job shops that perform the task of converting upholstery material into seating; and chain stores and mail order houses. In addition, products are sold directly to furniture manufacturers and small retailers.

At A&B, the actual production sequence is relatively simple for all products, although there is a slight difference in the processing sequence for yarn-dyed fabric and piece-dyed fabric. Yarn-dyed products are first dyed, then woven at the weaving looms. Piece-dyed products are processed through weaving before they are dyed. Otherwise, the processing steps are identical, are for the discussion of this case study, we will concentrate on yarn-dyed fabrics.

The basic production steps are yarn prep, dyeing, weaving, finishing, and cutting/sewing. At yarn prep, the raw materials, cotton and rayon, are combined in different percentages to form a variety of yarn materials. In dyeing, the properly prepared yarn can be dyed into a wide variety of colors and shades. At weaving, yarn is loaded onto looms where it may be woven into a number of different fabric types and patterns. At finishing, the fabric may be fitted with various thermal backing materials and sprayed with chemicals for durability and appearance. Finally, in cutting/sewing, the finished material is cut and sewn into a variety of sizes.

At each step, material is increasingly transformed into many distinct products. The product flow diagram for the A&B mill is shown in Figure 4.7. It clearly resembles the generic V-plant product flow diagram.

A key point to note is where there are major versus minor divergence points in the flow. For yarn-dyed fabrics, the major divergence points are at dyeing, weaving, and cutting/sewing. Finishing can only add some minor degree of divergence such as addition of thermal backing to drapery material. These major and minor divergence points are illustrated in Figure 4.8.

The Fundamental Problem

The complexity of the production/scheduling process is heightened by the following factors:

1. The number of end items is very large (thousands of distinct SKUs).
2. Since all products are processed in the same way, products compete for the same resources.

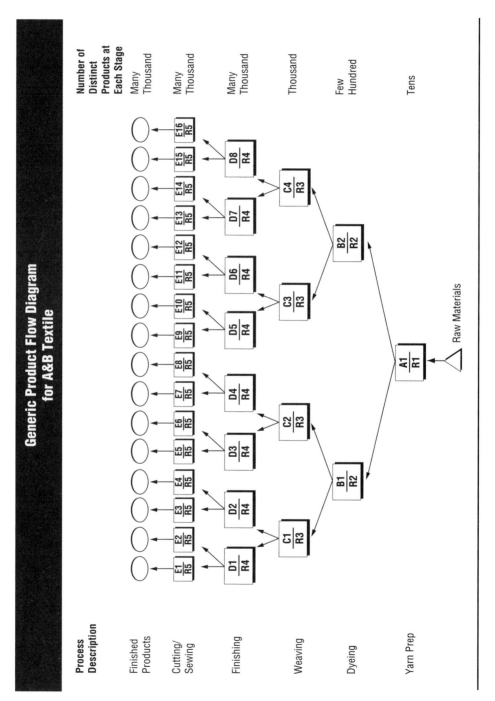

FIGURE 4.7

Generic Product Flow Diagram for A&B Textile

3. The number of individual units of a given resource is very large. For example, there are over 300 looms.

4. Although the required set-up time varies from one resource to the next, the equipment is quite complex and requires a considerable amount of set-up time (especially at critical resources). Moreover, depending on the nature of the change, the required set-up time at a given resource may vary from one setup to the next. For example, at the weaving looms, changing the pattern generally requires a lengthy setup. But changing the yarn type, filler, or color at the loom can be accomplished in much less time.

5. The various products exhibit a wide range of demand.

FIGURE 4.8

Major Divergence Points

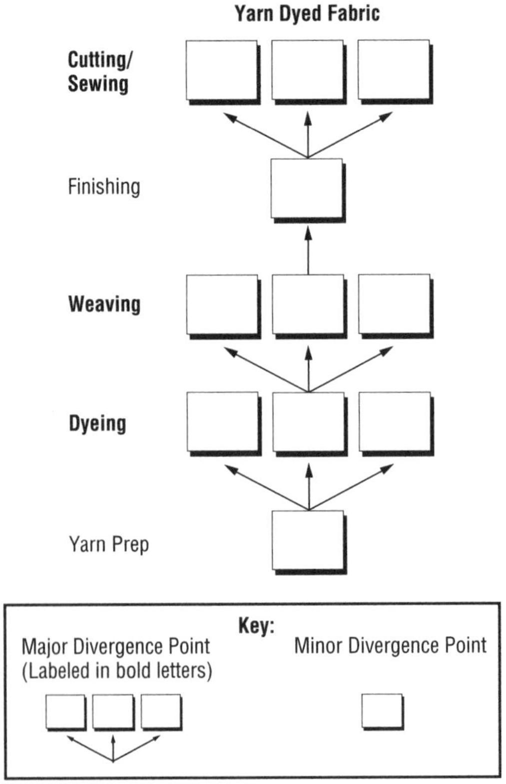

Yarn Dyed Fabric

Cutting/
Sewing

Finishing

Weaving

Dyeing

Yarn Prep

Key:

Major Divergence Point
(Labeled in bold letters)

Minor Divergence Point

All of this complexity creates the perception that it is not possible to use an order-by-order method to schedule the plant. Inventory is seen as the solution to achieving quick customer service. Customer orders are expected to be filled from finished-goods inventory, and the plant is expected to replenish the inventory using forecasted sales volumes.

This is a very old method that served A&B well in the past. It enabled the sales department to focus on selling without having to worry about product availability. At the same time, the manufacturing group could focus on producing products efficiently and at low cost, without having to worry about the need to be responsive.

However, intense competition from both domestic and foreign companies began to erode the customer base. The continuing struggle for market share in the industry created intense price competition, significantly reducing A&B's once healthy profit margins. The key business issues facing this plant now are clearly recognized by senior managers, most of whom are from the merchandising area. The task at hand is to make changes that will yield significant cost reductions and major improvements in customer service!

Failed Traditional Solutions

The A&B management team has already attempted to resolve these key business issues by implementing changes based on the "prevailing traditional management wisdom." These can be categorized as attempts to improve customer service or attempts to reduce costs.

Efforts to Improve Customer Service   Two distinct efforts were made to improve customer service. The first project was an attempt to upgrade the forecasting system, followed by computerizing the tracking system for work-in-process inventory.

It was perceived that the A&B forecasting system was outdated and inadequate. The rationale for focusing on the forecasting system was that the actual customer orders were invariably significantly different from the forecast. Since production planning was based on the forecast, this resulted in a large finished-goods inventory, shortages, and constant expediting. Significant time and money were invested trying to improve forecast accuracy, with no visible success. This proved to be a useless and frustrating exercise for two reasons. The forecasting algorithm in use was already sophisticated. Any attempt to fine-tune the algorithm would make it more complex and more difficult for planners to understand. Moreover, the basic forecasting problem was rooted in the rapidly evolving marketplace. As competitive pressures in the market increased, customers' delivery lead time requirements shrunk. Meanwhile, production lead times remained unchanged. This only acted to reinforce the inherent inadequacies of the entire forecasting process.

Another major project was to computerize the inventory tracking system, with particular emphasis on work-in-process inventory. This was considered appropriate because whenever the status of an order had to be determined or an order expedited, tremendous effort was needed to track down the material in question. Since expediting was a frequent activity, computerized lot tracking was seen as a major step in making this activity more efficient. Besides, at that time, computerized lot tracking and automated high-bay storage areas were generally accepted inventory system practices. Unfortunately, the computerized inventory tracking system did not have a significant impact on A&B's ability to meet customer service requirements. (Note that this action implicitly assumes that the disruptive expediting activity is unavoidable.)

Efforts to Reduce Costs   Cost-reduction efforts were attempted on three major fronts—automation, quality improvement, and equipment utilization.

A major thrust to reduce costs at A&B followed the classic industrial engineering approach. The first step was identifying the major cost elements (both labor and material) in the plant. Labor-intensive operations were systematically identified and attempts were made to reduce costs by planning the work more carefully to balance labor utilization, and by designing incentive schemes to extract more output. Of course, the cornerstone of this thrust was replacing skilled labor with automation.

This traditional view of labor as simply a cost element had three problems. One, the entire process at A&B was becoming progressively more inflexible, favoring long runs of standard products. Two, valuable technical skills were being lost. Three, the labor force was increasingly alienated. In the end, these changes generated such system-wide inefficiencies that costs actually increased.

A significant amount of money was spent on automation. In general, older pieces of equipment were replaced with faster equipment that required less labor. These equipment upgrades were made in the finishing area and in some of the material prep areas. Significantly, the decision was made that it was not cost effective to replace or upgrade the looms in the weaving department. (As you will see later, the plant's CCR was weaving.)

Also contributing to the inflexibility problem was an attempt to reduce unit cost by installing larger equipment. Dye tub sizes, for example, were increased from 50 pounds to 400 pounds, with even larger ones planned. The conventional wisdom behind such moves was that larger tub sizes increased both material and labor efficiency.

An additional effort to curb costs was implemented through an attack on quality problems. This approach consisted of identifying portions of the processes with quality problems (which turned out to be the entire process) and to use statistical process control (SPC) techniques to systematically identify and eliminate the causes. Existing infrastructure problems made this effort very slow going and ineffective.

The production planners attempted to keep the "cost" of production down through better planning. At the same time, operators were encouraged to lower costs by achieving positive labor variances. The natural result of such efforts is larger batches and keeping work centers supplied with material. As a result, customer service deteriorated even further, even as inventory grew. More frequent product shortages increased the level of expediting and unplanned setups throughout the plant.

Overview of the A&B Approach   Note the subtle separation of tasks in the traditional approach taken by A&B. Customer service was essentially considered to be a planning issue, and the responsibility for improving service rested with the planning group. Cost control was considered manufacturing's problem, and the approaches to reducing cost were deemed to be essentially shop functions. It was barely noticed by anyone in the organization that customer service and cost control are related and conflicting issues.

The fundamental difficulty facing A&B was that internal management methods and practices were in conflict with current market needs. On one hand, the market required quick service of a wide range of products. The variety of different fabrics, the diversity of colors, the number of finishes, and even packaging requirements were all increasing. With this increase in product diversity (customization), the size of the orders for individual products was decreasing. On the other hand, management tried to refine outdated mass production techniques designed to reduce production costs for high-volume standardized products. Any valid solution to the problem must address this basic conflict.

A&B Textile's Old Planning System   This section describes the planning process that was in place prior to the implementation of the Synchronous Management drum-buffer-rope logistical system.

The planning process began with a forecast. This forecast covered 12 weeks and was based on historical sales data for the preceding two quarters, construction industry forecasts, macroeconomic indicators, and a host of other parameters. The forecasting algorithm was quite sophisticated and did project the overall level of sales fairly accurately. However, as shown in Figure 4.9, the accuracy of the forecast for product families and especially for individual products (SKUs) deteriorated very

FIGURE 4.9

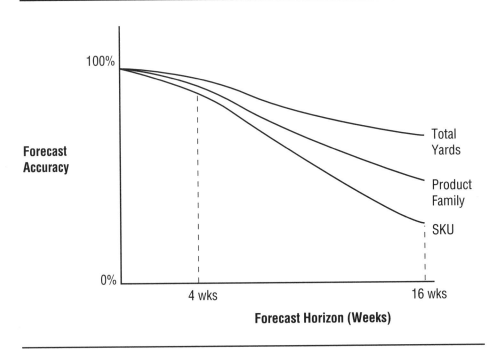

rapidly beyond four weeks. This rapid deterioration occurred because, for those products that were not ordered "off the shelf," the typical delivery lead time required by customers was about four weeks. And customers seldom placed firm orders further out than four weeks. Unfortunately, manufacturing activities have to be planned and executed at the detailed product level, not the aggregate level.

The projected sales volume for each SKU was used to establish the level of finished-goods inventory required to achieve a 90 percent customer fill rate. Comparison of this required inventory level against the current finished-goods inventory enabled planners to determine the mix and quantity of products to be produced in the next period. The projected quantities were then adjusted to reflect the established minimum run size at the looms. According to a long-standing policy, the minimum run size was 10,000 yards.

The production requirements planning was completed once each month and the results discussed at a joint meeting of senior managers from merchandising, manufacturing, and planning. In this meeting, production levels of the different fabric types for the different market segments were finalized. The negotiated production levels were used to determine capacity allocation by market segment. For example, 25 looms of a specific width might be allocated to drapery fabrics.

Actual scheduling was done by production planners. There was one planner for each major product type. The planner identified all products required to be produced during the next month. Then the various jobs were sequenced on the allocated looms. The sequencing took into account the job currently on the specific loom as well as the complex factors that influence a loom changeover time requirements. Jobs at the looms were sequenced so as to try to minimize set-up times, thereby increasing production efficiencies. Loom efficiency was the single most important measure at the mill, and was monitored daily.

The loom schedule was the driving force for determining the production requirements at the yarn preparation operations. In a sense, the loom schedule was being used as the drumbeat to determine yarn and filament requirements. The finishing operations basically processed the material that came off the looms. The only material accumulating ahead of finishing was due to variations in processing speeds and the desire to achieve economical lot sizes for the finishing operation. Lead times used in the old planning system are shown in Figure 4.10.

The planned lead times did not simply reflect actual set-up and run times for a job. They also included the typical amount of queue time a job was likely to experience at a given resource. This waiting time was primarily based on the number and composition of jobs normally in line at that resource. Experience indicated that these planned lead times at a resource were often inadequate. Therefore, additional "safety times" were added in an attempt to maintain the integrity of the planned schedule.

A Synchronous Management Overview Of A&B Textile

The discussion in this section focuses on those planning system and shop-floor procedures and policies that created the opportunity and the encouragement that resulted in misallocation of materials and capacity. These policies were the root causes of large inventories and long lead times that eventually led to poor customer service and excessively high costs.

At A&B Textile, misallocation was encouraged in at least three ways:

1. Planning lead times were overstated.
2. Minimum run lengths were too large.
3. Performance measures encouraged overactivation.

FIGURE 4.10

Old Planning System: Stock Buffers, Planned Lead Times, and Safety Times for A&B Textile

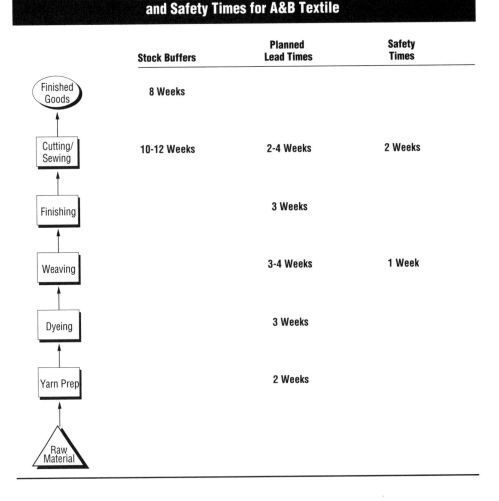

	Stock Buffers	Planned Lead Times	Safety Times
Finished Goods	8 Weeks		
Cutting/Sewing	10-12 Weeks	2-4 Weeks	2 Weeks
Finishing		3 Weeks	
Weaving		3-4 Weeks	1 Week
Dyeing		3 Weeks	
Yarn Prep		2 Weeks	
Raw Material			

Planning Lead Times Were Overstated   At A&B Textile, a batch of several thousand yards of material could be fully processed through the entire plant in only a few days. Yet the old planning system lead time was 12 weeks. The individual and total lead times were heavily padded because of the widely held, but mistaken, belief that adding extra production lead time increased the probability that orders would be shipped on time. What actually happened was far from the expectation. The extra lead time meant that the production floor was flooded with extra inventory, most of which was not needed to fill firm customer orders. The availability of this excess inventory increased the opportunity for misallocation.

The prevailing shop culture that encouraged misallocation then took over. For example, jobs were grouped at each stage of production. At the dyeing operation, jobs with similar colors were grouped together even though the dates or priorities were different. This enabled the dyeing operation to save setups and achieve a positive variance (a traditional indication of good performance). Even inspection was prone to group similar products in order to save the time required to change rolls at the inspection tables. The abundant supply of in-process material made all of this possible.

These types of actions were actually expected and encouraged by the traditional measurement system. Why else would supervisors be rated by variances? But overall plant performance suffered from the large number of "minor" adjustments constantly made to the plan at every stage of production.

In addition, the production planners received expedite requests from the merchandising people every day. These requests reflected the true customer requirements and were supposed to represent adjustments to the production plan. The percentage of the daily production that was affected by these adjustments clearly showed the wide disparity between the forecast (which was made months before) and the actual short-term requirements. In fact, the planner's primary task often became one of finding the "best" spot to run the required materials so as to satisfy merchandising without increasing setups at the looms to unacceptable levels.

Minimum Run Lengths Were Too Large   The minimum run length policy was designed to minimize setups at the looms and had been established many years before. However, it was totally inappropriate to current business conditions. Order sizes were now significantly below these minimum run lengths, and frequent design changes made carrying excess finished-goods inventory a risky and expensive proposition. In addition, the priority distortion created by minimum run lengths not only caused excess inventory, but also resulted in longer production lead times and product shortages.

Performance Measures Encouraged Overactivation   By their very nature, individual local performance measures provided a strong motivation for workers to keep making product. In fact, incentive systems even pressured the planning and materials groups to make sure that work was always available for every worker. Of course, this led to long lead times and excess inventory. What was not recognized was that local performance measures shifted supervisors'attention away from what should have been their prime concern— adhering to the production schedule and doing the right job. Supervisors' attention was directed toward monitoring individual efficiencies and making sure everyone had enough work to keep busy.

The planning system created opportunities for material and resource misallocations, and the shop culture encouraged taking advantage of these opportunities.

Unfortunately, in the A&B plant, the consequences of misallocation were very serious. The result was continuous rescheduling. Whenever a loom became available, the next job to be run was determined "on the fly," either by the planner or by the foreman. All of this rescheduling activity was highly disruptive on downstream operations. But it was equally disruptive to the upstream operations that were running smoothly. For example, the managers of the yarn preparation areas were asked to maintain high operator and equipment efficiencies while constantly reacting to highly unpredictable material demands from downstream operations. This put them in a no-win situation. The only chance yarn prep supervisors had to achieve both targets was to carry high levels of inventory. But the highly volatile nature of the forecast rendered this a futile tactic, leaving them with lots of inventory, unsatisfied downstream demand and/or poor efficiency performance.

V-PLANT CASE STUDY: IMPLEMENTING DRUM-BUFFER-ROPE

The ultimate objective of implementing a Synchronous Management drum-buffer-rope system at the A&B Textile plant is to improve profitability by improving customer service while reducing product costs.

Identifying Constraints

There are no material constraints at the A&B plant. This can be deduced from two facts. First, an analysis of product shortages and late shipments failed to reveal any common material as a potential source of delays. Second, no one in the plant seemed to feel that the availability of materials for the yarn was a problem.

The next step is identification of the capacity constraint resource, which starts with determining the inventory profile for the various stages of production. Figure 4.11 shows the inventory profiles, expressed in terms of the number of weeks' supply, of material available at each resource and as finished-goods. Inventory levels are averaged over time and rounded to the nearest week.

A quick glance at the inventory profile is a little confusing. There is a clear drop in the inventory level immediately after weaving. There is also a huge increase in inventory at cutting/sewing. The natural choice for the constraint appears to be cutting/sewing. But before accepting cutting/sewing as the CCR, let's perform a verification analysis.

FIGURE 4.11

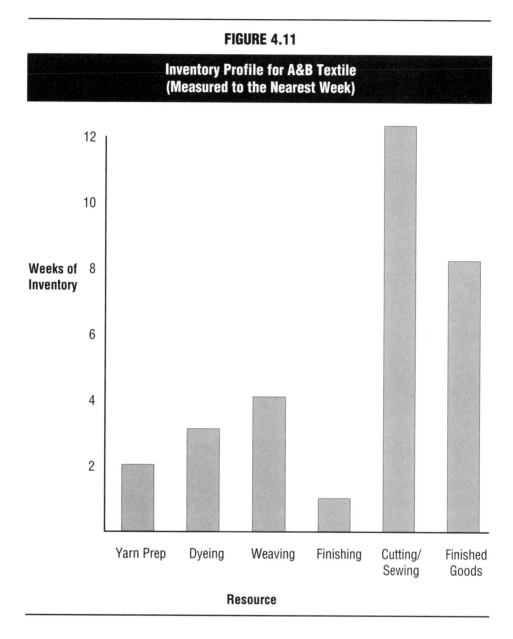

Inventory Profile for A&B Textile
(Measured to the Nearest Week)

The weaving looms operate three full shifts, five days a week. All other resources only operate partial second and third shifts. In addition, the looms are often scheduled to run on Saturdays to meet urgent customer orders. These facts are inconsistent with cutting/sewing being the capacity constraint, and the contradiction must be resolved.

Further investigation unravels the mystery. Managers at A&B are no longer managing the plant according to the generic V-plant model. They have deviated from the basic model to add an extensive stock buffer of inventory inventory immediately prior to cutting/sewing. This buffer is just one step removed from finished-goods. It is designed to help the plant respond to customer lead time requirements without adding to the extensive finished-goods stock buffer that already exists. In essence, if this material stock buffer in front of cutting/sewing is treated as an extension of the finished-goods stock buffer, the picture is clear. Cutting/sewing is not the capacity constraint. Without this planned material stock buffer, the inventory level at cutting/sewing would consist of one or two weeks' material.

As a result, it is clear that weaving is the CCR. This follows from the significant drop in inventory levels immediately after weaving and is also confirmed by the previous capacity analysis for the different work centers.

This case emphasizes the importance of performing a verification analysis in order to correctly identify the constraint. It also is a good reminder that every plant is unique, and will seldom fall neatly into a generic plant model.

One other thing is confirmed by the inventory profile. The very high level of finished-goods inventory (including almost-finished materials at cutting/sewing) is a good indicator that the production process involves at least some work centers with considerable set-up requirements. In fact, the weaving looms require setups that are quite lengthy, reinforcing the constraint status of weaving.

Setting The Buffers

Establishing a drum-buffer-rope (DBR) system requires a firm understanding of the nature of product demand and customer requirements. A key piece of information is that less than 10 percent of all SKUs are sold "off the shelf." The remaining products are ordered by customers with required delivery lead times of about four weeks.

Stock Buffers   Previous practice was to try to service all demand out of finished-goods inventory. However, this is not the most effective use of stock buffers. Finished-goods stock buffers are only required to satisfy those products that are ordered off the shelf, and are not needed for the vast majority of products. This allows for drastically reducing the finished-goods stock buffer.

The finished-goods stock buffer should service only off the shelf orders, and be set at four weeks' worth of product demand. Even this amount of inventory is somewhat excessive, but the A&B managers are uncomfortable with anything less than four weeks' inventory.

Appropriately located and sized material stock buffers service all other customer orders within the four-week lead time. (Note that material stock buffers are required as long as the production lead times exceed the customer delivery lead times.) These material stock buffers can, of course, be established at any point in the production process, from yarn prep through cutting/sewing.

Advantage is gained by stocking material in a partially processed stage if there are major divergence points after that stage of production. Since finishing is not a major divergence point, an appropriate material stock buffer location is after finishing–prior to cutting/sewing.

One additional material stock buffer needs to be established for all materials, at the capacity constraint, weaving. This mid-production stocking point allows fabric to be efficiently fed to the downstream material stock buffers and from there to the finished-goods stock buffers. The material stock buffer at weaving helps limit the size of the downstream stock buffers. (It is important to remember that the size of these stock buffers is dependent on the required replenishment time.)

Initially a six-week stock buffer is established at cutting/sewing. The size of the material stock buffer at weaving is four weeks. Figure 4.12 shows the initial composition, location, and size of all stock buffers.

It should be noted that the total level of inventory in the system (excluding raw-material stocks) can be roughly determined from the size of the stock buffers, planned set-up and run times, and time buffers. In the initial phase of the Synchronous Management system implementation, the total amount of work-in-process and finished-goods inventory is approximately 20 weeks. This compares quite favorably with the roughly 30 weeks' worth of inventory in the old planning and control system.

New Set-up and Run Times   In the DBR system, set-up and run times for each individual operation are not "padded." That is, instead of calculating a planned lead time for each operation, set-up and run time for the "typical" process batch at each operation is determined.

Figure 4.12 shows the set-up and run times established for each operation. The set-up and run time for weaving is two days, while for all other resources it is set at one day. Even these times are generous since virtually all process batches at most resources (except weaving) can be set up and run in one or two shifts.

In the DBR system, the planned lead time to move from one buffer location to the next is determined by adding the appropriate time buffer (at the receiving buffer location) to the calculated set-up and run times at the required resources. The time buffer must be set so as to ensure that the total planned lead time is *realistic*. Therefore, the time buffer must allow for all possible sources of time delays such as waiting time in the queue, schedule delays in order to perform related setups, machine breakdowns, quality problems, etc.

Time Buffers   Having established the stock buffers and the set-up and run times, the next step is to establish the size and location of the time buffers. Time buffers are required at several locations; at the CCR, at cutting and sewing, and finished goods. Figure 4.12 shows the location and size of all the time buffers.

The time buffer at weaving must be large enough to protect the planned product flow from scheduling problems and disruptions that affect yarn prep and dyeing. The time buffer at weaving is protecting the capacity constraint for the plant, and thus plant throughput. The time buffer for weaving is generously set at three weeks. Since the planned set-up and run times at yarn prep and dyeing are one day each, this means allowing three weeks and two days for material to be processed from the raw material stage to weaving. Since the material stock buffer at weaving is four weeks, it should remain adequately stocked.

Time buffers are also required to protect the material stock buffers located at cutting/sewing. The material that feeds this buffer comes from weaving. A four-week time buffer is adequate to protect the timely arrival of materials from weaving. Since material goes from weaving to finishing to cutting/sewing, the planned lead time for the cutting/sewing material stock buffer is four weeks and three days. This is the planned lead time from the material stock buffer to the cutting/sewing material stock buffer.

A time buffer exists at the finished-goods level to protect both the finished-goods stock buffer and the shipping buffer. Whether the products are headed for the finished-goods stock buffer or for the shipping dock is irrelevant in determining the size of the time buffer. Both categories of products need to be protected from the same fluctuations that occur at cutting/sewing, and a two-week buffer is sufficient. The planned lead time from the cutting/sewing operation to the finished-goods warehouse is two weeks and one day.

As the Synchronous Management DBR system is implemented, minimum and maximum run sizes are reduced and work-in-process inventory is drained from the system. The production priority sequence suffers less distortion from the demand-generated schedule, and more orders can be run in less total elapsed time. Inventory turns increases and production lead time decreases.

Set-up and run times, along with the relevant time buffers, basically determine total manufacturing lead time. In the initial phase of the Synchronous Management implementation, total manufacturing lead time is about 10 weeks. This represents a significant reduction from the previous manufacturing lead time, which varied from 16 to 19 weeks.

FIGURE 4.12

Initial Synchronous Management System: Stock Buffers, Setup and Run Times, and Time Buffers for A&B Textile

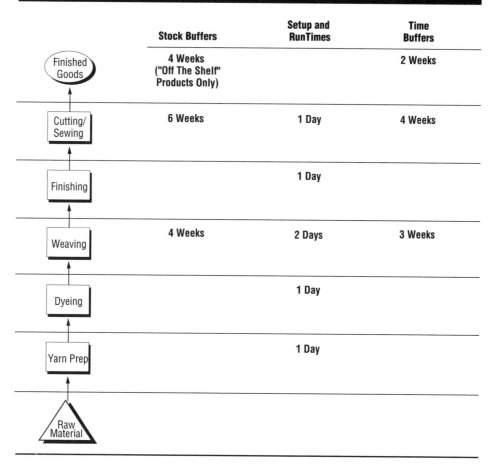

	Stock Buffers	Setup and Run Times	Time Buffers
Finished Goods	4 Weeks ("Off The Shelf" Products Only)		2 Weeks
Cutting/ Sewing	6 Weeks	1 Day	4 Weeks
Finishing		1 Day	
Weaving	4 Weeks	2 Days	3 Weeks
Dyeing		1 Day	
Yarn Prep		1 Day	
Raw Material			

Establishing the Master Schedule

The next step is to establish the plant drumbeat. Since weaving is the CCR, this step in setting up the DBR system consists of converting all customer requirements into a loom schedule. Weaving capabilities are critical in establishing the actual schedule. This is not a total revelation to A&B managers. However, there are major differences between the old planning system approach and the new DBR approach. The key difference is the nature of the policies and procedures used to establish the schedule.

Determining Material Requirements   Remember that a material stock buffer has been established at cutting/sewing. This stock buffer consists of finished materials that have yet to be cut and sewn and is used to replenish the relatively small finished-goods stock buffer for off-the-shelf items, as well as to provide a timely response to all other orders as they are received. *Thus, the primary objective of the weaving loom schedule is to keep the material stock buffers adequately supplied!*

The methodology for establishing the master schedule is described below. The first step in establishing the master schedule is to identify the finished (but not cut and sewn) fabric required to:

1. Replenish the "off-the-shelf" finished-goods stock buffer as products are sold from this buffer.
2. Fill the actual sales orders for all products not sold "off the shelf."

Remember, under the old system a new production requirements plan was developed every month. In a DBR process, it is imperative to update this plan more frequently, using the latest available information about inventory levels and customer orders. Thus, each week the updated information on products sold from finished goods and new orders received is reviewed and product requirements determined. (Eventually, the required materials are drawn from the material stock buffer at cutting/sewing, processed through cutting/sewing and sent to the finished-goods stock buffer for "off-the-shelf" products, or straight to shipping for the other products.) Since cutting/sewing is not a capacity constraint, replenishing the finished-goods stock buffer and order filling on an order-by-order basis presents no problem, as long as the required material is available at the cutting/sewing material stock buffer.

As soon as the material requirements from the cutting/sewing material stock buffer are identified, this information is converted to a production requirements plan at weaving. (Eventually, the needed materials will be pulled from the weaving material stock buffer, processed on the looms, and then sent to finishing and cutting/sewing.) Since weaving is the CCR and set-up requirements influence the priority sequence, greater care is required to develop an effective production schedule here.

Minimum and Maximum Run Sizes   The ideal loom schedule is to produce yarn-dyed fabrics on an order-by-order basis (similar to the schedule developed for cutting/sewing). However, due to the often lengthy setups at the looms, and the fact that some orders are for relatively small quantities, the prevailing management perception is that producing on an order-by-order basis is impossible. In fact, the old planning system philosophy was to make the batch size as large as possible without driving up finished-goods inventory to excessively high levels, based on the traditional view that every setup is evaluated in isolation. The traditional emphasis on efficient resource utilization encouraged larger batch sizes. But careful examination shows that the idea of producing on an order-by-order basis is not as far-fetched as it might seem, due to two factors:

1. In Synchronous Management, one is not interested in the individual batch sizes of the various products, only in the total time lost while performing setups. A mix of batch sizes, some large and some small, is perfectly acceptable. The orders received at A&B do consist of a mix of order sizes. Some products are ordered in sizable quantities every week and others are ordered infrequently and in small quantities.

2. The very complexity of the setups at the looms affords an advantage that can be used to produce very small batches. A key characteristic of loom setups is that some changeovers (such as only changing filler material) can be performed very quickly. Thus, a small order for a particular fabric type can sometimes be produced without significant penalty if there is an accompanying large order with similar set-up requirements.

In essence, small order sizes do not present a problem and need not be increased to arbitrarily established minimum run sizes as long as two conditions hold. One, the number of small orders is relatively small. Two, these small orders can be grouped with larger orders having similar set-up requirements. Note that this analysis holds without any change in set-up procedures as they are currently performed. And any significant set-up reduction program will only strengthen the argument.

While logically sound, this argument is at odds with management's deeply embedded beliefs, based on decades of experience. Technically, an order-by-order production scheme is possible. Psychologically, it represents too much change and trauma for management. It was decided to gradually reduce the batch size while simultaneously embarking on a set-up reduction program, and agreed that the starting point is to reduce the minimum run length from 10,000 yards to 6,000.

In addition to reducing the minimum run length, the new policy also affects the batch size in another way. The old policy was to produce in monthly quantities. In the new DBR system, the maximum batch size is limited to weekly quantities, with a 6,000-yard minimum. For example, a monthly requirement for 80,000 yards is broken up into four batches of 20,000 yards each. But a monthly requirement of 12,000 yards is run as two batches of 6,000 yards each.

This new procedure for setting the loom schedule does generate more planned setups than the previous procedure (monthly quantities with a 10,000-yard minimum). If weaving is the CCR, how can this not reduce system throughput?

The answer here involves the logic summarized back in Figure 4.6. The idea is to execute a production plan that minimizes total set-up time at the constraint while still satisfying customer demand. Total set-up time is a function of the number of planned setups, the number of unplanned setups, and the ability to execute an efficient sequence of setups that takes advantage of quick changeovers. The key factor is that if run lengths are too long, it can cause an excessive number of expedited orders and unplanned setups, which not only destroys the planned setup sequence but causes the actual number of setups to dramatically increase. Under the DBR system, expedited orders and unplanned setups are virtually eliminated and the total number of setups does not increase.

Once the priority sequence at weaving has been determined, then the raw material requirements can also be directly calculated. The needed materials are then released from raw material stocks, processed through yarn prep and dyeing, and then received at the weaving material stock buffer. Timely replenishment of the material stock buffer is achieved.

A New Role for Forecasting

Under the DBR system, the need for and the role of forecasting changes drastically, since the system is a replenishment system based on *actual customer orders*. The value of the forecast is now limited to predicting general trends and establishing seasonal variations in demand for various products. This information can then be used to help establish stock buffer levels. That is, if the forecast identifies a seasonal fluctuation that indicates that weekly demand for a product will increase by 25 percent for the summer months, corresponding stock buffers for this product will be adjusted so 25 percent more of the required product or material is held during the peak season.

Tying The Ropes – Establishing the Schedule Control Points

The next step in the DBR system is to establish the ropes to communicate to all resources what is needed to support the drum. Every resource at A&B Textile is a divergence point, and therefore, a schedule control point. This means that each resource must be provided with a job priority list that indicates the product to be produced, the quantity of product required, and the production sequence.

The procedure for converting the loom schedule into requirements at other operations is not the same as the procedure used in the old planning system, where planned lead times and safety times were used to develop resource work schedules. In the DBR system, typical set-up and run times are determined and coupled with a limited number of time buffers to determine material release and resource work schedules.

The average set-up and run times at each scheduled resource are summed to generate a "minimum" expected production lead time from one stock location to the next. But this minimum lead time does not allow for any delays or schedule slippage. That is the role of the time buffer. The time buffer quantity is added to the minimum expected production lead time to yield a realistic production lead time. This production lead time is not only realistic, but the fact that safety time is added to each step of the process results in shorter manufacturing lead times.

The technique for tying the rope may resemble the technique in use today. However, the rope system and the traditional system are fundamentally different in two ways.

First, in the DBR system, the basic idea is to release material into the system only as needed by the stock buffers, by the constraint or by the customer. Once the material has been released into the system (from raw material storage or intermediate stock buffers) it should be processed and moved to its final destination as quickly as possible. The time buffer associated with the material's destination is designed to account for any disruptions that occur as the material moves through the system.

Second, there is a big difference between traditional systems and Synchronous Management DBR systems as to how work centers utilize the job priority list information provided. The traditional system normally requires each individual supervisor to process the work in such a way as to optimize performance of the local work center. The DBR system requires that the supervisor adhere to the priority sequence, even at the risk of adversely affecting local work center optimization. In other words, in the DBR system, local resource optimization may be sacrificed (especially at non-constraint resources) in order to achieve a global optimum.

Monitoring Performance and Progress

As A&B Textile implements the DBR system, a number of additional actions are taken to reinforce the improvements being made.

A set of detailed operational measures are developed and used to evaluate critical performance aspects. Some of the specific measures include throughput at the CCR (weaving), scrap and yield reports at the finishing and cutting/sewing work centers (since they work on material already processed by the constraint), on-time delivery performance, and inventory turns.

Also developed and implemented is a key measure that determines whether a resource is following the required priority sequence. Since the new DBR policies run counter to traditional procedures, which emphasized local optimization, close monitoring is necessary at the beginning of implementation. This helps eliminate material misallocation that had previously plagued the entire plant.

Process improvement programs have also been implemented. For example, a critical obstacle to achieving a higher level of responsiveness was the set-up time requirement at the weaving looms. Reducing set-up time at weaving has a greater impact on bottom-line performance than any automation program at any other operation. Therefore, one of the first actions taken was to implement a set-up reduction program that first focused on the weaving looms. In short order, this led to reduced set-up time requirements and more productive capacity at the looms. It also reduced the waiting time before orders could be processed at the looms. This and other process improvements, along with the elimination of material misallocation, enabled a reduction in the size of the required time buffers. This, in turn, allowed a reduction in stock buffer levels. As a result, overall inventory levels dropped significantly even as responsiveness increased.

As the implementation of Synchronous Management progressed, A&B's performance improved dramatically. Figure 4.13 gives an indication of the plant-wide improvements. The figure identifies the values of the stock buffers, required set-up and run times, and time buffers less than one year into the implementation.

As the process at A&B Textile has become more synchronized, the nature of the DBR system has continued to change. Production planning meetings are now held, and production schedules set, twice a week instead of once a week. As the various process improvements took hold, production lead times were reduced to the point where materials consistently flowed from cutting/sewing to shipping in one week and from weaving to shipping within three weeks. Remember that the standard customer lead time requirement as set by the market is four weeks. Consider the implications. A&B has a choice of two very nice alternatives.

FIGURE 4.13

Synchronous Management System: Stock Buffers, Setup and Run Times, and Time Buffers for A&B Textile (Less than One Year into the Implementation)

	Stock Buffers	Setup and RunTimes	Time Buffers
Finished Goods	2 Weeks ("Off The Shelf" Products Only)		1.5 Weeks
Cutting/ Sewing	3 Weeks	1 Day	2.5 Weeks
Finishing		1 Day	
Weaving	3 Weeks	2 Days	2.5 Weeks
Dyeing		1 Day	
Yarn Prep		1 Day	
Raw Material			

A&B has the ability to promise and deliver any product to customers (from cutting/sewing material stock buffers) in one week. This could mean a real competitive advantage in the marketplace and could translate into a higher sales volume for the plant. (Of course, any additional throughput could only be sustained if weaving can generate the additional needed capacity.)

Alternatively, A&B could establish a three-week delivery lead time, less than the current market standard, and still eliminate the material stock buffers at

FIGURE 4.14

**Restructured Synchronous Management System: Stock Buffers,
Setup and Run Times, and Time Buffers for A&B Textile
(More than One Year into the Implementation)**

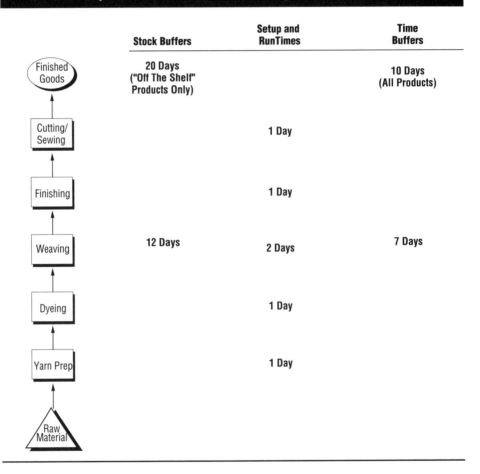

cutting/sewing and finishing, and supply finished-goods and shipping directly from the material stock buffer at weaving. This places the only material stock buffer at a relatively early divergence point in the product flow, increasing material flexibility and reducing the amount of inventory carried in material stock buffers.

Figure 4.14 illustrates the second alternative, chosen by A&B. In the restructured drum-buffer-rope system, after more than one year into the implementation the sole material stock buffer is located at weaving.

Note that all time units in Figure 4.14 are expressed in days instead of weeks. This change to shorter time increments is a reflection of the significantly shorter lead times and is a natural outcome of implementing a DBR system. The total production lead time at A&B Textile can be calculated by adding all setup and run times with the value of the two time buffers. Total production lead time is 23 days, or just under five standard five-day weeks.

Recall that the primary objective of this Synchronous Management implementation was to enhance company profitability by improving customer service while reducing product costs. In a relatively short period of time, A&B dramatically reduced inventory, drastically shortened production lead times, and generated extra capacity at the looms that allowed for a larger production (and sales) volume. Needless to say, the company's bottom-line financial performance improved sharply as the DBR system was implemented and continuously enhanced.

Chapter 5

IMPLEMENTING SYNCHRONOUS MANAGEMENT IN A-PLANTS

Genius, in truth, means little more than the faculty of perceiving in an unhabitual way.

– William James, 1890

OVERVIEW OF A-PLANT ISSUES

As discussed in Chapter 3, an A-plant is a manufacturing plant whose behavior is dominated by the presence of assembly operations. Moreover, those operations are convergent assembly points, where the material flows of two or more component parts converge to form a single parent item.

A-plants are commonly found in industries that manufacture specialized equipment and low-volume capital intensive products. The main characteristics of A-type plants were presented in Chapter 3 and are summarized below:

1. The distinguishing characteristic is the assembly of a large number of manufactured (and purchased) components into a relatively small number of end products. In a typical A-plant, there are a number of assembly points in the process where multiple components are sub-assembled to create one new part. As a result, there are many more raw materials and purchased components than end products.
2. The various component parts are unique to specific end items. In A-plants, each specific end item is normally designed according to different product specifications. Therefore, for different end items, even similar looking or similar functioning components will generally incorporate unique design specifications.

3. The production routings for the various manufactured components are typically different, and may be highly dissimilar. Any given manufactured component may require anywhere from one to several dozen different processing operations. And the manufactured components needed for a given assembly will seldom utilize the exact same production resources. Even when production resources are shared by two or more components, these resources are not generally used in the same processing sequences.

4. The machines and tools used in the manufacturing process tend to be general purpose equipment. In A-plants, a specific piece of equipment may be used in the processing of a wide variety of different materials and components. In addition, a given part may be processed by the same equipment several times in the course of its routing. Therefore, of necessity, most A-plant equipment must be quite flexible.

Figure 5.1 shows the product flow diagram of a typical A plant.

We have described the problems found in A-plants that are not managed in accordance with basic Synchronous Management principles. In such non-synchronized environments, production bottlenecks often appear to wander about the plant, overall resource utilization is poor, and unplanned overtime is often required in an attempt to stay on schedule. As a result, production costs are too high. But despite management's best expediting efforts, parts shortages often result in late shipments and poor customer service.

The two most problematic performance issues in A-plants are generally considered to be:

*   Keeping production costs under control.
*   Improving customer service levels by improving control of the system.

A-plant managers often incorrectly conclude that production costs can effectively be reduced by limiting the use of overtime and improving labor efficiency through work force reductions and automation. They also often conclude that the observed control problems are primarily caused by a lack of information and the inability to track the status of materials throughout the process. Reaching this conclusion usually leads to implementation of the latest computer-based information and control system.

Unfortunately, implementing a new computer-based information and control system will not resolve the A-plant problem the old dysfunctional policies and operating rules used to manage the operation are transferred into the new system.

FIGURE 5.1

Product Flow Diagram of a Typical A-Plant

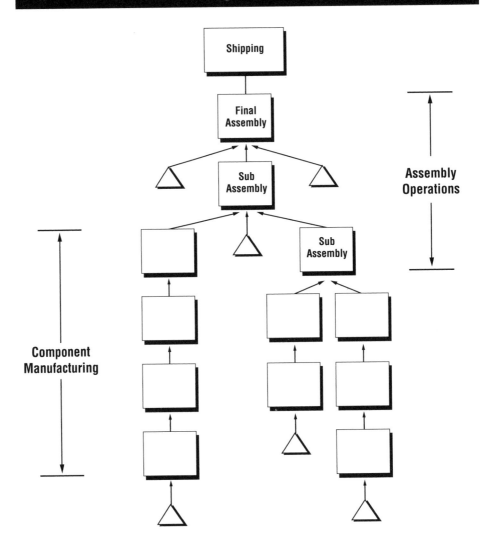

What the new information system can deliver is constant updates that describe in great detail how poorly the manufacturing system is still operating.

Implementing a new computer-based information and control system is also costly, in both time and money. However, the greatest cost is not often recognized. Managers do not actively look for better solutions because they are too busy implementing the new computer-based system.

In Synchronous Management, the critical performance issues are addressed by improved synchronization of the component production operation. This synchronization is accomplished through implementation of a drum-buffer-rope logistical system, accompanied by the necessary changes in policies, operating rules, and performance measures.

Synchronizing the manufacturing process reduces operating costs through two different mechanisms. One major reduction occurs as inventory levels are reduced, since this directly results in reduced carrying costs. Synchronization further reduces operating costs by significantly cutting the wasteful expenses associated with planned and unplanned overtime, premium freight, rework or scrap caused by time pressures, and excessive material handling.

Improved synchronization also improves customer service levels by ensuring that all required component parts are processed through the fabrication and assembly operations quickly and smoothly. This not only improves on-time delivery performance, but also shrinks the manufacturing lead time to customers. As customer service improves, the company's competitive advantage in the marketplace improves. This should lead to an increase in throughput.

In Synchronous Management terminology, the key business performance issues and the objectives of any planning and control system implementation should be to simultaneously:

- Increase Throughput.
- Reduce Inventory.
- Reduce Operating Expense.

THE DRUM-BUFFER-ROPE IMPLEMENTATION PROCESS

Identifying the Constraints

The first step in a drum-buffer-rope implementation for A-plants is identification of the physical constraints–both material constraints and capacity constraints.

Material Constraints   Material constraints are materials that in some way limit the plant's ability to serve marketplace needs. In other words, a material constraint either causes higher levels of inventory, higher operating expense, or lower throughput.

There are two basic reasons for a material constraint to exist. One, the material is simply not available in the quantity needed at the time needed. Two, the quality of the material is substandard. Let's examine each of these cases further.

Material availability may be a problem for several reasons. In some cases, the vendor's capacity to supply the constraint material is simply insufficient. That is, the vendor may have a true production bottleneck. In other cases, some specialized components have extremely long vendor lead times. In such cases, it is sometimes difficult to forecast material requirements with sufficient accuracy to guarantee availability. Even when vendor lead times are not excessively long, availability can be a problem if the vendor is unreliable. Sometimes the required material is not available because the vendor did not deliver the material when promised, or in the quantity promised. Either case can cause the production schedule to slip, causing a loss of throughput or excessive expediting costs. To compensate for such vendor unreliability, the plant may resort to holding larger stock buffers of certain materials than otherwise would be necessary.

Material quality is a problem if it generates excessive scrap or rework, or causes operators to spend an excessive amount of time processing. If substandard material causes scrap, the ultimate result is a quantity of usable material insufficient to meet downstream requirements. Extra time spent processing substandard material or performing rework can cause operating expense to go up if, for example, overtime is required.

Whenever a true material constraint exists, it should be dealt with decisively. Managers should never let unavailable or poor quality material limit the performance of the manufacturing system. A comprehensive material control program that monitors vendor performance and material quality throughout the process will help pinpoint material-related problems and provide a clear indication of the identity of any material constraint. However, consistent with our definition of constraint, to be classified as a constraint the material must be a chronic problem, not just a one-time situation. Therefore, any worthwhile monitoring system should continuously track material availability and quality.

Material unavailability caused by poor vendor delivery performance is relatively easy to track. The straightforward way to do this is to identify those materials that are consistently released late to manufacturing. Identifying substandard materials is a more difficult task because such materials can cause a variety of problems such as scrap, rework, poor yield, or excessive processing time requirements. And these problems can be difficult to quantify and accurately trace back to poor material quality as the cause

Capacity Constraints   In this section, we begin by discussing the problems encountered trying to identify capacity constraints. We then develop a systematic procedure to identify capacity constraints in A-plants.

Problems Identifying Capacity Constraints   In V-plants, capacity constraints are identified by developing an inventory profile and identifying the resource that marks the dividing line between high inventory and low inventory levels. Unfortunately, this relatively simple and straightforward approach does not work in generic A-plants because there is work-in-process inventory everywhere!

The reason for this abundance of in-process material in A-plants lies in the nature of the product flow. Since A-plants are organized functionally, and the routings for the different products are highly dissimilar, each department or work center receives material from many different work centers. Some of these materials may be processed by a CCR, but many are not. Thus, even work centers that work on parts already processed by a CCR will not be totally starved. They can be well supplied with parts by work centers that are not CCRs. Hence, any work center in an A-plant may possess large work-in-process inventories.

As with V-plants, the use of capacity planning systems is not a viable alternative to identify capacity constraints in A-plants. In spite of its appeal, this approach has one major and fatal flaw. The calculation of required work loads is based on the information contained in the manufacturing data base. And the integrity of most such data bases is far from acceptable. The information concerning set-up and processing times, specific work centers that are actually used, and the identity of alternate resources and processes, is not accurate in most cases. The problem of obtaining accurate data from the information system is compounded by the large number of component parts and resources in A-plants.

Hence, neither inventory profile nor computer-based information systems can be used to identify capacity constraint resources. Instead, an understanding of A-plants and the expected effects of CCRs must be used to develop a procedure to identify the CCRs in A-plants.

A Procedure For Identifying Capacity Constraints   Because capacity constraint resources are those resources whose available capacity limits the plant's ability to meet the product volume, product mix, or demand fluctuations required by the marketplace, it follows that parts requiring these resources are often in short supply. Hence, an analysis of part shortages should contain the necessary clues to identify capacity constraint resources.

By definition, CCRs have difficulty processing the parts required in a timely fashion. In contrast, non-CCRs should not have consistent difficulty meeting required production. This difference in capability shows up at assembly points as a mismatch in the availability of parts that require CCRs and parts that do not require CCRs.

However, a single snapshot taken at any specific point in time can be misleading, due to the existence of "wandering bottlenecks" created by the tendency to overactivate resources. This can cause shortages of all parts, even those not processed by a CCR. In addition, the large batch sizes often found in A-plants can temporarily create a sizable amount of inventory anywhere in the plant. To weed out "wandering bottlenecks" and identify the true CCRs necessitates taking multiple snapshots of inventory queues over a period of time.

This systematic procedure for identifying CCRs has two major phases. First, identify all resources that are likely CCR candidates. Second, subject each candidate CCR to a rigorous validation process.

The candidate identification analysis is conducted with information taken from the component stores area just prior to assembly. This phase includes three steps:

1. *Develop a list of parts that are chronically late arriving to the assembly stores area.* This is the list of parts that show up frequently on the assembly expedite or shortage list. These parts may involve CCRs.
2. *Develop a list of parts that are chronically in excess.* These are parts that do not appear on the shortage list and are plentiful in the stockroom. These parts clearly do not involve CCRs.
3. *Review the routings for the parts found on the two lists.* Identify those resources that are involved in the processing of parts found on the shortage list and are not involved in the processing of parts on the excess list. The CCR candidates are those resources that process parts that are chronically short but do not process parts that are chronically in excess.

The true CCRs have to be extracted from this candidate list. To identify the true CCRs, as many of the following validations as possible should be performed:

1. *Verification that a sizable work-in-process queue at a resource is typical.* If a candidate resource is a true CCR, material should naturally

accumulate at that resource. But remember that inventory can be found ahead of many resources in A-plants. What we are looking for is the periodic absence of a sizable queue. This would cast doubt on the resource being a true CCR.

2. *Verification of overtime worked.* If a resource is a true capacity constraint, it should experience a high degree of difficulty keeping pace with demand. CCR's must generally resort to overtime on a regular basis to meet assembly schedule requirements and keep up with other resources.

3. *Discussion with expediters.* Expediters can be used to confirm whether or not a part is frequently short. Expediters also can usually point out the resource where short parts are usually "stuck."

4. *A general check of processing and set-up times.* The processing and set-up times of the candidate resources should be examined as a spot check for inconsistencies. This analysis is only performed to further validate that the processing and set-up time requirements of the candidate resource are consistent with it being a CCR.

A-plants may be organized along product or component lines rather than the more typical functional organization. In this case, the routings within the component "lines" will be similar and require the same resources. Therefore, once the chronically late components have been identified, developing an inventory profile similar to that used for V-plants can be used as an additional validation of the existence of a CCR.

Some A-plants do not have a true bottleneck, or even a CCR. In such cases, the problems meeting delivery requirements are not due to limited available capacity, but rather ineffective management of available capacity!

The purpose of performing the validation process is to either confirm that a resource is a CCR or to expose an inconsistency. An inconsistency occurs when a resource that is initially identified as a capacity constraint is shown to be a non-constraint. Whenever an inconsistency is revealed, it is critical to fully understand the underlying reasons.

Fully analyzing every inconsistency will help managers understand the difference between what is expected in generic A-plants operating under traditional management guidelines and their own specific plant. This process reveals many of the critical distinguishing features that make their specific plant different from a generic plant. Highlighting these distinguishing features is imperative because this knowledge should be used by managers to guide the Synchronous Management implementation.

Setting the Buffers

Once the constraints have been identified, the next step is to determine buffer requirements. What types of buffers are appropriate? Where are the buffers needed? How large should the buffers be?

Stock Buffers   The key to understanding how stock buffers can be used in A-plants is based on the distinction between what we refer to as a *product stock buffer* and a *component stock buffer.*

Product stock buffer
Stock buffer composed of either finished goods or partially processed material that, by itself, can be fully processed into finished goods.

Component stock buffer
Stock buffer composed of component parts that must be assembled with other component parts in order to produce finished goods.

The stock buffers utilized in V-plants, as described in chapter 4, were product stock buffers. That is, they were stock buffers of finished or partially processed products. The purpose of these buffers is to enable the plant to satisfy market demand in less than the normal production lead time. In V-plants, the general product structure lends itself very nicely to product stock buffers at intermediate stages of production to achieve substantial benefits.

Product stock buffers are not generally appropriate for A-plants. In the case of product stock buffers of finished goods, the nature of product demand in A-plants does not typically lend itself to holding stocks of finished goods in anticipation of off-the-shelf demand. (Although this would be possible in an environment where the volume of demand for specific products is sufficiently high and predictable.) Product stock buffers of partially processed material are not appropriate for A-plants because finished products in A-plants are never composed of just a single material.

Component stock buffers of partially processed material are not generally utilized in A-plants to improve market responsiveness for three reasons. One, specific component parts that exist at intermediate stages are not common to multiple end items. Two, a very large number of parts are generally needed to produce each unique end item. Three, the volume of product demanded is usually not sufficient to support holding inventory of all needed parts.

However, component stock buffers can be used very effectively in A-plants to simplify the problem of establishing detailed control over the many different parts required for the assembly operation. The final assembled product may contain tens, hundreds, or even thousands of components. Some of these components are manufactured or subassembled in the plant while others are purchased.

The many components required to produce products in A-plants can be segmented into two broad subsets. One subset consists of manufactured or subassembled components that are totally unique to specific products. The other subset includes all other parts, primarily common parts or components that are used in the assembly of multiple end products. This second subset generally contains the majority of parts used in the plant.

Significantly, only those components in the first subset–those that are unique to specific products—are considered to be the "key" components in an A-plant. *It is this minority of key components that establish the A-type nature of the entire plant.* The procurement and production of these key components must be carefully monitored and precisely controlled.

Fortunately, in most A-plants, the (sometimes vast) majority of components are common to several end items. These components may range from very high-volume, low-cost items (such as bolts, nuts, and standard gauge wire) to items of lower volume or higher cost. A simple way to control these items must be established because devising a detailed monitoring and control system for hundreds or thousands of different parts is not feasible.

Component stock buffers can be developed for the non-key items. Once the component stock buffers are set, purchasing and production need only be managed in the simplest way possible that will keep these stock buffers sufficiently replenished. For example, for purchased parts, these buffers could be maintained by using the old two-bin system. (In this system, parts required for production are taken from the first bin. When the first bin is totally empty, a replenishment order is placed. Meanwhile, production needs are satisfied from the second bin. When the order of parts is received, the second bin is refilled, and the remainder of the ordered parts go into the first bin. Production needs are once again satisfied from the first bin.) For parts that are processed internally and placed in stock, a modified two-bin system could be used. This system can be seen as a kanban system, where the kanbans are established at the stock buffer point and the entire production routing for these parts is managed like as a single kanban work center.

Time Buffers   Stock buffers can be used to take care of the problem of detailed control for non-key material in A-plants. But time buffers are needed to protect system throughput from the internal variability inherent in the A-plant's manufacturing and assembly environment.   This internal variability includes equipment breakdowns, absenteeism, temporary work overloads, yield problems, etc.

In A-plants, three different categories of time buffers may be required:

- *Constraint Time Buffer.* This buffer is established at CCRs. Allowing extra time for parts to arrive at CCRs ensures that disruptions that occur at other resources earlier in the routings of CCR parts do not jeopardize CCR production schedules and plant throughput.
- *Shipping Time Buffer.* This buffer is established at the shipping department, after the final assembly operation and any final preparation processing such as packaging. This time cushion protects the customers' promised ship dates from disruptions that occur at operations beyond CCRs, at the final assembly operation, and at final preparation or packaging operations. This is not a revolutionary concept. Almost all companies inherently allow for a shipping buffer, although they don't recognize it as such. For example, suppose a plant is scheduled to ship an order by 5:00 P.M. Thursday. Who in their right mind would schedule final assembly for the order to be completed at 5:00 P.M. Thursday?
- *Assembly Time Buffer.* This buffer is established at the assembly operation itself. This buffer is designed for any part that is not processed by a CCR, but is assembled with a CCR-processed part. This buffer is provided to make sure that the assembly operation can be performed as soon as the CCR parts are available. It protects the assembly operation and the overall plant throughput from the disruptions that affect non-CCR parts. The assembly time buffers and the constraint time buffers work together to keep the assembly operation on schedule.

Figure 5.2 shows the appropriate locations for both time and stock buffers for the A-plant shown in Figure 5.1.

Buffer Sizes   The size of a given component stock buffer depends on a number of factors, including the component usage rate, desired service level, and replenishment time. Usage rate variability and replenishment time variability may also be considered. However, since the idea of component stock buffers is to simplify control, avoid complex monitoring and replenishment systems.

FIGURE 5.2

Appropriate Time Buffer and Stock Buffer Locations in an A-Plant with a Capacity Constraint and Common Purchased Components

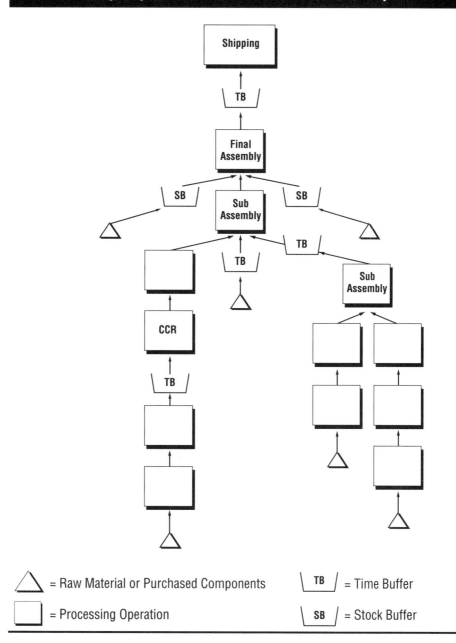

△ = Raw Material or Purchased Components   TB = Time Buffer

▢ = Processing Operation   SB = Stock Buffer

The appropriate time buffer size is unrelated to usage and desired service levels, which were important factors in determining the size of component stock buffers. It is determined instead by the inherent variability of that part of the production process covered by the time buffer. In principle, the size of a time buffer can be established by analyzing the nature of the disruptions and performing statistical analyses. In practice, experience indicates that a reasonable starting point is about one quarter of the current production lead time. Depending on the location of the CCR and the complexity of the assembly operation, the total amount of allocated buffer may have to be redistributed between the different time buffers.

Establishing the Master Schedule

In A-plants, the master production schedule (MPS) is the assembly build schedule. This schedule has to be established in such a way that it satisfies customer promises while creating a smooth material flow consistent with the availability of capacity and material. This generally means that the MPS will be different from the customer orders as they are received. The pattern of customer orders often exhibits peaks and valleys (heavy demand on some days/weeks and light demand on others). If the MPS simply reflected customer orders, it would cause periodic overloads and dead time throughout the production system—an undesirable situation. This uneven load can best be smoothed by "level loading" the assembly schedule.

In most A-plants, the available capacity at final assembly (which we will simply refer to as assembly) is closely controlled so there is just slightly more capacity than needed to satisfy expected customer demand. In other words, assembly capacity is generally adjusted in such a way that this operation is a borderline CCR. Assembly capacity is therefore an excellent choice for setting the drum beat or MPS. This is done by planning the assembly schedule in such a way as to meet customer demand while level loading assembly. Of course, sometimes there are material or capacity constraints, and to have a workable schedule the assembly schedule has to be adjusted according to the limitations of these constraints.

The inclusion of material constraints into the master scheduling process is straightforward. The total amount of products scheduled in any given time frame cannot exceed the availability of the known material constraint. For scheduling purposes, the constraint is based on the quantity of available material, not the timing of its availability. Most timing problems can be accommodated through use of appropriate buffers at the raw material stage and through reduction of production lead times.

The existence of a capacity constraint complicates the process of developing the assembly schedule. The degree of complexity depends on whether or not setups are required at the constraint. If the CCR does not require setups, then the desired sequence at assembly should not be affected. However, the overall load of the assembly schedule may have to be adjusted to accommodate the limited capacity at the constraint.

If the CCR requires setups, the situation changes. If the total load at the CCR exceeds its available capacity, process batches at the CCR may have to be adjusted. The adjustment should be made to reduce total set-up time so the planned CCR load does not exceed its available capacity (see Chapter 9, Volume 1). The frequency with which setups can be performed at CCRs determines the modifications that need to be made to the assembly schedule. If very few setups are possible, the assembly schedule reflects this limitation. The assembly schedule may have to group orders of a given product and build the entire grouping of orders before switching over to another product. This is equivalent to assembly having process batches based on the CCR.

In some cases, savings in set-up time can be realized by scheduling the CCR so similar products are processed back-to-back, taking advantage of faster dependent setups to create additional processing capacity. The tradeoff is that true priorities are usually distorted, and variability of production lead time increased. That is, some parts are produced earlier than required, while other parts have to wait for the right grouping. This adversely affects the plant's ability to respond to customer demands. Grouping orders according to dependent setup requirements should only be performed when the additional capacity generated is absolutely critical. The general philosophy should be to modify the true order sequence as little as possible and only then to align the planned work load to with the limits of available capacity

Tying the Ropes - Establishing Schedule Control Points

Once the master production schedule has been established, the next step is to ensure that all resources run in accordance with the needs of this overall plan. A key feature of the drum-buffer-rope system is that scheduling, communication, and production control is simplified by limiting the need for detailed control to the schedule control points. The list of potential schedule control points - where detailed schedules specifying quantity and sequence/timing are necessary - were identified and discussed in Chapter 9, Volume 1.

The schedule control points of interest in A-plants are material release, capacity constraints, and assembly. In general, for A-plants this means that the total number of schedule control points is a very small fraction of the total number of work centers. The problem of control is thus greatly simplified in A-plants. If the two-bin system component stock buffers are used to handle the non-key components, the control problem is further simplified.

There are three key outcomes that result from establishing a good rope system in A-plants. They deserve some elaboration.

1. *Eliminating the need for detailed control.* Traditionally, the major problem in A-plants is a lack of effective control. This usually translates into a perceived need for tighter and more detailed control of each work center. The rope system actually results in the exact opposite!

   Since the majority of work centers do not fall into the schedule control point category, they do not need, and will not receive, detailed schedules. Remember that in a rope system, only material required to fill customer orders is released. And this material is released according to planned lead times that are much shorter than previously experienced. As a result, the number of jobs and amount of material in the system are significantly reduced. Since non-CCR work centers, by definition, have more capacity than required to process the scheduled work, most of the time they have two or fewer jobs in queue. This allows a very simple priority work rule to be implemented, work centers that are not schedule control points are simply directed to process jobs in the order that they arrive at the work center–First In, First Out (FIFO).

2. *Process batch sizes at non-CCRs are drastically reduced.* In many traditional A-plants, the batch size to be used in the production of most components is established using economic batch quantity (EBQ) logic, and is determined independently of the detailed assembly schedule or MPS. If the MPS requires a particular part to be produced, this part is produced in a quantity determined by its lot sizing rule. But in the DBR approach, the lot size of parts for non-CCRs is simply the quantity required by the MPS. The MPS, not an independent rule, controls the production quantity of these parts. Of course, if the resulting setups transform the resource into a CCR the process batch size will be modified.

3. *Small transfer batches are encouraged.* In many traditional A-plants, the batching mentality is so pervasive that process batches are often moved intact from one work center to the next. This clearly impedes the fast movement of material through the system. In DBR systems, transfer batches are usually much smaller than process batches. This often allows downstream work centers to begin processing jobs much sooner. This has

two major beneficial effects. One, it helps smooth the flow of material throughout the system, which in turn allows better utilization of available work center capacity. Two, it reduces overall production lead time.

The combined effect of smaller process and transfer batches, coupled with elimination of the need for detailed scheduling, is significant in A-plants. The usual outcomes include faster material flow, elimination of the feast-or-famine syndrome, elimination of wandering bottlenecks, elimination of frustration caused by the inability to generate or execute a detailed schedule, and elimination of overtime (at non-CCRs) caused by falling behind schedule.

In addition to the control established at schedule control points, the flow of material into the time buffers should be monitored. Analyzing the causes of deviations of the actual flow from the planned flow into these time buffers provides the information necessary to implement process and procedural improvements.

Monitoring Performance and Progress

When implementing a drum-buffer-rope system, new sets of operational measures are usually necessary to properly evaluate manufacturing managers at various levels. Appropriate performance measures also support and encourage the transition to a Synchronous Management system. There are a number of operational measures that can be used to monitor and measure the progress of the implementation. The ones discussed here have the advantage of recording the improvements directly and immediately (before the benefits have been registered in the bottom line), and are relatively easy to measure on an on-going basis.

1. *Severity of shortages.* This can be measured by the number of items on the shortage list as well as by their degree of lateness (relative to the due date of the affected order). As the flow of material becomes increasingly synchronized, this list should shrink and the average lateness should decrease.

2. *Applicability of production to orders.* A key objective of Synchronous Management is to reduce the disparity (both in quantity and time) between what is produced and what is sold. As Synchronous Management is implemented, an increasing proportion of production should be targeted for near-term orders. This means that due date performance should improve and finished goods inventory should decrease.

3. *Overtime usage, particularly at assembly and non-CCR operations.* As the wave-like flow of material is replaced by a smooth, synchronous flow,

the load at most work centers, and at the assembly area in particular, should become more uniform replacing the feast or famine situation. This should reduce the need for overtime caused by product overloads.

4. *Throughput at CCRs.* In the absence of Synchronous Management methods, there is usually insufficient recognition of the crucial role of capacity constraint resources. In unsynchronized plants, CCR capacity is often wasted, which in turn causes a loss of throughput. For example, sometimes CCRs simply run out of material to process. At other times, the constant expediting typical of unsynchronized plants forces a CCR to incur additional setups for "hot" parts. Wasted CCR capacity should be significantly reduced or eliminated as the DBR system is implemented.

5. *Scrap/yield of constraint materials.* Any loss of constraint material, no matter where in the process it occurs, is a loss of throughput. As the importance of this material to throughput becomes increasingly recognized, yield improves–both as a result of greater care in processing and through process improvements targeted to achieve this objective. To encourage these improvements, the scrap/yield of any constraint material should be closely monitored.

6. *Scrap/yield of materials processed by a constraint.* Any loss of material that has already been processed by a CCR is a waste of valuable CCR capacity and of system throughput. Therefore, the scrap/yield of CCR-processed material should be closely monitored.

Many more operational measures are possible. The relative importance of any and all chosen measures varies as the implementation proceeds and with the particular needs of the business. These measures do not replace the financial measures of how well a company is doing. But they do provide valuable feedback of progress, and are a more intuitive set of measures that identify critical aspects of system performance as Synchronous Management is implemented.

A-PLANT CASE STUDY: AN OVERVIEW OF THE C&D PLANT

Background Information

The C&D Company is a manufacturer of pumps for the aerospace and defense industries. The plant is located in New England and employs several hundred people. C&D manufactures less than 30 end items, and each has a very specific and specialized application. Each end item is assembled from about 40 components, and only the key components—an average of about 10 per end item—are produced in the plant. The key components, such as housings, shafts, blades, and sleeves, involve significant amounts of machine and manual work. There is little commonalty of these components between the different products. The product flow diagram for a typical pump produced by this plant is shown in Figure 5.3. The product flow structure clearly indicates that C&D is an A-plant.

The C&D plant is organized by functional areas. The different areas include the turning department, milling department, drilling department, grinding department, heat treat and other batch processing departments, manual bench work, subassembly, final assembly, and testing. In addition, several specialized processes are performed by outside vendors.

Compared to the A&B mill described in Chapter 4, the parts manufactured at C&D have long and highly variable routings, with the manufactured components having between 10 and 50 different operations. The actual manufacturing operations are performed by general-purpose machines that work on a wide variety of products. For example, the same milling machines process both shafts and sleeves for all of C&D's different pumps. In addition, most parts are routed through one or more departments several times during processing (e.g., green grind to heat treat to finish grind), and the specific sequence varies from one part to the next.

C&D has a relatively small customer base. But business has been very solid the past few years and sales have increased at a rate of about 15 percent per year. However, all is not roses at the C&D Company.

The Fundamental Problem

The plant manager of the C&D facility would describe a typical day as follows. The plant did not ship the products expected to be shipped today. For order XYZ, the shafts were not available. They are still at an outside vendor and are being expedited to the extent possible. No other products were assembled because at least one required part for each scheduled product was unavailable.

Despite the fact that assembly is underutilized due to parts shortages, the vice-president of finance indicates that in-process inventory is much higher than it should be and must be reduced. A visit to the shop floor shows piles of material everywhere, most of which have a red "expedite" sticker on them. In spite of all this in-process material, end products cannot be assembled in a timely manner.

Labor utilization has been running low. (Remember, assembly did not work today, just like several other work centers.) Yet there are frequent requests for overtime from many departments, including assembly. The same pattern repeats

FIGURE 5.3

Partial Product Flow Diagram for One Type of Pump in the C&D Plant

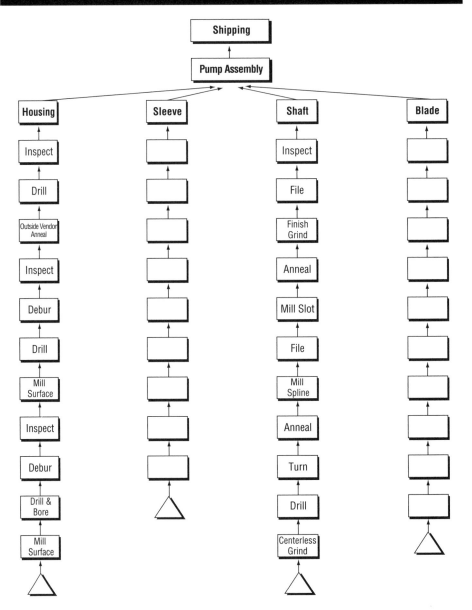

Note: Each type of pump has a different product flow diagram.

every month, with the result that overtime expenses are out of control.

The sales department is continually bombarded with irate customers because, in a typical month, the plant ships only about 80 percent of the orders promised that month. Furthermore, the cost of attaining even that level of delivery performance is absurdly high. Nothing ever seems to get produced without significant fire fighting and considerable overtime.

In summary, despite long lead times allowed by their customers, the plant is having difficulty shipping products within two weeks of the promised dates. Furthermore, expenses are alarmingly high. In fact, profits are on the verge of disappearing completely. C&D's managers recognize that they must improve their shipping performance and control expenses.

An Overview of the Traditional Management Approach at C&D

The C&D plant appears to be plagued by every problem known to manufacturing managers. In addition to generally poor on-time shipping performance and high operating costs, other symptoms include excessive scrap and rework, shortages of needed manufactured components, crucial machines breaking down at inopportune times, and untimely absenteeism.

Every past attempt by management to isolate a few fundamental causes for the problems has been unsuccessful. To help understand the causes for the problems, it is important to summarize the primary driving forces for this plant.

Shipping the product on time is a major problem. However, the fault does not lie with customers' required lead time. In fact, customers generally provide more than the quoted lead times. Like many similar facilities, this plant tries to achieve shipping targets by allowing a generous lead time to produce the product. Management has always believed that this more than adequate lead time, coupled with a careful monitoring of schedule attainment and resource utilization, should enable the company to profitably meet customers' delivery requirements.

It is precisely this assumption that has created the current situation. To the uninitiated, it may be difficult to understand how playing it safe (by allowing plenty of lead time) and being economical (by attempting to reduce unit costs) actually precipitates the crisis. The answer lies in the basic nature of manufacturing operations, that is, in the cumulative effects of variability and dependencies. Remember there are as many as 50 operations in a routing, using common resources, with a back and forth flow of materials between some resources. And then there is the final ultimate dependency that occurs at assembly, where a shortage of any single component disrupts the assembly schedule.

By trying to play it safe, C&D's managers flooded the shop floor with material. Priorities are easily distorted as each work center tries to take advantage of the often large work queues to achieve good local performance. Typically, this is done by combining like parts, by cherry picking (choosing the best or easiest jobs to work on first), or waiting until sufficient loads are available before assigning workers to operations. All of these actions occur with the intention of being locally cost efficient. However, this introduces many distortions because in the C&D plant, as in any typical A-Plant, the dependencies are extremely high. As we saw in Volume 1, when this high level of dependency is combined with high levels of variability, the effect is complete degradation of the original plan and the material flow falls completely out of synchronization.

The problem is further aggravated by the desire to keep the assembly operation active. In most A-plants (including the C&D plant), the available capacity at assembly almost makes it a CCR. And if products are not assembled, they cannot be shipped, and revenue cannot be collected. Thus assembly capacity is not to be wasted by being idle.

The desire to assemble something at C&D motivates managers to evaluate what components are in stock, and hence the most expedient product to assemble. For example, suppose that the products scheduled for assembly for the next two days cannot be assembled because they are missing one or more components that will not be available for at least two more days. Then the scheduler will examine the assembly schedule to find the best available alternative product to build. If all of the necessary components except shafts are available to build a specific pump, then the expediters move into overdrive to get the required shafts to assembly. The fact that this specific pump was not due to be shipped until next week (or even next month) is secondary to being able to build and (hopefully) ship some product.

Unfortunately, expediting has a significant harmful side effect. It throws all priorities aside and introduces its own significant disruptive effect into the plant's operation. Once started, the expedite mode becomes the rule. Production status and component stockroom are reviewed daily to identify the parts that are worth expediting so some pumps can be assembled that day. Since the routings do not follow any specific flow, every work center is subject to the expediter's short-sighted demands. In effect, expediting becomes the plant's *de facto* material control system. This is exactly the case at C&D!

C&D also has some quality problems. The reason is that when a batch of parts for one component is set aside because of quality problems, there may not be another batch of parts in the process at that time that can be easily substituted (unlike the case with repetitive manufacturing plants). In such cases, a new batch of parts must be expedited from the beginning through the long routing process and through all of the work-in-process queues.

The result of all of this economizing (batching, combining, and waiting for full loads) and expediting (to keep assembly busy and because of quality problems) is that material flows at the C&D plant (as in almost all traditional A-plants) are erratic and exhibit the wave-like feast-or-famine syndrome. Any work-center can be starved for material to process one day and then be inundated with large amounts of work the next. Whenever there is a large pile of work-in-process inventory at a work station, there is a strong tendency to assume the station is a (wandering) bottleneck resource, and use overtime to work down the inventory. This overtime is easy to justify since the work center is likely to be behind schedule. The result is a wave-like flow of materials, coupled with a hurry-up-and-wait syndrome for both operators and batches of component parts.

The problems in the C&D plant are the result of too much material (caused by excessive lead times) being processed in an uncoordinated and uncontrolled manner (due to local economizing factors). Any effective solution must directly address this issue.

A-PLANT CASE STUDY: IMPLEMENTING DRUM-BUFFER-ROPE

A Synchronous Management DBR system was implemented at the C&D plant in order to allow the plant to meet customer promises and get costs under control. By achieving these two objectives, management expected that plant profitability would increase significantly. These objectives were quickly met and exceeded.

The implementation process at C&D began with the identification of the constraints.

Identifying The Constraints

Material Constraints　　A systematic analysis of the component part shortages and late shipments to customers showed that they were almost never the result of purchased component availability. In fact, vendor delivery performance was generally very good. This is partly due to the fact that the delivery lead times required by C&D customers were generous enough to allow C&D more than enough time to procure the needed material from vendors. The few times vendor deliveries were a problem were due to such rare circumstances as a strike at a vendor's plant. In general, all material required for C&D manufacture were available as needed for material release to the shop floor. Likewise, all purchased components needed at the assembly operation were generally available in required quantities.

In addition, the quality of the raw materials and component parts did not appear to be a problem. No one at the plant could recall a significant production problem caused by substandard material.

Investigation of orders delayed due to material unavailability showed that there were two primary causes. One was processing errors by C&D operators. The other was schedule changes initiated not by the customer but by C&D's own scheduling department. The clear conclusion is that there were no true material constraints at C&D. Pseudo-material constraints were created by schedule changes and quality problems.

Capacity Constraints   The systematic procedure outlined earlier in this chapter was utilized to identify capacity constraint resources at C&D. Specifically, an analysis was conducted that identified potential CCR candidates and then subjected each candidate CCR to a thorough validation process.

The objective of the first stage of the analysis was to identify the list of parts that were chronically in short supply. The logic is that only those parts that require processing at a capacity constraint resource should be chronically late.

The starting point for the first stage of the analysis was the daily shortage lists created by material control personnel at the assembly component stores area. Two lists were created–one of parts that *continually* showed up on the parts shortage list, the other of parts that rarely (or never) appear on the shortage list.

This stage of the analysis was very straightforward at C&D. Pump housings (every one of the nearly 30 different housings produced) clearly stood out as the only category of part that was chronically short. On the other hand, there were several parts that did not appear on any of the shortage lists examined.

Every resource involved in processing housings was identified. Each of these resources became a suspect for being a CCR. However, logic indicates that any resource that processes parts that are chronically in excess (the second list) is not a CCR. Using this logic, one by one, resources were eliminated from the suspect list. Eventually, every resource was eliminated except one. The lone remaining candidate CCR was a CNC machine center (CNC-X) that performed the drill and bore operation on the housings.

The CCR status of CNC-X was validated through all of the checks discussed earlier. The work queue at this work center was measured in weeks (typically, two to four weeks of work-in-process inventory would be available). CNC-X had worked overtime every weekend in the past six months. Both shop supervisors and production control people were unanimous in their belief that CNC-X was the most severe bottleneck in the plant.

As a side note, the shop supervisors and production control people thought that several other work centers, especially outside vendors, were also bottlenecks. However, a careful analysis proved that what they were describing were temporary or wandering bottlenecks. These were pseudo constraints—the victims of the feast-or-famine syndrome at C&D. They were not true constraints. CNC-X was the only true capacity constraint resource at the C&D plant!

Setting the Buffers

In the C&D plant, constraint time buffers, assembly time buffers, and shipping time buffers were all required. Figure 5.4 illustrates the recommended time buffer locations.

Stock Buffers   There is no need for stock buffers for any of the major components required in the C&D plant. Remember that stock buffers are only required when the material procurement and/or manufacturing lead times exceed the customer lead time. But all customer orders at C&D are received with apparently more than sufficient lead time to purchase all needed materials and to manufacture and assemble the final products. Therefore, stock buffers would serve no purpose except to increase inventory.

There is one minor exception. It is prudent to keep component stock buffers of the most common, inexpensive parts such as screws, nuts, bolt, etc. (These components are not represented on the product flow diagram.)

Constraint Time Buffer   There is only one CCR at the C&D plant—CNC-X—which performs the drill and bore operation on all pump housings. Therefore, only a single constraint time buffer is required. The purpose of this time buffer is to make sure that CNC-X receives the required housings in sufficient time so that it can adhere to its production schedule, which is synchronized with the assembly build schedule.

Assembly Time Buffers   Time buffers are also required at the final assembly operation for all of the various final assembly components except pump housings. The components that need time buffers at final assembly can be conveniently divided into two categories—manufactured and purchased components. The first category includes all key components manufactured at C&D, except pump housings. The second category includes all purchased components that do not undergo any processing at C&D.

The assembly time buffers developed for both categories provide the same function. They are designed to make sure that the components needed for

FIGURE 5.4

Recommended Locations of Time Buffers in the C&D Plant

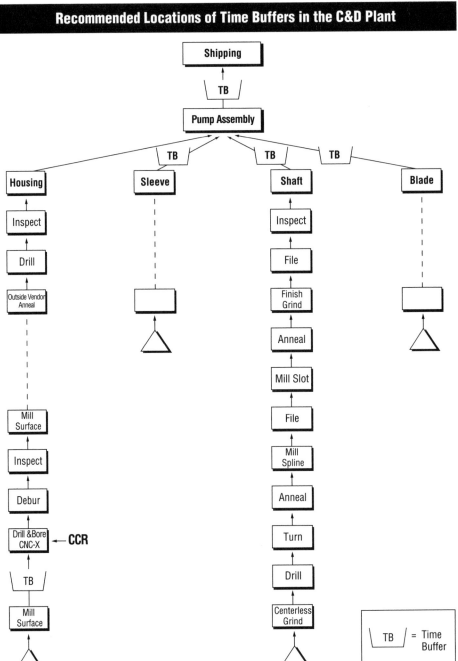

assembly are available to meet the assembly schedule. Even though the location and purpose of the buffers for these two categories are the same, determination of the buffer size is based on totally different factors.

Remember that buffer times are only one component of total planned lead time. For manufacturing processes, the other components are the expected processing and setup times. For procurement, the other component is expected procurement time.

In the case of each manufactured component, the appropriate buffer size is the amount of time needed to make sure the raw material is purchased, delivered, and processed through its entire routing. Of course, the various disruptions that occur throughout the manufacturing environment randomly cause some components to fall behind the planned schedule. The time buffers must be large enough to allow final assembly to have the full array of needed components on hand so pumps may be assembled as scheduled. Given the length of some routings (50 operations) at C&D, the high degree of variability, the contention for resources, etc., the buffer size required for a specific manufactured component can be quite large. In the initial stages of drum-buffer-rope implementation, the assembly buffer times for manufactured components ranged from four weeks to as much as 10 weeks.

The size of some of these manufactured components' time buffers appears to be quite large. However, with no other planned WIP queues in the operation (except at the CCR), the resulting total manufacturing lead times for orders is greatly reduced.

For each of the purchased components, the time buffer must only account for variability in procurement. That is, the buffer must account for only the variability of the vendor and the C&D purchasing department. At C&D, the majority of buffer time was needed to protect against late vendor shipments. Initially, buffer times for purchased components ranged from two days to three weeks.

Shipping Time Buffer   A shipping buffer is established at the end of the process. This buffer includes all pumps and provides a time cushion from when pumps are scheduled to be finished at final assembly until the time they are scheduled to be shipped. The shipping buffer protects the integrity of the shipping dates promised to customers.

Establishing The Master Schedule

The master schedule in A-plants is the schedule for final assembly that meets customer demand, is consistent with capacity and material constraints, and results in a smooth flow of material. Since the only constraint in the C&D plant is CNC-X, creating the master schedule is relatively simple. All that is needed is an assembly schedule consistent with the capacity at CNC-X that meets customer requirements.

In order to effectively synchronize CNC-X capacity with any given assembly schedule, all relevant CNC-X data had to be verified and corrected. The routing file for housings was quickly cleaned up, particularly for the operations involving CNC-X. The processing time per part, setup times, expected yields, etc., for each housing were all verified with shop personnel and engineering. This cross-functional data verification process resulted in a minor change to the processing sequence on some housings that resulted in a 2 percent time savings at the CNC-X resource. This seemingly insignificant change effectively increased CNC-X's capacity by 2 percent. As has been emphasized before, the translates directly into a 2 percent increase in capacity for the entire plant.

The next step was to establish the proper process batch at the CCR. It was quickly determined that processing housings on an order-for-order basis was not possible at CNC-X. While the total required processing-time at CNC-X was less than the available capacity, the inclusion of set-up times created an overload.

It soon became clear that some combining of orders would be necessary at CNC-X. The idea was to sufficiently reduce the total required number of CNC-X setups so its total workload no longer exceeded its available capacity. It was finally decided that all orders for the same end product due within the same two-week period would be combined. This freed up enough CNC-X capacity to meet the assembly schedule and customer demand.

Establishing the MPS in this plant is now a very straightforward task. Customer orders are converted into an assembly build schedule, which loads the assembly operation in uniform daily buckets (x number of pumps assembled per day) in the sequence specified by the order due dates and in quantities that reflect two weeks' worth of orders. This procedure loads the assembly operation while satisfying customer due dates. Even though the CNC-X machine is treated as a CCR, it does not introduce any additional modifications to the MPS because it has sufficient capacity to execute the MPS.

It was essential to ensure that the CNC-X operation runs as smoothly as possible. To this end, several directives were issued:

1. Expediting will not be allowed to interfere with the CNC-X schedule. Expediting generates additional setups and destroys CNC-X's overall ability to execute the schedule.
2. All necessary actions should be taken to ensure that CNC-X is not starved for material at any time. Establishing the constraint time buffer at CNC-X is a major first step.

3. CNC-X capacity must not be wasted by processing defective parts. Therefore, all incoming parts must be inspected for defects before being processed by CNC X.
4. No authorization is needed to run overtime at this work center if it is needed to maintain schedule integrity.

Tying the Ropes

The last element of the drum-buffer-rope system is the rope. Implementation of this aspect of the DBR system is a major departure from the previous system used at the C&D plant, and at many A-plants.

The previous system was an MRP system that established generous allowances for queue times, move times, and other delays at each and every resource. Remember that the resulting increase in the planned lead time at C&D was simply viewed as a necessary, but minor, penalty to pay. The result was expected to be a realistic production plan, but this was never achieved under the old system.

In the drum-buffer-rope system, the planned lead times are calculated differently. The planned lead times are composed of the processing times and setup times for the various resources in the routing of a part, plus any time allocated for a time buffer. The entire routing is buffered, but each individual resource is not buffered at all. That is, the processing and setup times used in the planning process are designed to reflect the actual processing and setup times. No delays are added at individual resources.

In addition, the process batch size at all resources was set to the MPS quantity. As discussed in the previous section, this resulted in all process batches being reduced to two weeks' worth of orders for a given product. Again, this was a significant departure from previous practice, where the standard process batch size was one months' worth of orders for most parts. However, for several products, some of the resources required long and difficult setups. For these products, the batch size was typically two months' worth of orders.

At first, some C&D personnel could not believe that cutting the batches would not cause the system to explode from all of the extra setups required. However, the almost complete absence of expediting meant that the total number of setups actually performed under the new system did not increase. The additional planned setups caused by smaller process batches were completely offset by the huge reduction of unplanned setups caused by the virtual elimination of expediting.

Another major change was the implementation of smaller transfer batches. Under the old MRP system, the transfer batch was typically the same as the process batch, unless the batch was being expedited. But in the DBR system, the goal is for all materials to move through the system as quickly as possible. In a sense, it is like "expediting" every batch through the system by using small transfer batches. The small transfer batches not only move material through the system faster, but eliminate the feast-or-famine syndrome.

The effectiveness of small transfer batches can be seen another way. In the old MRP system, where the transfer batch was equal to the process batch, only one resource at a time worked on a given batch. With transfer batches that are much smaller than process batches, several resources work on the same process batch at the same time.

At first, old-line supervisors thought this new approach was the "craziest idea" they had ever heard. They thought that running smaller batches would be too "inefficient," that shorter planned lead times would "wreck the plant schedule," and that trying to run a plant without significant expediting would "be a disaster." Only the proof of actual experience eventually convinced them (and even then it took six months) that the DBR system was a major improvement.

Finally, to make the entire system workable, the schedule control points had to be implemented. At the C&D plant, as in all drum-buffer-rope systems, strict control begins at the material release point. This is a critical control point. Under C&D's DBR system, no batches were released to the production floor before the planned release date. In addition, assembly was not allowed to expedite parts for any pump that was not on the schedule for the current week.

Additional schedule control points in the C&D plant were established at CNC-X and assembly. But this was not enough. This was because of the extremely long routings of most parts. Without additional control points, once parts are released, no systematic scheduling or monitoring would be performed until the part was due at either the constraint buffer or an assembly buffer. That is, the part could go without tracking for several months. To avoid this situation, several monitoring points were introduced. Outside vendor processing points provided natural monitoring points. In addition, resources that were shared by all manufactured parts were good candidates for a monitoring point. In the C&D plant, an internal heat treat operation and shipping to outside vendors were sufficient to provide each part with at least four schedule control points.

A simple FIFO system was used at the non-CCR manufacturing operations. In a plant that had been accustomed to detailed schedules, with a four-week look–ahead dispatch list, this was quite a shock. After all the effort that had gone into establishing and then attempting to use the MRP system, it appeared that the whole MRP system was being abandoned. When training sessions first introduced the logic of the new system, skepticism was high. However, once shop personnel understood the powerful simplicity of the new system, they quickly adopted the new operating methods.

Monitoring Performance and Progress

The basic performance measures for Synchronous Management are throughput, inventory, and operating expense (T, I and OE), and the goal is to increase throughput while simultaneously reducing inventory and operating expenses. However, at the operating level, several day-to-day measures were used as proxies for T, I and OE. These included on-time shipments, appropriate release of material to the drum, timely arrival of material to buffer locations, work-in-process queues, overtime expenses, and scrap levels. The most important of these intermediary measures was the actual output at the CNC-X constraint resource.

Continuous improvement efforts were focused by conducting constant analyses of the buffers, and by using statistical process control (SPC) techniques to continually measure quality and process improvement. By focusing on changes that affected the constraint and the buffers, key gains in productivity and processing efficiency were achieved.

The results experienced at C&D were typical of most A-plant implementations, specifically:

1. Several months into the implementation, average production lead time had been cut by 45 percent. After that, lead times continued to decline steadily.
2. Inventory levels were reduced by almost 50 percent. The generation of new obsolete inventory was virtually eliminated because parts were only procured and products only produced as needed to satisfy actual orders.
3. On-time delivery performance improved from 80 percent to 94 percent.
4. Overtime expenses were slashed by over 80 percent. Overtime was focused at the constraint and mostly eliminated everywhere else.
5. Production volume was stabilized, first on a weekly basis, then on a daily basis. As the system became increasingly synchronized, total plant volume increased. Within six months, total plant throughput had increased 10 percent.

The bottom line result was that plant performance increased dramatically and this catapulted C&D from a very weak financial position into a strong one.

Chapter 6

IMPLEMENTING SYNCHRONOUS MANAGEMENT IN T-PLANTS

Where sense is wanting, everything is wanting.
– Benjamin Franklin, 1754

OVERVIEW OF T-PLANT ISSUES

As discussed in Chapter 3, the behavior of both A-plants and T-plants is dominated by the presence of assembly operations. However, whereas the assembly operations in A-plants represent convergence points, the final assembly operation in T-plants is a divergence point in the product flow. That is, final assembly operations in T-plants generate a very large number of different end items from a relatively small number of common components. Plants that assemble highly optioned products fall in the T-plant category. In addition, plants that produce products that have a variety of packaging options are usually T-plants. T-plants often manufacture consumer products, electronics, and other high-volume goods. The main characteristics of T-plants can be summarized as:

1. Several common manufactured and/or purchased component parts are assembled together to produce the final product.
2. The component parts are common to many different end items.
3. The production routings for the component parts do not include significant divergent or assembly processes.
4. The production routings for any fabricated component parts are usually quite dissimilar.

The product flow diagram of a typical T-plant is shown in Figure 6.1. The diagram illustrates the structure of a "pure" T-plant that does not include any manufacturing divergence points or convergent assembly points. Figure 6.1 clearly indicates the component manufacturing operations, component stores area, the final assembly operation, and finished goods.

FIGURE 6.1

Partial Product Flow Diagram of a "Pure" T-Plant

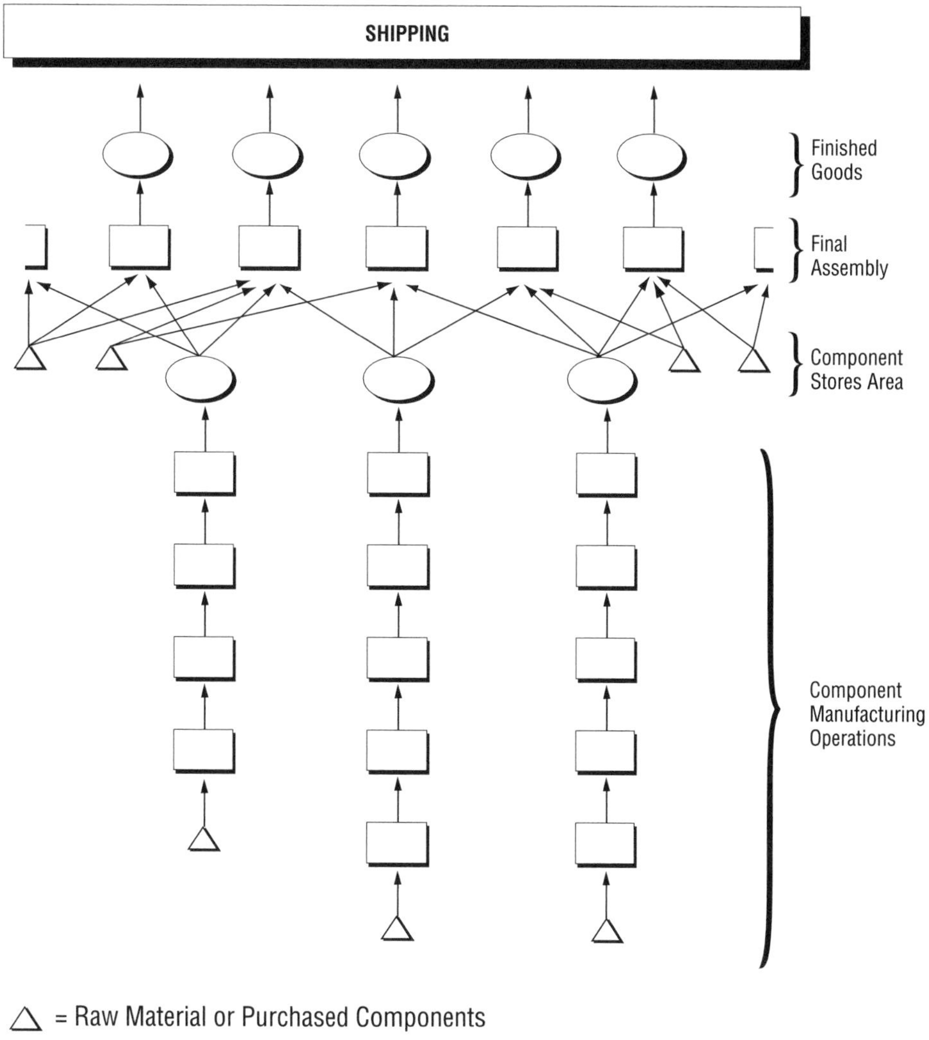

△ = Raw Material or Purchased Components

Since the number of different possible end items in a typical T-plant is extremely large, trying to maintain sufficient inventories to sell "off the shelf" is not usually a realistic option. Thus, T-plants are usually assemble-to-order plants, often in markets where demand is difficult to forecast and customer lead times are relatively short. Unfortunately, component and raw material procurement times, as well as component manufacturing times, can be quite lengthy. It is therefore necessary to master schedule and stock the various purchased and manufactured component parts at a component stores area prior to final assembly.

The various interactions that take place between the available common components, the required product mix, and the utilization of assembly capacity dominates the T-plant environment. Limited manufacturing resource capacity and lengthy manufacturing and procurement lead times further complicate the problems.

The main business issues facing traditional T-plants are:

1. Large finished-goods and component-parts inventories.
2. Poor delivery due date performance.
3. Excessive fabrication lead times.
4. Unsatisfactory resource utilization in fabrication.
5. Fabrication and assembly act as separate non-synchronized plants

The conventional approaches to resolving these problems include developing better forecasting techniques, improving inventory planning and control, and reducing the product cost by improving the efficiency of fabrication resources. However, conventional solutions do not address the root cause of the problems. They are typically ineffective and often contribute to the problems.

The root cause in traditional T-plants is material misallocation that occurs at final assembly. Interestingly enough, in most traditionally managed T-plants, this "stealing" is not only allowed, it is unwittingly encouraged by the existing set of operating policies and locally focused performance measures.

From the Synchronous Management perspective, the primary problem can be restated in bottom-line business terms as poor delivery performance. Excessive inventories and an inability to respond quickly to a dynamic market are often important secondary business issues.

The key to addressing these business problems is to eliminate material misallocation at the assembly operation and to improve the synchronization of the assembly and component manufacturing operation. Improved synchronization will improve on-time delivery performance by improving the timely availability of component parts to the assembly operation.

Major reductions in inventory are also made possible by a more synchronized material flow. Inventory reductions slash operating costs by cutting carrying costs and by significantly reducing unplanned and wasteful expenses associated with overtime, premium freight, rework, quality costs associated with excessive handling, etc.

In the terminology of Synchronous Management, the objectives of a material control system are to simultaneously increase throughput and reduce inventory.

THE DRUM-BUFFER-ROPE IMPLEMENTATION PROCESS

Identifying the Constraints

Our previous discussions of V-plants and A-plants emphasized how the effects of overactivation complicates the identification of constraints in two different ways:

1. When there is a divergence point, shortages of products beyond this point are caused not only by lack of material but also by material misallocation. To correctly identify any true material shortages, these artificial shortages must be weeded out.

2. When the opportunity for resource misallocation exists, the plant is often deluged with excess inventory. In addition, sporadic shortages are caused by the resultant creation of wandering bottlenecks. These system distortions have to be accounted for in order to correctly identify any true resource constraints. The constraint identification problem is particularly acute in T-plants since both of these complicating phenomena exist.

Material Constraints   Any material whose limited availability adversely affects the plant's bottom-line performance is a material constraint. Whenever a true material constraint exists, the products requiring this material are in short supply. It would appear that knowledge of orders that are late should provide an indication of material shortages. But it is not that easy.

A snapshot of late orders at any time may indicate that some products are late because of a constraint material. But orders can be assembled late for a number of other reasons. It is therefore necessary to review the pattern of late orders over a period of time to find the products that are consistently late and in short supply. Only these products could involve a material constraint. From the end products, the common material(s) can be traced. Any common materials are potential candidates for material constraints. If no common material is identified, then there is no true material constraint. But any potential material constraint must be subjected to a thorough validation process.

Any potential constraint material should be reviewed with the purchasing/materials group to confirm whether these are materials that are in short supply in the marketplace. If the identified material is known to be in plentiful supply, then it is not a true material constraint.

In some cases, quality problems may affect the availability of a material. Let's consider two different cases.

First, consider the case where a specific material used at assembly is a purchased component. If purchased components include an excessive number of substandard units, then the limited availability of usable parts may cause late orders or shortages. By strict interpretation, this is a constraint material. However, the real underlying cause of substandard quality might also be traced to inadequate purchasing/certification policies and procedures. Thus, managing the material procurement system better could eliminate this material problem.

Second, consider the case of purchased materials that are further processed internally and then used at assembly. Assume that the materials are initially available in sufficient quantity and quality. But during the manufacturing process, excessive scrap or yield problems occur. By the time the material reaches the component stores area for final assembly, there is no longer sufficient material to assemble the required orders. Once again, there is a real shortage of material, but the underlying problem does not lie with the material itself. The problem is the processing capability of the manufacturing system. If the manufacturing capability problem can't be resolved, then the procurement policies should be modified.

In a T-plant, as in a V-plant, material misallocation (stealing) is the major problem. That is, common materials that are scheduled for product A are instead used to assemble product B. Thus, product A cannot be produced on schedule and is late. Often, product B is not even needed to satisfy an immediate customer order.

Experience indicates that stealing is the most common reason for late orders in T-plants. And when significant stealing occurs, even products for which there should be plenty of material are often short or produced late.

Fortunately, there is a quick, reliable way to determine if significant stealing is occurring in T-plants. If stealing is a significant problem, two phenomena are observed. One, a large number of orders are routinely assembled late. Two, either a significant number of customer orders are assembled earlier than required or a significant number of unordered products are assembled.

In summary, limited availability of material can be a constraint. However, in many cases, the root cause does not lie exclusively (or even partially) with the vendor, but with the assembly plant's systems and policies.

Capacity Constraints   The technique used in the case of V-plants to identify capacity constraints—analyzing the inventory profiles of resources—is not effective in T-plants. The primary reason is that T-plants (like A-plants) typically have inventory everywhere!

As was the case with V-plants and A-plants, capacity constraints cannot generally be identified by analyzing data taken from the capacity planning system. The availability and accuracy of the required manufacturing system data used in most planning systems is simply inadequate. The continual updating due to engineering changes alone makes current data accuracy a real problem. The problem of accurate computer-based data is compounded by the high degree of commonalty of parts and the wide variety of end products. This only increases the likelihood of errors in the bill of material. The order book is also likely to have a whole host of canceled orders and other erroneous information.

The approach used to identify CCRs does not depend on inventory profiles or computer data base accuracy. Instead, an intuitive understanding of T-plants, along with the expected effects CCRs would have in a T-plant environment, drives the analysis.

When a CCR exists in a T-plant, the plant's ability plant to produce certain component parts needed for assembly is limited. It therefore follows that the supply of products that require these limited-availability component parts is typically less than the quantity demanded. Thus, in T-plants, a product-by-product analysis of delivery performance should provide the information needed to identify any capacity constraints.

The recommended procedure for identifying CCRs in a T-plant is somewhat similar to the one used in A-plants. First, identify any and all potential CCR candidates. Then, subject each CCR candidate to a thorough validation process. The identification process has five steps:

1. *Identify end-item orders that are late.* Unlike the recommended A-plant procedure, the starting place is not identifying shortages at the component stores area, because component shortages can be caused by material misallocation at assembly. If there is widespread stealing, the component shortage list will be extremely volatile, making it virtually impossible to uncover any consistent pattern of resource-generated component shortages. Therefore, it is necessary to analyze the end items to begin identifying the resource-generated component shortages.

2. *Identify the manufactured components responsible for the late orders.* Start with the end items that are chronically late and derive the list of manufactured components required for these items.

3. *Identify the manufactured components that are chronically in excess.*

Start with the end items that are chronically in excess and derive the list of manufactured components required for these items.

4. *Eliminate from the component-shortage list any components that also belong to the excess list.* The remaining components are the chronically short parts.

5. *From the routings for the chronically short components, identify the resources involved only in the production of these components.* These are the suspected CCRs.

To verify the existence of any true CCRs, as many validations as possible should be performed. The suggested validations for T-plants are essentially the same ones recommended for A-plants:

1. *Determining whether or not a sizable work-in-process queue at a resource is typical.* If a resource often does not have a significant inventory queue, it is probably not a CCR.

2. *Determining whether or not overtime is commonplace at the resource.* Overtime at true CCRs is generally higher than for other resources.

3. *Ask expediters to confirm the causes of shortages.* Of all the people in the plant, expediters are the ones most familiar with the location of troublesome resources.

4. *Perform a general check of processing and setup times to help spot any inconsistencies.* For example, the likelihood that a resource is a CCR will be greatly diminished if it has a faster processing time and a shorter setup than another resource on the suspect list (all other things equal, such as the same number of both types of resources).

The objective of these validations is to either confirm or disprove the existence of a capacity constraint resource. If the identification and validation processes indicate that there are no CCRs, this indicates that problems are not caused by limited availability of capacity, but ineffective management of capacity.

Our experience indicates that in many T-plants, there is no true bottleneck or CCR. This is because the complexity posed by the wide variety of end items and the high degree of commonalty of component parts makes the T-plant difficult enough to manage without a CCR. If capacity shortages were added to the inherent complexity of a T-plant, the plant's ability to assemble and deliver products on time would be severely degraded. The severity would typically be sufficient enough to force management to resolve the capacity shortage.

On the other hand, traditionally managed T-plants that do have a true bottleneck or CCR will typically exhibit very poor delivery performance, significant lost sales opportunities, and a high level of chaos accompanied by continuous fire fighting. The good news for such plants is that very dramatic improvements in bottom-line performance can be quickly generated with Synchronous Management.

Setting the Buffers

Once the plant has been checked for constraints, the next step is to determine stock and time buffer requirements.

Stock Buffers   Stock buffers are often appropriate in T-plants because lead times requested by customers are usually much less than the normal production lead time. In T-plants, as in V-plants, the product structure lends itself to the use of stock buffers at intermediate stages of production to achieve substantial benefits. Product stock buffers are possible in T-plants if the decision is made to stock inventories of finished end items. However, in most T-plants, the primary stock buffers should be component stock buffers composed of the various component parts required at the assembly operation.

There is always a choice as to the type and location of stock buffers in any plant. But in T-plants, the logical choice is to stock material at the component stores area. This is because final assembly, which is after the component stores area, is the divergence point in a pure T-plant. (Even in modified T-plants, final assembly will be the major divergence point.) Because forecasting accuracy is better prior to divergence points, a given level of customer service can be achieved with less inventory if stock buffers are located at component stores rather than at finished goods.

Thus, in T-plants, stock buffers should be held at the component stores level. Product stock buffers of finished goods are only required if products can not be assembled and delivered quickly enough to satisfy customer requirements. In such cases, a very small amount of finished-goods inventory should be held in product stock buffers. The actual amount of finished goods held in the product stock buffers should be the minimum necessary to accommodate customer orders during the replenishment lead time from the previous stocking point—the component stock buffers.

Component stock buffers are also useful in T-plants to establish detailed control over the many different parts required for the assembly operation. The final assembled product requires many different components, some manufactured in the plant and others purchased. The manufactured components generally require more control than the purchased components. But the procurement and production of all key components must be monitored and controlled in detail.

(Low-cost items like screws and standard gauge wire require very little control. As discussed in chapter 4, such items can be adequately controlled with a simple stock buffer system such as a two-bin system.)

The size of the various component stock buffers will vary depending on the component usage rate and the replenishment cycle time. Once stock buffer locations and sizes are established, procurement and production of materials will have to be managed in concert with the demands of these stock buffers.

Time Buffers   In T-plants, stock buffers can be implemented to help satisfy customer demand and to take care of problems of detailed control. But there is still a need for time buffers to protect system throughput from the inherent disruptions and variability of the manufacturing environment. In T-plants, three categories of time buffers are needed:

1. *Constraint time buffer.* If there is a capacity constraint in the T-plant, it must be protected by a time buffer. This buffer protects the CCR schedule from disruptions at upstream operations.
2. *Stock replenishment time buffer.* Stock replenishment time buffers are established to ensure that all component parts are available at the store room when needed in spite of disruptions in the procurement process and fabrication operation. For parts that do not require the CCR, this is the only time buffer in their entire routing. (Assembled products also have the shipping time buffer.) Parts processed by the CCR have one additional time buffer, at the CCR itself. This fact should be considered in establishing the size of the individual time buffers.
3. *Shipping time buffer.* A relatively small shipping time buffer is needed to protect customer promise dates from disruptions and scheduling distortions at assembly.

As in V-plants and A-plants, the sizes of the various time buffers are unrelated to factors such as usage rate, service level desired, and replenishment rate, which are used to determine the size of the stock buffers. The appropriate sizes for time buffers are determined by the frequency and severity of disruptions and scheduling distortions that occur in the relevant part of the process.

Figure 6.2, shows appropriate locations of time and stock buffers for the pure T-plant shown in Figure 6.1.

FIGURE 6.2

Appropriate Locations of Time Buffers & Stock Buffers for a "Pure" T-Plant

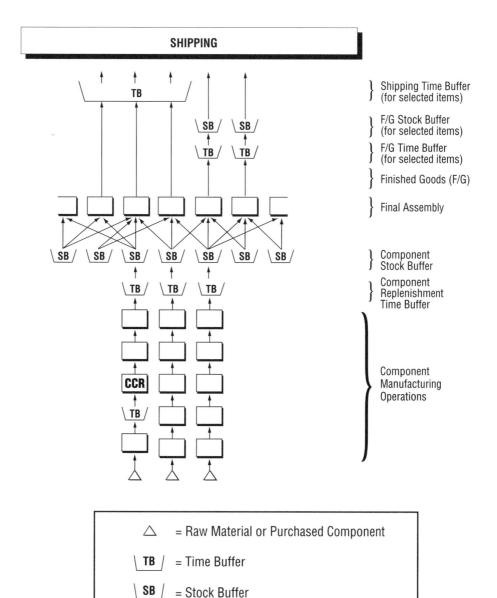

Establishing the Master Schedule

A T-plant should be run essentially as two separate plants–an assembly plant that produces finished products from components made available by the component stock buffers in the component stores area, and a fabrication plant that keeps the component stores area replenished with the required component parts. (The procurement process for non-manufactured components are included as part of the fabrication plant.)

Master scheduling rules are different for the two areas.

Scheduling Assembly   In some T-plants, off-the-shelf service may be required to satisfy some demand. For off-the-shelf products this requires a small stock of finished-goods inventory. In such cases, finished-goods stock buffers should be established and assembly scheduled as needed to replenish those buffers.

In most T-plants, the assembly area is essentially operated as a build-to-order system. But it may not always be possible to assemble products according to strict customer order priorities for at least two reasons. One, if there is a capacity or material constraint in the component fabrication process, this restricts the options at assembly. The constraint limitations will have to be considered when developing the master production schedule. Two, assembly work loads based strictly on customer orders may show extreme fluctuations of alternating overloads and idle periods. These work load peaks and valleys at assembly can be smoothed by allowing assembly to build some orders ahead of schedule.

The "build-ahead horizon" is defined as the length of time by which orders can be built early for the specific purpose of filling in and smoothing out the assembly work load. The existence of a build-ahead policy presents a small dilemma. A longer build-ahead horizon improves assembly operation efficiency, but at the cost of greater variability in assembly lead times. That is, with longer build-ahead times, some orders are produced way ahead of schedule while other orders are delayed. This reduces the overall level of customer service and increases inventory. On the other hand, a shorter build horizon allows greater fluctuation in the assembly work load, but does result in better customer service and lower inventories.

The most serious problem with a lengthy build-ahead horizon is that it formally allows stealing—misallocating material needed for a current order to instead assemble a future order. Since stealing is *the* major problem in most T-plants, this practice must be stopped. Therefore, it is essential to establish a simple, but critical, assembly scheduling rule—the assembly operation can only build products for orders within a very limited time horizon! This means there can be no stealing of components to make future orders just to keep the assembly operation busy. If all of the required components needed for the products scheduled within the permitted time horizon are not available, the assembly process simply has to temporarily shut down! The orders will have to be processed when the material is available using whatever normal (or overtime) assembly capacity is available.

Since stealing is the primary cause of the delivery and inventory problems in a T-plant, the benefits of the new assembly scheduling rule are quite dramatic. To prevent stealing, assembly goals must be reoriented from volume output (whether in units or dollars) to customer satisfaction. New performance measures need to reflect whether or not the right products are built in the right quantities at the right time.

It is relatively easy to agree with the need to change measures and assembly build practices, but it can be relatively difficult to do. This is primarily because the assembly operation is at the end of the process, and assembling units literally "ring the cash register." This sometimes makes shutting assembly down, for even a short period of time and for perfectly valid reasons, very painful. However, without stopping material misallocation at assembly, significant improvements in bottom-line plant performance and customer service are virtually impossible.

Scheduling Component Fabrication   The component fabrication operation should be operated in a build-to-stock mode. The objective of the fabrication operation is to replenish the component stock buffers with the shortest possible production lead time and minimum possible expense. Components that involve capacity or material constraints have to be master scheduled in a way consistent with optimizing the performance of the constraints. The master scheduling process is simply one of determining the batch sizes to be used for the various parts. As has been thoroughly discussed in these two volumes, the process and transfer batch sizes used in most plants today are too large. The best way to proceed is to establish aggressive batch reduction targets and systematically move toward these targets.

Tying the Ropes - Establishing the Schedule Control Points

The next step in the drum-buffer-rope system is to establish a good rope system. A good rope system should ensure that four things happen:

1. Purchased components are procured and available at the component stock buffers to support the assembly schedule.
2. Materials that are to be processed by a CCR must be procured and released to support the CCR production schedule.

3. Materials that are to be processed through non-CCR routings in the fabrication operation must be procured and released to replenish the component stock buffers in a timely manner.

4. All resources (especially assembly) must produce in accordance with the needs of the overall plan.

The schedule control points in a T-plant are material release, capacity constraints and the assembly operation. Since the most serious problem is the misallocation of parts at assembly, the most important schedule control point in a T-plant is the assembly operation. Thus, managers must be vigorous in enforcing the limited build-ahead horizon at the assembly operation so that stealing does not occur.

In a pure T-plant, there are no divergence points (as found in V-plants) and no convergent assembly points (as found in A-plants). Thus, in a pure T-plant, the only resource-based schedule control points are CCRs and the assembly operation. A key advantage of the DBR system in pure T-plants is that control in the fabrication operation is simplified because the only fabrication resources that qualify as schedule control points are CCRs (if any).

If the proper functioning of the rope limits the material releases to the right resources at the right time in the right quantities, then controlling the resources that are not schedule control point resources is simple. These resources only have to process the materials that are routed to them, in the sequence that they arrive. Furthermore, if a two-bin replenishment system is used to handle the non-key components, the problem is further simplified.

When a good rope system is implemented in T-plants, three key changes, similar to those that occur in an A-plant, generally occur. They are:

1. *The complete elimination of detailed schedules for almost all resources.* Control in traditional T-plants usually means a detailed schedule for each work center. In DBR systems, the exact opposite is true. Since almost all work centers are not schedule control points, they receive no detailed schedules at all. They are simply required to process material on a first in, first out (FIFO) basis.

2. *Process batches are drastically reduced.* In most traditional T-plants, in an attempt to be "cost efficient," batch sizes are often based on "economic batch quantities" (EBQs) and are much too large. Component stock buffers are replenished according to such lot sizing rules that ignore the need for synchronized flows and do not consider projected usage rates and replenishment rates. However, in DBR systems, the objective is to

produce only what is needed in very short time horizons.

3. *Small transfer batches are encouraged.* In DBR, to help ensure smooth movement of material through the system, small transfer batches are encouraged. This reduces the likelihood of feast-or-famine cycles and allows better capacity utilization. It also helps shorten fabrication lead time.

Monitoring Performance and Progress

The flow of material into the stock and time buffers is monitored by analyzing the deviations between the planned flow and the actual flow into these buffers, which helps focus attention on the parts of the operation where the need for process and procedural improvements is the greatest.

The move toward Synchronous Management helps the company's competitive position and quickly improves bottom-line financial performance. To monitor implementation of a DBR system in a T-plant, an intuitive set of operational measures is needed that is readily available and easy for everyone to understand. Moreover, they should have the effect of encouraging appropriate behaviors and discouraging dysfunctional behaviors. Some measures that meet these criteria are:

1. *Due date performance.* As the assembly operation is brought under control there will be a significant improvement in the plant's due-date performance. This will be evident in the decreasing age of past due orders as well as the number of past-due orders.

2. *Build-ahead time horizon at assembly.* This is the driving force for the business problems of T-plants, since longer horizons allow more stealing. As the build-ahead time horizon is reduced, finished-goods inventory, material shortages, expediting, and overtime requirements will all decrease, and due-date performance will improve.

3. *Applicability of component stocks.* A key objective of Synchronous Management is to reduce the disparity (both in quantity and time) between what is produced and what is sold. As a drum-buffer-rope system is implemented, the availability of component parts will be better matched to satisfy near-term orders.

4. *Throughput at CCRs.* In most conventionally managed T-plants, there is no explicit recognition of the crucial role played by capacity constraint resources. As a result, there will be periods when, because of normal manufacturing system disruptions, a CCR may simply run out of material to process. In addition to this forced idle time, constant expediting often forces a CCR to incur additional setups for "hot" parts. These and other

causes of lost throughput at CCRs will be drastically reduced as the DBR system is implemented.

Many other operational measures are possible in T-plants. The relative importance of any measure is a function of the specific plant environment and the industry's competitive characteristics. Remember that the chosen measures should not only act as key feedback measures of progress, they should encourage the behaviors that hasten the movement toward Synchronous Management.

T-PLANT CASE STUDY: AN OVERVIEW OF THE E&F PLANT

Background Information

The E&F Company is a manufacturer of industrial air tools. The company is located in the Southwest and employs about 500 people. The company's catalog consists of nearly 3,000 items. The plant was recently relocated from the North, purportedly in order to take advantage of cheaper non-union labor.

Delivery lead times demanded by customers varies by customer and product. For most products, the market is willing to accept two-week delivery. However, for some products, some customer orders must to be shipped in less than one week. On occasion, a few customers even require that certain products be shipped within 24 hours.

The production process at E&F is fairly typical of a T-plant. All of the various tools produced at the plant use a common family of motor assemblies. The motor assemblies consist of a handle housing (of which there are four types - pistol grip, in-line, angle, and push start), a motor (of which there are two types - reversible and non-reversible), and a gear mechanism (of which there are two types - single and double). Any single item from one of the three major components for the motor assemblies can be assembled with any item from the other two component categories. Thus, there are 16 different (calculated by multiplying 4 x 2 x 2) possible motor assemblies produced at the E&F plant. (We identify these 16 different motor assemblies as MA-1, MA-2, MA-3, . . . , MA-16.) Figure 6.3 illustrates the key component requirements for the motor assemblies identified as MA-5 through MA-11. For example, MA-5 is assembled with a non-reversible motor, a pistol grip handle housing, and single-gear gear mechanism; while MA-8 is assembled with a reversible motor, an in-line handle housing, and a double-gear gear mechanism.

The motor assembly is secured to the tool attachment by a coupler assembly. The company currently offers about 60 different tool attachments—screw drivers,

FIGURE 6.3

Representative Combinations of Motors, Handle Housings, and Gears for Motor Assemblies in the E&F Industrial Air Tool Plant

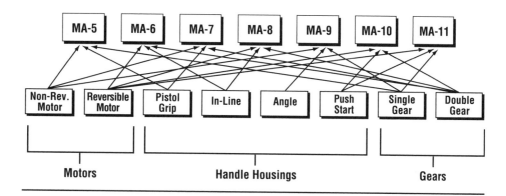

nut setters, or wrenches. (We identify these 60 different tool attachments as TA-1, TA-2, TA-3, . . . , TA-60.) There are three different coupler assemblies. They include a positive clutch assembly, a cushion clutch assembly, or a direct drive assembly. (We identify these three different coupler assemblies as CA-1, CA-2, and CA-3.)

Figure 6.4 illustrates part of the product flow diagram for the tool end items. In summary, there are 79 major components—16 different motor assemblies, 60 tool attachments, and three coupler assemblies. Since any of the three major components can be assembled with any of the other two major components, the total number of end items at the E&F plant is 16 x 60 x 3 = 2,880 different tools. That is, 2,880 different end items can be assembled from a mere 79 different common components.

Figure 6.5 shows the product flow diagram for the E&F plant. This product structure clearly is dominated by the existence of divergent assembly points. We have already noted that the 16 different motor assemblies share many common components. The same is true of the three different coupler assemblies. Thus there are two divergent subassembly operations, one for the motor assembly and one for the coupler assembly. However, the major divergence point occurs at the final assembly operation.

FIGURE 6.4

Representative Combinations of Motor Assemblies, Coupler Assemblies, and Tool Attachments to Produce End Items in the E&F Industrial Air Tool Plant

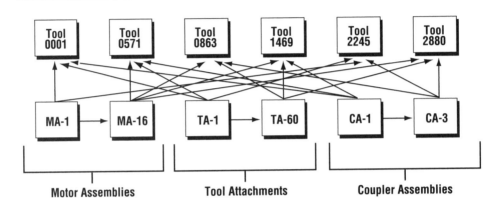

The Fundamental Problem

The E&F plant has experienced many problems. On-time delivery performance was very poor. Unit cost of products was considered to be way too high, and this had severely cut into profit margins. Inventory levels were out of control, with the plant averaging only two inventory turns per year.

According to top management, the primary problem at E&F was an inability to provide timely delivery of the right products to its customers. In fact, this poor performance had eroded E&F's customer base. This problem existed in spite of the fact that the finished-goods warehouse had nearly a three-month supply (measured in dollars) of products. All previous attempts to improve customer service resulted in increased inventory levels, but failed to solve the delivery problems. It seemed that no matter what E&F had in finished-goods inventory, the customers always wanted something else.

These problems also existed when the plant was located in the Northeast. Top management had suspected that many of the problems in the plant were caused by union work rules, poor work habits, poor supervision, and a poor overall company culture. Top management had hoped that relocating the plant—getting a fresh start with non-union workers, new supervisors, and even mostly new management—would solve the problems. They were wrong!

FIGURE 6.5

Representation of the Product Flow Diagram for the E&F Industrial Air Tool Plant

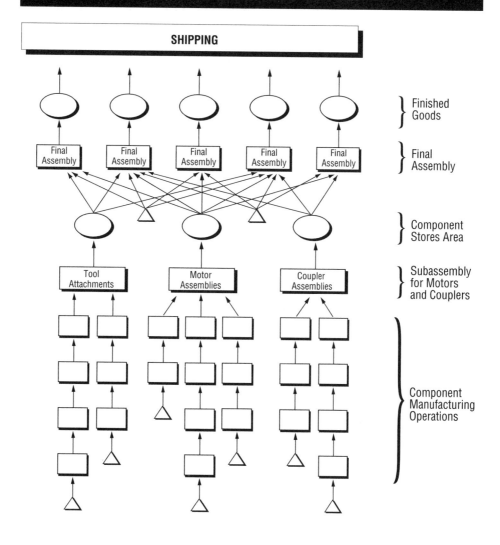

= Raw Material or Purchased Component

Top management didn't know what to do next. They were at a loss to identify the real root problems at E&F. But they had plenty of suggestions from the different functions.

The marketing managers believed their forecasts were as accurate as possible. They also felt that they usually allowed sufficient time for manufacturing to build the products. They blamed manufacturing for simply being unresponsive.

The manufacturing managers thought the marketing forecasts were terrible, that there was an unnecessary proliferation of products, and that an excessive number of small orders were accepted that the plant was not equipped to handle. They argued that heavy investment in automation, cell technology, etc., was the only long-term solution. Naturally, the manufacturing managers felt that, in the meantime, a smaller product line, more accurate longer-term forecasts, coupled with larger order quantities, would take care of the problems.

The new plant manager found the situation at E&F thoroughly confusing. Both the component-parts stock room and the finished-goods warehouse were bursting at the seams. The actual total production from the assembly department seemed to match the required total output. But on-time delivery performance only averaged about 65 percent. Assembly claimed that it only made products for which there was demand. But the plant manager recalled seeing large quantities of obsolete products in both the component stock room and in the finished-goods warehouse. Marketing and engineering design changes were blamed for these obsolete inventories. The plant manager wondered how there could be such delivery shortfalls in the midst of all that inventory!

An Overview of the Traditional Management Approach at E&F

E&F's sales group, like sales departments in most companies, wanted to be able to ship products from finished-goods inventory. The planned lead time for products scheduled at final assembly was less than one week. This was facilitated by short assembly changeover times. Furthermore, when necessary, most fabricated parts could be produced within two weeks. Based on these stated standard production and assembly lead times, marketing had developed a fairly sophisticated forecasting module to establish a finished-goods inventory plan for each end item. The quantity of a given product required in inventory varied from just a few units to several thousand.

Assembly was manned to achieve a daily production quantity of 2,000 units. This production target was sufficient to meet the market forecast. The total daily output (in units) at assembly was closely tracked and became the primary performance measure for assembly.

The final assembly operation was scheduled to replenish the finished-goods inventory based on the planned usage. Since component parts tended to be common across many different end items, replacement quantities had been established for each component part using an ABC rule. Large usage items (A items) were run in two-month quantities, medium usage items (B items) were produced in six-month quantities, and small usage items (C items) were produced in annual quantities.

The production people felt that these batch quantities were already too small to achieve really good resource efficiencies. They also viewed the proliferation of low-volume items as a serious problem. This was partly due to the fact that the low-volume parts were processed on the older conventional machines while the high-volume parts were produced on recently acquired CNC machines. The older and slower conventional machines caused the calculated cost per unit of parts to increase, thus causing manufacturing's performance to look even worse. Manufacturing was primarily measured on resource efficiencies and manufacturing cost per unit.

A Synchronous Management Overview of the E&F Plant

The root cause of the problems at E&F, as in the previous two case studies, lies in the inherent conflict between the need to achieve a good material flow (with high customer satisfaction) and the need to run an efficient operation. This conflict is intensified by the performance measurement system used at the E&F plant. Assembly is measured on total daily output and manufacturing is measured on efficiencies and cost per unit. Where are the performance measures that encourage excellent customer service? Of course, on-time delivery is measured, but it is not used to gauge the performance of either assembly or manufacturing.

Consider the assembly operation. The chaos at E&F is triggered by the fact that the focus is on total output to the exclusion of the appropriate mix of products. There is a strong relationship between operating the assembly area according to total output quotas and the existence of activation without utilization throughout the plant. The fact that stealing occurs at E&F is evidenced by 35 percent late deliveries coupled with the large amount of finished-goods inventory, including a significant amount of build-ahead products.

To improve performance, the stealing phenomenon must first be controlled. To achieve this control, a strict rope system must be implemented in the plant. In addition, the performance measures should be drastically changed to support a more synchronized assembly and manufacturing environment. Instead of emphasizing gross output, the new performance measures should focus on customer satisfaction and producing according to the desired product mix. Producing units for which there is no firm demand just to keep assembly "busy" must be strongly discouraged through this new set of measures.

Manufacturing performance must also be synchronized with the needs of assembly. This means making sure that the appropriate component parts are available as needed to support the planned assembly schedule. If the right components are available so assembly can build the scheduled products, there will be no motivation for stealing at assembly. This means the performance measures for manufacturing must change. Efficiency measures must be eliminated and replaced by measures that determine whether or not manufacturing is fully supporting assembly's needs in a timely manner.

While overall operating expense cannot be ignored, decisions should not be made on the basis of traditional cost measures. If the manufacturing operation is run according to the Synchronous Management philosophy, inventory levels, overtime, and operating costs will all decrease.

T-PLANT CASE STUDY: IMPLEMENTING DRUM-BUFFER-ROPE

The overall challenge at E&F is to improve customer service significantly while dealing with the fact that the forecast is unreliable today and will be unreliable tomorrow. Improving on-time delivery performance and improving the plant's ability to respond quickly to unique specifications from customers will afford E&F the opportunity to increase total sales, total throughput, and net income. To achieve this additional throughput, E&F must be able to produce more varieties of products with shorter lead times. This will be made possible with the implementation of a drum-buffer-rope system.

Identifying The Constraints

Material Constraints   A systematic analysis of late orders showed no pattern to indicate that lack of a common material was responsible for late shipments. This suggested that there were no material constraints. This was verified by both the planning group and the purchasing group. Raw materials needed for fabrication and purchased components needed at the assembly operation were both readily available in sufficient quantities.

Although there were frequent component shortages at assembly, they were the result of internal problems, primarily material misallocation. Less frequent causes of component shortages were poor manufacturing priorities, design changes, or rush customer orders.

The conclusion was that there were no true material constraints at the E&F

plant. Pseudo-material constraints occured continually, but they were typically the result of material misallocation.

Capacity Constraints   Following the systematic procedure for identifying capacity constraints in a T-plant outlined earlier, a list of "short or missing" component parts that were responsible for late orders was created. This list of parts did not indicate any unique common resource as a problem. As part of the verification process, the "where used" feature of the MRP bill of material file was also used to identify other end items that used components found on the list of short parts. Finished-goods inventory was then checked to determine whether or not there were excess stocks of end items these parts.

In the case of every short part, at least some of the end items using the part were found to have an excess of finished-goods in stock. This led to the conclusion that there was no capacity constraint at E&F. This conclusion was verified with supervisors and by overtime records. Both indicated that no single resource could be identified as consistently overloaded.

The phenomenon of wandering bottlenecks was observed throughout the plant. However, this was the result of misallocation of material and poor control systems. Thus, there were no true capacity constraints at E&F, only pseudo-constraints.

Setting the Buffers

In the E&F plant, both stock buffers and time buffers are required.

Stock Buffers   Both finished-goods stock buffers and component-stock buffers are needed. These two different types of stock buffers work in concert to satisfy customer requirements. Finished-goods stock buffers are needed for two reasons; because some customer orders for some products must be shipped in less than the assembly lead time, and because daily and weekly demand peaks exceed assembly capacity.

In the first case, as stated earlier, the required customer lead time for most tools is two weeks. Since assembly lead time is less than one week, it is therefore not necessary to carry finished-goods inventory for these tools. However, recall that for some products, customer orders may have to be shipped in less than a week (some within 24 hours). These orders can only be serviced from finished-goods-stock buffers. But since the replenishment lead time from component stocks is one week, only a small amount of finished-goods inventory is actually needed.

The second case that argues for establishing finished-goods inventory is the volatility of daily and weekly demand. No hard data was available at the time, so it was decided to monitor customer orders by request date. This would allow the tracking of the actual volatility of demand as well as the plant's performance to customer expectations. This information would then be used to help determine an appropriate level of finished-goods stock.

To get the process started, it was decided to keep four weeks of finished-goods inventory in stock buffers of "A" items only (regular-demand, high-volume, standard-configuration products). Note that this is a significant reduction from the three-month's worth of inventory of all products previously held.

Component stock buffers are vital at the E&F plant because the component-part stores area provides a better location for stock buffers than the finished-goods warehouse. Establishing a stock buffer at the component-part level provides two key advantages:

1. Since there are only 79 "key" common components, the forecast accuracy at the component level is much higher than for each possible variation of finished tools (2,880 different tools). This is simply the result of the fact that positive and negative forecasting errors for individual items cancel out at the aggregate level, making the aggregate forecast much more accurate.
2. The component-stock buffer provides a great deal of flexibility in meeting highly volatile customer demand. A finished-goods stock buffer provides no flexibility.

The primary stock buffer in the drum-buffer-rope system at E&F is the component-stock buffer. The size of this buffer is determined by three factors:

1. *Replenishment lead time.* That is, the time it takes for the manufactured components to be processed through the fabrication operation and reach the component stores area. The longer the required replenishment lead time, the bigger the component stock buffer needs to be.
2. *The expected usage rate.* The higher the expected usage rate for a given component, the bigger the needed stock buffer for that component.
3. *The volatility of demand.* As the volatility of demand increases, more components must be carried in the component stock buffer to accommodate the "spikes" in demand for components.

Initially, most fabricated parts could be produced in two weeks or less. However, as a safe starting point, a component stock buffer of eight weeks was chosen for all components.

Time Buffers   As previously discussed, there are no physical constraints at E&F. All problems were related to policy constraints, not to physical constraints. Therefore, there is no need of a constraint time buffer. Time buffers are needed for only three cases:

1. *Replenishing the component stock buffers.* Time buffers are needed to ensure that all manufactured components are released to the shop floor at the appropriate time. This time buffer allows sufficient time in the production routings to compensate for the disruptions of the manufacturing operation so the component stock buffers will not run out of parts.
2. *Replenishing the finished-goods stock buffers.* This time buffer ensures that products have enough time to be processed by assembly and arrive at the finished-goods stock buffers to maintain the desired stock level.
3. *Establishing a shipping time buffer for those products for which there is no finished-goods stock buffer.* This time buffer covers the lead time from the component stores area to the shipping department. This buffer protects the integrity of the promised delivery dates of those products for which there is no finished-goods stock buffer.

Figure 6.6 illustrates the location of the various recommended stock and time buffers in the initial Synchronous Management drum-buffer-rope solution for the E&F plant. The diagram for Figure 6.6 is based on the product flow diagram for the E&F plant developed in Figure 6.5.

Establishing the Master Schedule

With a sound stock buffer strategy, the E&F plant operates as two separate but well-synchronized plants. The assembly department operates primarily in a build-to-order mode (except for those products that have finished-goods stock buffers). The fabrication process operates in a build-to-stock mode. The fabrication operation essentially replenishes the component stock buffers ahead of assembly. Therefore, two master schedules must be developed—an assembly master schedule and a component fabrication master schedule.

Assembly Master Schedule   The assembly master schedule is derived from weekly customer orders. If the load created by those orders is less than the capacity of the assembly area, the anticipated load for the next three weeks is checked to determine if any orders should or could be pulled in. If after this step the assembly load for the week is still below a predetermined minimum

FIGURE 6.6

The Location of the Time Buffers and Stock Buffers for the E&F Industrial Air Tool Plant (Initial Synchronous Management Solution)

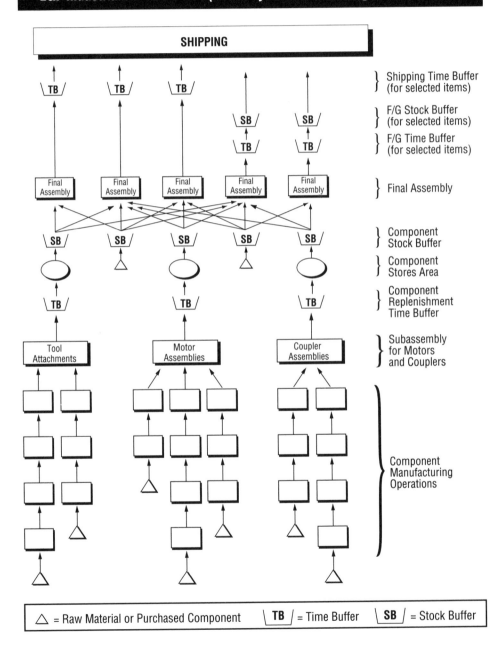

△ = Raw Material or Purchased Component   TB = Time Buffer   SB = Stock Buffer

production level, (based on the low end of projected sales) standard items kept in finished-goods stock buffers would be added to the production schedule. The standard items to be assembled are selected based on current inventory levels and projected needs.

The goal of this scheduling procedure is to smooth out the peaks and valleys in the assembly work load, not to keep assembly busy. Strict discipline is necessary to make sure assembly does not produce unscheduled items, even if it means standing idle when there is plenty of component materials in stock.

Fabrication Master Schedule   The master schedule for the fabrication area consists of the components needed to replenish the component-stock buffers. In the initial stages of implementation, the batch quantities for all components was established as two months' worth of parts. This maintains the same batch sizes for "A" items under the old ABC rule. But this is a significant reduction in the previous batch sizes for both "B" items (formerly six month quantities) and "C" items (formerly 12 month quantities).

The logic of using lengthy time horizons, even for the little-used "C" items, does not work well in reality due to the highly inaccurate forecasts for these parts. For example, producing an expected year's worth of parts in a single batch creates an excessive amount of component inventory and adds to the problem of obsolete inventory as design changes are introduced. Besides, since the E&F plant does not have a capacity constraint, decreasing the process batch sizes is appropriate. All of the fabrication resources have the extra capacity to absorb any additional required setup time.

Tying The Ropes

The final step in implementing the drum-buffer-rope system is to establish the rope system. The strict control of the rope system was quickly implemented in the component fabrication areas to ensure that all production priorities would be followed. The process batches were already established through the master scheduling process discussed above. The next requirement is the determination of the planned lead times, so that material release schedules can be established.

In the E&F plant, the lead times for the fabrication of component parts was significantly reduced. This was accomplished by setting all move and wait times at each resource to zero. With this change, the lead times calculated by E&F's MRP system would essentially be the sum of the expected process and setup times for all resources in the routing of a component. To this time, a time buffer was added to account for all of the disruptions that might be encountered during the process. This time buffer should account for any and all delays that might reasonably be expected as the components move to the component stores area.

The rope system also makes provisions for improving schedule execution. This is done primarily by establishing strict control at the schedule control points. In the E&F plant, schedule control points are limited to material release and assembly.

Significant changes were implemented in the amount of discretion allowed planners and supervisors. Under the previous system, the schedule window (the total time horizon for which activities were reviewed and acted upon) was 30 days. This meant that planners and supervisors looked at all the jobs they were supposed to perform in the next 30 days and were given the freedom to release materials and execute tasks in any way deemed appropriate to improve local efficiencies.

However, under the drum-buffer-rope system, local efficiencies are irrelevant. Thus, the schedule window was reduced from 30 days to zero; planners and schedulers were no longer allowed to pick and choose jobs to meet some outdated notion of efficiency. Instead, priorities were established by the planning system and those priorities had to be strictly followed. Materials were released as determined by the fabrication master schedule and the planned lead times. Production priorities were established on a FIFO basis. It was simple and effective.

Monitoring Performance and Progress

At E&F, several intermediary operational measures were developed to help track the day-to-day performance of critical areas. These measures acted as proxies for T, I and OE, and provided immediate and highly visible feedback. Of prime importance was a "performance to schedule" measure implemented at final assembly. This new measure replaced the old "total units assembled" measure and was instrumental in eliminating the stealing problem. Other key Synchronous Management measures monitored on-time delivery performance and inventory levels at the finished-goods and component-stock buffers.

As the drum-buffer-rope implementation progressed, planned lead times decreased, and the level of synchronization between the assembly operation and manufacturing improved. As part of the implementation, some equipment was rearranged into cellular configurations to help reduce lead times. As the implementation proceeded, the volatility of demand became better understood and managed.

As a result, within an 18 month period, all stock buffer quantities were reduced. The component stock buffers were reduced from eight weeks to four weeks, and the finished-goods stock buffers were reduced from four weeks to two weeks. With less than half the inventory, due-date performance improved from about 65 percent to over 90 percent. At the same time, overtime fell by 60 percent.

Chapter 7

A FRAMEWORK FOR IMPLEMENTATION

Important principles may and must be flexible.
– Abraham Lincoln, 1865

INTRODUCTION

In previous chapters, we have developed the techniques and methodologies needed to effectively manage product flow in complex plants. The remaining challenge is implementing these techniques to realize benefits.

For the purpose of our discussion, we assume that the target plant is managed by traditional rules and procedures rather than Synchronous Management concepts. We also assume that the plant is "typical" in its performance and the competitive issues it faces. For instance, we assume the plant has come through a period in which quality was the dominant competitive factor and is now facing the challenge of achieving superior on-time delivery performance and a high degree of responsiveness to customers. Of course, these new challenges must be met while maintaining (in fact, improving) previous quality gains.

Our discussion of critical Synchronous Management implementation issues is based on a general framework that guides the process of continuous improvement. We discuss in detail the most critical issues that must be faced when moving from a traditional management approach to Synchronous Management.

FIGURE 7.1

A General Framework for Synchronous Management Implementations

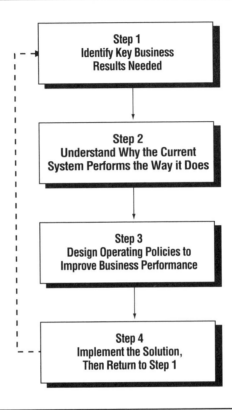

GENERAL FRAMEWORK FOR IMPLEMENTATION

A Synchronous Management implementation to improve company performance should follow a logical four-step process. The general framework is presented in Figure 7.1 and summarized below:

Step 1. Identify Key Business Results Needed.

This is the starting point for any analysis of performance, particularly in light of the need to carefully link local performance with business-level results, and to make it clear that specific local improvements do not necessarily lead to business improvement. At the same time, the desired objective should be something more specific than "making money."

To return to the analogy of a football team (used in Chapter 1), in this step the team determines what major performance factors must improve. Remember that the team was losing by an average score of 10 to 3. The specific objective should be stated as "scoring more points," and not just simply as "winning more games."

Step 2. Understand why the Current System Performs the Way it Does.

A systematic cause-effect analysis should be performed to identify the root causes for poor business performance with respect to the key measures identified in step 1. This analysis must encompass understanding what the current processes are and why they result in the specific performance the company is trying to improve.

In the case of the football team, the coaching staff needs to understand what it is about the offensive team and/or game plan that results in an inability to score points. Using carefully compiled game statistics and review of game films, the coaches try to identify the root causes of the team's offensive woes. This understanding is critical to any successful changes.

Step 3. Design Operating Policies to Improve Business Performance

The next step is to develop operational strategies and policies that will improve performance. To the football team, this means developing a new game plan consistent with the team's capabilities. Of course, if trades and free agent signings can be executed to acquire new players and improve team capability, these things should be done first. To improve the team, individual players may be assigned to different positions. The game plan should then be constructed to fully capitalize on the team's new strengths.

A business begins this process by analyzing its constraints to see which ones can be immediately resolved and which should be managed. Then an operating system is designed that optimizes performance within the remaining constraints.

Step 4. Implement the Solution, then Return to Step 1.

The final step is to implement the solutions developed in step 3. This is the hard step. In the case of the football team, this is the step of putting the new game plan with the new team to work. It includes explaining the new game plan to all players and explaining the role of each individual. Playbooks have to be modified and updated, and practices must be conducted before the weekend game. At game time, the plan is executed, and then performance can be evaluated using measures (statistics) and game films. This information is used to repeat the process and improve the team for the next week's game.

Implementation issues in business organizations fall into two major categories. The first can be described as project management issues. These include development of detailed actions plans, documentation of procedures, allocation of resources, and so on. The second can be described as culture-change issues. Culture-change issues related to changing company mindset and measures are what make Synchronous Management implementations different from simply installing automated equipment, building a new facility, or undertaking other complex tasks. We will focus on the culture side of the implementation issue in our discussion below.

APPLYING THE GENERAL FRAMEWORK

Step 1: Identify Key Business Results Needed

As noted earlier, the objective is to identify specific improvements that need to be accomplished at the business level. This must be more specific than "increase profits." We know that in today's global and highly competitive markets, almost every company needs to improve performance with respect to two key elements: *customer satisfaction and asset productivity.* Within these two broad elements, each company must identify the specific factors that must be improved and answer two basic questions:

1. What improvement in performance must we achieve so we can sell more?
2. What improvements in asset utilization do we need so we can be more productive?

The answer to the first question may be improvement in a single performance element, for example on-time delivery performance. More commonly, improvements in different elements are required for different customers and different market segments. In fact, the answer to the first question should force a company to fully understand what value each customer is buying from the company and what the customer would like to buy in the future. Answering these questions, with more feedback from the customer, is the first step to identifying what improvements are required.

A manufacturer of high-tech products for the aerospace industry embarked on a Synchronous Management initiative with an initial intent to reduce working capital requirements by reducing inventory. Management felt that this would be a nice complement to the company's quality initiatives, and together the two initiatives would improve operating efficiencies. In traditional management style, the company's viewpoint when it came to improvements was internal. The company first looked to improving efficiencies, even though the problem was loss of market share. When forced to answer the first question, managers realized that they really did not know why the company was losing market share. After careful investigation, it was determined that customers no longer made buying decisions based on technology and quality. Customers demanded and received from all their suppliers significant improvements in quality. Quality was now simply the "entry fee" to the game. On-time deliveries and responsiveness had become important buying criteria for all four of this company's key customers. Needless to say, improving on-time deliveries became the focus of the Synchronous Management implementation.

In another case, a manufacturer of wood furniture products initiated a program to improve on-time deliveries. Customer complaints had been inappropriately correlated with internal measures of on-time shipments, and it was incorrectly concluded that poor on-time delivery performance was at the heart of customer complaints. But what this company was trying to improve was performance against the internal measure of on-time shipments, with an objective of shipping all standard products from finished-goods inventory. If the company could not ship from finished-goods stock, it would count as a missed shipment. When a standard product was not in stock, a promise date would be acknowledged to the customer. Non-standard products were promised based on the scheduling cycle (or 'cutting schedule' as it is called in the furniture industry). Performance against the promise dates was measured for both standard and special-order products.

What customers were upset about had little to do with either performance criteria. Customer's were upset at not receiving the product when they requested the product be delivered. The first task in this Synchronous Management implementation was to understand when customers would like to receive the product.

After careful review, it became clear that all customers did not have identical delivery requirement for products. A small number of customers wanted products shipped within 24 hours. The vast majority of customers, whether they were ordering standard products or specials (minor variations in construction and finish), usually requested shipment in about four to six weeks. By attempting to ship all standard products within three days, no customer was happy and the company carried excessive finished-goods inventory. Since manufacturing lead time averaged 16 weeks, not even the few customers who ordered specials were satisfied. The core problem from the customer satisfaction side for this company was a lack of understanding of the differences in these customer segments. Different strategies would be needed to satisfy different customer segments.

Before deciding that a specific improvement in performance will result in improved customer satisfaction, and hence provide opportunity for increasing revenues, make sure to answer two specific questions:

1. Which specific customer will (or is likely to) buy more of a specific product if we improve performance in a particular manner?
2. How do we know this?

The key is to make sure that customers' real needs are being addressed.

The second area of business performance that can be improved is operational effectiveness, or asset management. The idea is to identify what performance outcome (for the entire unit) is needed so the company's financial performance will improve. In Synchronous Management terms, productivity is measured in terms of the three operational measures—throughput, inventory, and operating expense. But which of these is the most important to business performance?

In the Synchronous Management philosophy, the most significant operational measure is throughput. Throughput increases have the maximum financial leverage and are the direct link to customer satisfaction measures. Improvements in the chosen customer satisfaction measures should result in increased T.

Second in importance is inventory, because of its impact on competitive edge. Finally, operating expense, while definitely providing opportunities for improving profitability, has less leverage than throughput, rarely improves competitive performance factors, and often has a negative effect on morale. The overall financial impact of changes in T, I, and OE can be computed and priorities set for improvement.

The organization must focus on the most important results needed at the business level. These business results should drive actions at all levels of the organization. In the case study discussed in the next chapter, throughput is clearly the operational performance measure that was the focus of Synchronous Management initiatives.

Step 2: Understand Current Process and Performance

The next step in the implementation of a new, more synchronized process is to clearly understand the current organization and current management process, with the objective of identifying the key issues responsible for current business performance. In implementing a major change, it is important to not only understand what must be changed and why, but also what must be left unchanged and why. Every business performs well on certain elements and poorly on others.

When improving performance on the weak elements, it is important not to lose or degrade performance on the strong elements.

Overall business performance is the result of the individual processes that make up the business (activities involved in the flow of information and material from order receipt to shipment) and the management rules that govern these business processes. To understand current performance it is necessary to understand the process map of the activities involved, and the management policies that drive these activities. Just as a doctor examining a patient limits the detailed examination to aspects that are likely to be the cause of the patient's specific ailment, it is necessary to limit detailed analysis to those aspects most likely to be the cause of the weak business results identified.

Begin by constructing a map of the activities that make up the business operations. This essentially consists of the flow of products and other information necessary to create the Product Flow Diagram (PFD). Even for a relatively small organization, a complete and detailed PFD that includes most activities will be too large and complex to serve as a meaningful tool for detailed root-cause analysis. The usual technique is to start with a business-level "block" diagram and explode down to the necessary level of detail in the required areas.

The next step in understanding current processes is to identify the specific management policies that drive the activities. Synchronous Management is concerned with four major groups of management policies:

1. Policies that result in the misalignment of the Three Ms: mindset, methods and measures.
2. Policies that result in complexity and lack of a streamlined flow.
3. Policies that result in misallocation of assets.
4. Policies that result in mismanagement of constraints.

The analysis of these causes is greatly facilitated by realizing that root-cause issues can be classified into two categories:

1. Generic causes based on plant type. This is the list of causes expected from an understanding of whether the plant is a V-plant, A-plant, or T-plant. Earlier chapters of this book showed how the traditional cost-focused management system of production results in problems that are generic to plant type. Understanding the plant-type also helps to develop the cause-and-effect connection to make sure the suspected cause is actually a valid explanation of the business-level problem.

2. Organization specific issues. This list includes issues peculiar to the industry in general, and to the organization in particular. For example, most companies in the electronics industry share some practices and policies, but each electronics company has some unique policies related to its history, technology, and culture.

Some examples of organization specific issues we have encountered include:
- The factory is a set of old buildings and the machinery is spread out over several floors, and in different buildings, creating unique material flow issues.
- The scheduling (or shift crewing or purchasing) rules were established by the current company president. Although the rules are now 10 years old and everyone can see the need for changes, people's behavior reflects a sense that these rules are cast in concrete.
- Stock-room and production-control clerks share in the output-based bonus program. Any attempt to control material release meets with "lip service" at best.
- The company president has developed a habit of asking "how many parts did we press yesterday?" as he walks past the press room supervisor's office each day.
- A key piece of equipment was developed in house (by retired technical wizards) and is not flexible, but those who use it are emotionally attached to it.

Clearly, plant type issues can be very quickly developed from knowledge of V, A, and T plants. Understanding 3M-related issues requires detailed analysis of the specific mindset, measures, and methods of the particular organization.

Described below are some key concepts to keep in mind when evaluating mindset, measures and methods.

Mindset   The importance of mindset in bringing about change has been repeatedly emphasized in this book. Identifying the prevailing mindset and determining whether or not it presents an obstacle to change is not easy. Observation of what actions receive priority, what gets done, what does not seem to get done (even though there appears to be general agreement) and discrepancies between words (such as those in mission statements and posted slogans) and actions, all provide a picture of the organization's mindset. Formal surveys can also be conducted to provide more detail of the organization's mindset.

Measures   It is important to find the measures that drive localized, non-synchronous behavior in the organization. The collection of reports and measures used to evaluate performance at all levels of the organization should be carefully analyzed to see which measures are key and drive decision making. Observation and discussions with people at all levels and in all functions provides additional information on key measures. Another way to find clues to the prevailing mindset and the culture measures is to review successful and unsuccessful appropriation requests.

Methods   Methods are the actual rules and procedures used in the execution of job activities. The major areas that should be reviewed include:
1. Demand management
2. The planning process
3. Interactions with manufacturing support areas
4. Shop floor/production operations
5. Plant layout and organizational structure.

Information should be analyzed to help provide a clear cause-effect linkage between specific sets of management policies and the weak business results identified in the previous step.

Demand Management   Key questions may include: What are the markets and what is the nature of the demand? What are the process inputs and outputs? How much massaging of information is done and how is information communicated?

It is important to look at all communication channels with customers, including customer incentives and other marketing programs that alter ordering patterns from true customer needs; distribution and warehouse needs versus those of the end user (the true customer); forecast-generated demand versus build to order; and order-entry issues, such as timeliness of order entry, speed in reflecting internal demands, and completeness and usefulness of information.

The Planning Process   Key questions to ask about the planning process include: What does the planning process involve? Does it promote stability? What logic and parameters drive it?

The philosophy (mindset) regarding the use of assets is important. Does the old mindset of keeping capital assets running and not letting labor have idle time still apply? Or has the mindset begun to change to a Synchronous Management mode, where the use of assets is determined by the system's constraints, and the goal is to effectively utilize assets in order to make the right product at the right time.

Part of this planning mindset is the planning logic, including lead times used, how they are developed, and how often they are reviewed; inventory policies including how much, where, and why; and lot-sizing rules. It is also important to know the time lines allowed within the plan, including the time between order receipt and order planning, the rescheduling frequency, and system response time.

Some plans are more realistic than others. This depends to a great degree on the integrity of data and the stability of the plan from one planning cycle to another. A stable plan with good data integrity yields planning output that is actually used, while a plan that everyone knows is "fudged" is not used.

Finally, it is important to understand the degree of integration within the plan, how many different sources of data are needed to produce the plan, and what impact these data sources have on the timeliness and quality of the planning process. This gets back to the issue of data integrity and ultimately to integrity of the plan itself.

Interactions with Manufacturing Support Areas   Quality assurance, engineering, and materials management are all integrally connected to the manufacturing process. Quality assurance activities are a good indicator of the company's mindset; is it one of prevention or one of inspection and detection? Engineering has an important voice in the process description, product specifications, and process and product improvements. Materials management controls material release policies, movement of material from and to stockrooms, and is involved with supplier performance and supplier management methods.

Another important adjunct is information systems, which link all of these critical areas. If the information systems are antiquated or ill designed, artificial communication barriers between manufacturing and its supporting areas will exist to such a degree that even good methods can be stymied.

Shop Floor/Production Operations   This is an area where mindset and measures really do set the tone for methods. About the only objective issue to consider is process and equipment limitations. After that, shop floor issues are quite subjective.

It is important to understand the key drivers and measures of supervisory activities. These include both the ways supervisors are measured and the way supervisors measure operators.

There are usually more informal rules on the shop floor than there are formal rules. Determining work sequence may be an informal rule, and one that is often driven by the desire to please the "best" customers. Effects of ignoring formal rules include the "end-of-month push" and most expediting.

Some of the key shop-floor methods to be analyzed relate to who conducts material transfer, when and in what quantities, the validity of standards and setup data, and inventory profiles, with particular attention to chronic piles and shortages. But from the Synchronous Management perspective, the most important shop-floor method issue is how the shop-floor personnel view the issue of constraints. Do they see a constraint as something to be "worked around" or something that creates the schedule to be worked within? Do they try to "beat down" a constraint by pushing more material at it, or do they allow the constraint to be the limiting factor and adjust up-stream activities to the constraint? Do they focus improvement efforts on the constraint?

Plant Layout and Organizational Structure   The physical layout of the plant should be conducive to a smooth product flow. An easy way to check this is to actually trace the product routes from material release to shipping by walking. Is it an efficient path or is there significant unnecessary backtracking or movement? Are there excessive non-value-adding activities required because of the physical layout?

The organizational structure should also be designed to facilitate a synchronous operation. It is useful to determine whether the different functional areas work together as a team, or whether there are significant boundaries that cause dysfunctional behaviors and activities.

Step 3: New Process to Improve

Discussion in this book has focused on the design of material flow management techniques. This chapter, however, highlights the fact that implementing Synchronous Management requires realigning the mindset, measures, and methods of the organization. In this section, we discuss some of the the key mindset-, measure-, and method-related issues that should be considered when designing and implementing a Synchronous Management system.

Mindset   Mindset changes over time. If you are working to implement Synchronous Management, then you have already changed your mindset. Management must continue to articulate to all employees what it is about the old mindset that has changed and what the new mindset is. This must be made explicit and constantly reinforced through management actions and through new measures. Employees must not feel they are being told one thing and then measured against another.

Measures   A balanced set of Synchronous Management measures has to be developed to replace the typical cost-based measures used in most companies. The new set should include four categories of measures: customer satisfaction measures, operational performance measures, constraint measures, and activity-outcome measures.

- Customer satisfaction measures:

    A basic need in any business is to assure that there is a steady flow of revenue from satisfied customers. In today's marketplace, the critical issue is not simply price. Customers are demanding fast, on-time delivery, at parts-per-million quality, before they even ask about price. Thus, a company must establish customer-focused measures that measure the critical aspects of product features, delivery reliability, lead time, quality, and service.

- Operational performance measures:

    Once the external, customer-focused measures are in place, a set of operational performance measures can be created that will drive improvement. Synchronous Management uses throughput, inventory and operating expense.

    The T, I, and OE measures encompass all of the spending under a manager's control, not just the direct labor force. This encourages a balance between labor reduction and reduction in the other elements of cost, such as scrap, inventory, and overtime. It is well known that simple labor-cost reduction often hinders improvements in some competitive elements. Thus, as part of the overall set, these measures keep both improvements in the competitive elements and labor-cost reductions in perspective.

- Constraint Measures:

    Ensuring proper constraint management is critical if the organization is to achieve optimum performance. The measures that help manage and control constraint performance to the best advantage of the entire business are called constraint measures. For example, if material availability is the constraint, a logical constraint measure is the yield for this material through the process.

    To underscore the importance of constraints, and to provide crucial managerial focus, we elevate constraint measures to the rank of "global" measure. Therefore, Synchronous Management's global measures includes customer-focused measures, the operating measures T, I, and OE, and the company's constraint measures.

- Activity-Outcome Measures

    Customer-based and operational measures provide information on how well the business is performing. The measures that help evaluate performance of individual activities are called local measures or activity-outcome measures.

    Tying these local measures to total system performance is difficult.

Consider for example a department that provides two components, both required at a subsequent assembly operation. The number of matched sets produced is an example of an activity-outcome or local measure. Simply counting the number of units produced (or the equivalent standard hours) does not create a good activity-outcome measure, since a unit without its matching component is useless.

At the individual operator level, it must be determined what aspects of performance have the greatest impact on the business. This is equivalent to identifying the activity-outcome measures.

Methods   The methods for managing resources and materials in a manufacturing operation should follow the mindset that "manufacturing is a sales driver." This means they should support a Synchronous Management approach that utilizes drum-buffer-rope to optimize system-wide performance. In step 2, system constraints were identified and a process map (product flow diagram) was developed.

When designing the new process flow in step 3, it is useful to synchronize operations, including appropriate time and stock buffers. Then management's attention can be focused on improving the performance of the system's constraints. Specific recommended actions vary depending on whether the constraint is physical, policy or market-based. These recommendations have been well documented throughout both volumes of this series.

Step 4: Implement The Solution, Then Return to Step 1

Culture change is an enormous part of the transition to Synchronous Management. A successful implementation must incorporate three key elements

1. *Managerial support expressed through "talking the talk" and "walking the walk:"*

    This is usually accomplished through a steering committee, which also serves to guide and support the implementation team. Even if all of the top executives do not serve on the steering committee, it is important that they are briefed on steering committee business at executive meetings and show their support during their day-to-day interactions with all company personnel. If executive attention wanes, this sends a message throughout the business that Synchronous Management isn't very important.

2. *Buy-in from key members of the user group.*

    This applies to all steps in the process. Just because there is initial buy-in doesn't mean it will last. Support for the implementation of Synchronous Management must be continually reinforced by all managers and supervisors to those who work for them.

3. *A clear champion who drives the implementation activities forward.*

This champion must work at a sufficiently high level in the organization to be able to identify and remove barriers. He or she must be willing and able to push for rapid decisions to be made that remove the barriers and maintain the necessary implementation momentum.

These three elements are valid for any large organizational change initiative. But there are some key points that are peculiar to the implementation of Synchronous Management:

• Implementation activities should follow a step-by-step approach. It is not necessary that the full magnitude of the solution developed in step 1 be implemented all at once. For example, if the initial plan includes reducing the batch size to one half of its current value, this can be done in two or three phases.

• Simple, visual methods are preferable to complex and sophisticated ones.

• The nature of the required changes (related to the existing mindset, measures, and methods) should determine the activities undertaken to close the gap. For example, activities that change the method of operation and are still consistent with the mindset of the organization, can be accomplished in a "just do it" mode. On the other hand, activities that require a change in mindset require additional effort. Education and pilot projects may be necessary in order to sell the organization on the validity of the new approach.

One final note. Once Synchronous Management has been implemented, that is not the end of the story. As anyone who has worked in a manufacturing environment knows, the process of correcting problems is somewhat similar to squeezing a balloon. If you squeeze the top of a balloon, the bottom bulges. Squeeze the bottom and the top and the bulge appears somewhere else.

Fix a problem, and this allows another problem to become more visible. Find a constraint and resolve it, and this allows the next constraint to be discovered. Synchronous Management is an iterative process. Every system will always have at least one constraint. The key to not being overwhelmed by the knowledge that constraints will always exist is to understand that every newly discovered constraint will be less disruptive than the previous ones. We know this because the entire process is designed to continuously identify the most disruptive constraint. Understanding that more pressing and more difficult constraint issues already have been successfully resolved should inspire you to rub your hands together and say "piece of cake."

Chapter 8

IMPLEMENTATION CASE STUDY

The world we have created today has problems which cannot be solved by thinking the way we thought when we created them.
— Albert Einstein, 1950

In Chapters 4, 5, and 6 we described and illustrated how to develop and apply a drum-buffer-rope system to manage product flows in different types of plants. In chapter 7, we developed a general framework for implementing Synchronous Management in a company. This framework identified some of the more critical issues that must be addressed during implementation. In this chapter, we illustrate the general framework for implementation with a detailed case study of an actual implementation. Given the complexities and dynamics of a real organization, this case study provides excellent insights into some of the critical issues often encountered during an implementation. The actual company shall remain anonymous, being referred to as SportIt, Inc.

CASE STUDY DESCRIPTION

SportIt, an autonomous division of a large corporation, manufactures and sells to the consumer sporting goods market through a variety of dealers and retailers. The typical finished product is an assembly made up of approximately 100 components. Normally, about 70 of these components are purchased from outside suppliers. The remaining 30 or so are manufactured at the plant. The facility is quite old and most of the equipment is more than 20 years old, some dating back to the 1930's. There are some new pieces of equipment, including a multi-million dollar Flexible Machining System (FMS).

The plant recently weathered a very turbulent period. Bad business conditions had resulted in significant work force reductions. The surviving work force numbered about 2,000. Labor is unionized, with a long standing "us versus them" attitude. Trust between labor and management, or for that matter between senior managers and supervisors, was virtually non-existent. In addition, a series of key management changes had generated a significant amount of chaos and intensified existing feelings of insecurity.

The past few years had brought about major changes in the industry. Overall growth rates had slowed. Meanwhile, both domestic and foreign competition had intensified as more players competed for the same customers. In response, SportIt had adopted an aggressive marketing strategy to increase market share. This consisted of introducing sorely needed new products to stimulate purchases, broadening the market base through segmentation of products, and entering into selected niche markets. The strategy also called for reliable and responsive deliveries as a key competitive advantage in the marketplace.

The new products were well accepted by the market and annual demand increased from 765,000 units to 950,000 units over two years. Forecasts for the coming year targeted a potential market of 1,275,000 units. But production was having difficulty coping with the heavier workload. This was partly due to the increase in unit volume, but also partly due to the additional complexity caused by a greater number of different products, more unique order configurations, more rush orders, and significant deviations from the forecast.

Just prior to the start of the Synchronous Management implementation, the previous year's production and profit targets were not met and the plant was significantly behind schedule by the end of the current quarter. The delivery and profitability issues were serious enough that the plant was on the corporation's "critical review list."

It is interesting to contrast the views of the different players in this business. The customers' view was that the company made good products. The problem was that SportIt never seemed to have the right products available, and promised delivery dates were excessively long and totally unreliable. Given these negative service factors, customers felt the products were over priced.

Company managers, being focused on asset productivity, saw the issue as one of insufficient return on sales. Despite the fact that nobody lived within established budgets, production and delivery problems were rampant. Managers believed they had heard every excuse under the sun for why there were constant cost overruns, production problems, and missed deliveries.

Plant employees saw a chaotic situation run by managers who seemed to be clueless. Product priorities changed daily and conflicting instructions were often issued by different managers. Targets and budgets did not seem to matter one day and the next day became the Holy Grail. Most employees were resigned to going in whatever direction the wind was blowing that day. SportIt was very much a typical, traditionally managed factory!

The company made repeated attempts to resolve its problems. None yielded any notable success. Meanwhile, pressure from dissatisfied customers and corporate headquarters intensified. The management team reacted to the pressure by calling more and more meetings.

Every morning there was a managers meeting to review the previous day's production, listen to excuses for poor performance, list the shortages for the current day, revamp the plan for the current day's build schedule, and so on. The managers would then meet with their line managers to update them on the day's game plan. At the end of the shift, managers would again meet with their line managers to receive the latest production status updates to take to the end-of-day meeting.

There were also field crisis review meetings, where the numerous product shortages and relatively few quality issues would be reviewed. The most critical product shortages would be checked against the current day's plan and the daily build rates. From this "on the fly" analysis, new delivery promises would be made. Of course, decisions made in these crisis meetings could, and often did, override the morning meeting decisions.

Daily MRP meetings were attended by the manufacturing manager, purchasing manager, and second-level line managers. They reviewed parts and material shortages, obtained re-promises for missing materials and parts, and used the new "need by" dates to create the MRP expedite list for the following day.

Of course, there were weekly meetings to review specific issues—quality review meeting, corporate asset review meeting, budget performance meeting, and so on. Most of the time, people in the meetings would not have the answers to questions that arose. This gave rise to the feeling that if more information were readily available, they would be able to make better decisions.

Everybody was working hard. Managers worked 10 to 12 hours per day and many routinely came in on Saturdays as well. Overtime for the hourly force had reached the point where it was considered more of a pain than a bonus. The increased volume of newly designed products added to production process complexity with more part numbers, more tooling, more setups and more opportunity for mistakes. The daily grind of long hours, the increased pressures, and schedule chaos all added up to a poor quality of work life.

Significant investments in new equipment had recently been made. Much of the investment was spent on multi-axis Computer Numerical Control (CNC) equipment. While it succeeded in reducing labor content in the product, the new equipment added to the work load in support departments such as engineering, NC programming, and maintenance. The centerpiece new investment was an addition to the factory that housed a series of CNC machines that constituted the FMS work center. Each CNC machine replaced an entire series of operations with a single operation. Once machined, the parts were moved by an AGV (Automated Guided Vehicle) to an automatic coordinate measuring machine. This device would inspect each machined part, accept or reject it, and provide feedback to the computer that controlled the entire FMS area. Tooling was also delivered from an automated tool storage system to the individual machines and loaded by the AGVs. In other words, the FMS work center was designed to run as a "lightless factory."

Unfortunately, the FMS work center cost a lot more than planned, exceeded its implementation timetable, and could not run the desired volume of parts. Of course, this was a sore spot and issue of great concern to both corporate and plant managers. The employees were also unhappy because vast sums of money had been spent on this state-of-the-art work center while they had been denied raises due to the company's lack of profitability.

The bottom line was that, under the old system, extraordinary effort was required just to survive. Furthermore, huge investments in technology only aggravated the situation. SportIt was in deep trouble. A totally new approach was needed!

In the remainder of this chapter, we describe how Synchronous Management techniques were implemented to turn the situation around–to transform SportIt from a loser to a winner. The implementation process follows the general framework developed in Chapter 7.

APPLYING THE GENERAL FRAMEWORK

Step 1: Identify Key Business Results Needed

SportIt had problems everywhere. The company was losing money, production volume was insufficient to meet customer demand, on-time delivery performance was poor, production costs were out of control, quality problems were pervasive, and the warehouse and factory floor were full of component parts and unsold product.

The ultimate objective of transforming SportIt was to dramatically change the perception of both customers and corporate leaders. The president wanted the customer to perceive SportIt as the company with "good new products that are delivered promptly." This would enable SportIt to command a premium price and not get caught in inventory clearance price wars. At the same time he wanted

SportIt to go from the corporate "dog house" to a "best practice showcase." To his credit, the president realized that this transformation would not be achieved by some magical new technology. In fact, he coined the phrase "continuous improvement through continuing hard work."

The president clarified his overall vision by specifying expected performance levels and operating conditions to be achieved within two years. Target performance levels were established from both the customers' perspective and the internal asset productivity perspective.

Specific customer performance targets included:

- Introduce four new models per season (up from the current average of one or two).
- Ship all standard products in five days, with popular models shipped within 24 hours of order placement (reduced from the current average of four weeks).
- Fill at least 98 percent of customer orders according to the above time parameters (not currently measured).

Asset productivity targets included:

- Increase throughput rate to yield 1,275,000 units annually (from current 850,000 units annually).
- Slash working capital requirements by reducing inventory at least 60 percent.
- Achieve all of the above targets with the current work force (which would require about a 50 percent improvement in output per employee.)

It was determined relatively quickly that the problems had to be dealt with in a sequential manner, and that the most significant problem was the volume of output. In Synchronous Management terminology, the most critical problem was identified as increasing throughput.

Increasing throughput would address three critical issues at the same time; it would relieve the immediate pressure from customers, improve profitability and asset productivity, and do so from a positive viewpoint rather than the negative approach of cost cutting. The positive approach was particularly important for employee morale, given recent downsizing and outsourcing decisions.

Once the key business issue was identified as increasing throughput, the next step was to evaluate current processes to understand how they affected throughput.

Step 2: Understanding Current System Performance

Plant Classification Type and Characteristics   Developing an in-depth understanding of current system performance is greatly facilitated by knowing the plant characteristics and classification type. SportIt manufactures four families of products, with multiple models in each family. Of the approximately 100 components required for each product, only three are considered to be "key components." Two metal components require significant fabrication and are considered key components. A purchased wood housing component qualifies as the third key component. The fabrication routings of the remaining manufactured components are limited to a few steps each such as drill, heat treat, and color. They are not considered key components.

One year earlier, the wood housing was manufactured in-house, but had been outsourced for cost reasons. Now there is an availability problem. Depending on the product model, this outsourced component still has two or three final machining operations performed at SportIt.

Figure 8.1 shows the product flow diagram for one specific model series. Since it is the plant type that we are interested in at this time, the diagram does not include details of specific machines, runtimes, etc.

Different models within a product family have a large number of non-key manufactured and purchased components in common. Moreover, each of the key components are common to a number of different models within a product family. But significantly, no two models share all of the key components. In fact, the key components are the product differentiators.

Figure 8.2 shows a schematic product flow diagram that includes two product models (models A1 and A2) from a single product family (product family A). The diagram shows that, except for the wood housing component, all of the key components and purchased components are common between models A1 and A2.

Much information about the product and production process was gathered during the initial investigation. Some of the key pieces of information are:

- Models within a product family typically share many common components.
- Key components are product differentiators.
- Some key components have long routings.
- Some of the key manufactured components share common raw materials and diverge at an early stage in the production process.
- Some key components are dedicated to specific models early in their fabrication routing.
- Demand is seasonal and different models and product families have widely

FIGURE 8.1

Simplified Product Flow Diagram for One Particular Model Series (Type A)

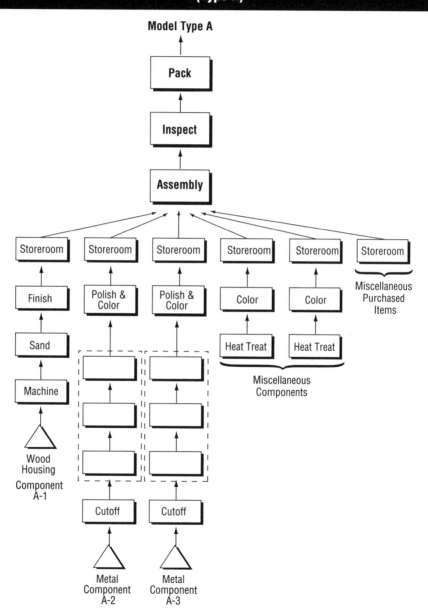

Note: The dashed lines in the flow of components A-2 and A-3 represent component machining cells.

FIGURE 8.2

Simplified Product Flow Diagram Showing Shared Components & Purchased Items Between Models A1 & A2

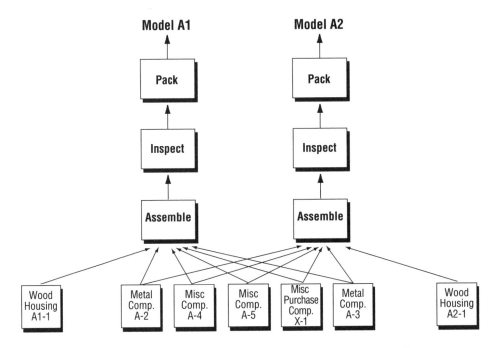

Note: Models A1 & A2 belong to the same series — Type A. They share all components except the Wood Housing.

varying levels of demand.

- Despite the fact that delivery performance is poor and total volume is less than needed to satisfy demand, some items are built and stored as finished-goods inventory.
- Many products require rework.

In Synchronous Management terminology, the product flow structure at SportIt is best described as a T-plant, with some critical divergence points in the fabrication process. SportIt also exhibits all of the symptoms of assembly-driven material misallocation that characterizes T-plants. The misallocation problems had been aggravated by recent changes in market conditions and the decision to significantly increase the number of products (over 150 new models in the past three years). This caused the average unit volume for models to drop significantly. This proliferation of products was in direct conflict with the economy-of-scale manufacturing practices that characterized the plant. The result was constantly changing priorities, chaotic expediting, high inventory, frequent shortages, and late shipments.

The generic T-plant issues were compounded by a number of issues unique to SportIt:

- Many of the machines are shared resources that were used to process multiple key components. Moreover, many of these machines (particularly the older generation machines) had difficult and lengthy setups. The long set-up times encouraged large batch sizes that typically average two-months' worth of components. This provided ample opportunity for material (and resource) misallocation.

- Some resources (polish, color and heat treat) were shared across many components from all product families. The high commonalty of resources created a high level of dependency. Thus, any disruption or misallocation had immediate and serious consequences for many products and customer orders.

- Finished products had a high failure rate for visual/surface finish defects. Setting aside a finished product at final inspection and sending it back for rework has the same effect as T-plant "stealing." Good components were tied up in the rework pile and were not available to produce products the customers wanted.

- The plant used an extremely cumbersome level-by-level planning system. Planners had to create firm planned orders for each level of the bill of material to generate shop paper. Once the work orders were created, the MRP explosion from assembly would stop and essentially disconnect changes in assembly or end-item schedules from the work orders. It was up to individual planners to maintain the connection between the work orders on the floor and actual end-item requirements. But this was not typically done. Long fabrication lead times that averaged about 20 weeks—another T-plant legacy—meant that there were many work orders on the floor, and many revisions to assembly schedules had occurred since the work orders were issued. All of these factors simply increased the opportunity for material and resource misallocation.

- Cribs or stock rooms for storing products had been established at many different stages of processing. Initially done as part of the MRP implementation for better control of in-process inventory and control of execution, they were now just holding areas with generously padded inventory stocks. This added unnecessary steps, inventory, and time to the process.

- The physical factory was an old building that had grown to its current size and form through many small additions over time. It was now a maze of departments with no logical material flow whatsoever. The poor layout not only prevented a streamlined flow, it provided numerous opportunities for covering up problems. Defective components could be hidden in all sorts of places. Sometimes even good components were hard to locate. Often, a search party was required to physically locate misplaced material.

- Finally, matters were made worse by the work force reductions and the constant stream of new management teams with different solutions and styles. The work force had resigned itself to hear talk of the latest plan of salvation, followed by a spurt of activity that yielded minimal results. Each failed plan of attack was typically scrapped and soon followed by the formation of a new team and the start of a new program. This factor had to be acknowledged when planning the implementation activities.

Constraint Identification   The next critical issue is the identification of constraints. It was quickly determined that there was no capacity constraint. This conclusion was primarily the result of two key observations. No single work center consistently worked overtime, and the "bottleneck" shifted constantly.

There was a material constraint. The wood component used to make the wood housing was not available in the quantity needed to support the necessary production volume. The wood component had recently been outsourced, and the new supplier had not been able to ramp up to meet the delivery requirements.

A verification analysis confirmed that the wood component was a material constraint. The gap between the number of units required to meet commitments made and the number of housing units received was significant, and knowledge of this shortage was widespread. For some high-volume product families, there was a tendency for housings to be processed in large batches. This caused a wave-like flow of housings that created pseudo-constraints of other components. However, the wood housing was the only constant member of the hot/expedite list across all product families.

It is important to note that, although the wood housing was widely recognized as a constraint, the organization did not manage it as a constraint. Consistent with the local optimization perspective encouraged by the traditional management system, the housing was just another component. In fact, its short supply gave everyone a convenient external excuse to explain why production was below targeted levels.

In addition, there was significant and widespread mismanagement of the constraint material. For instance:

- Wood housings were often damaged during handling or assembly. No extra precautions were taken to prevent damage to the constraint material.
- Good housings were assembled with metal components whose color finish was suspect. This meant that the constraint component would be sent to the rework pile when the assembled product was rejected. Meanwhile, perfectly good metal components were available but left unused in the component crib. If better care had been exercised in the selection of the non-constraint metal components used for assembly, the entire assembled product would have been immediately shipped.
- Typical T-plant material misallocation at assembly—driven by the traditional "units packed per shift" measure—resulted in misallocation of the constraint material. That is, wood housings were used to build models for which no current demand existed.
- Mismatched components at assembly also created the situation where wood housings could not be used as they became available due to the non-availability of non-constraint components.

Step 3: Design New Process to Improve Business Performance

It was conservatively estimated that proper synchronization and constraint management would increase throughput at SportIt by 15 percent. Other relatively modest changes in work organization, processes, and product design could increase throughput by an additional 10 to 15 percent. The president whole-heartedly agreed. He also bought into the idea that a sustained series of improvement steps was preferable to the risky "hit a home run" approach.

It was clear that SportIt would have to be significantly transformed into a very different operating entity. An 18-month period was selected as an appropriate time frame for the transformation. The restructured vision would have to be sufficiently defined to provide clear guidance. However, trying to spell out every detail would be futile and in all likelihood result in "paralysis by analysis."

Once the basic framework was defined, the step by step transformation process could be developed in detail as needed. We now describe some of the key elements that were specified at the onset of the SportIt implementation.

Assembly areas would be clean, well lit, and uncluttered. Major components would be released in matched sets on specially designed carts. Unused components would be returned to the finished-component stock room on these same carts for disposition. Shared and inexpensive components would be managed by a basic bin system. The work area and tools would be designed to minimize possible damage to the product. Assembly schedules and appropriate performance measures would be clearly posted, and each person in the assembly department would know what was to be built. (Improved lighting, along with additional training for assembly personnel, should reduce final inspection rejections caused by cosmetic blemishes.)

The company would be organized along product lines, with each product manager responsible for final assembly as well as fabrication of key components. Shared resources and materials would come under a single support resource manager. The rules for the use of shared resources would be developed in joint meetings with all product managers. Shared resources included the color and polish operation just prior to assembly. Assembly supervisors would pull needed components through the polish and color operations in matched sets in two-hour increments. Matched, finished components would be sent directly to the assembly area, minimizing the chance of damage as well as mismatched components.

The logistical organization of material flow would be as shown in Figure 8.3. The entire plant would be scheduled on a fixed two-week rolling schedule, including a daily assembly-build schedule. This would serve as the drum beat for the plant. Component parts could be fabricated in one week. The entire polish, color, and assembly processes could be completed in one day (three shifts). The two-week rolling schedule allowed for a time buffer of two days ahead of polish and another of two days prior to shipping.

The rope mechanism for major components would consist of releasing material in daily lots to match the assembly-build schedule for day 10 of the rolling schedule. The fixed schedules would drastically reduce the level of expediting, and mismatched components at assembly would be a distant memory of the chaotic past. Compared to the current 20-week lead time and two-month lot sizes, the proposed lot sizes and fabrication lead times were considered by most SportIt personnel to be a "pipe dream."

Before releasing any material from the time buffer location prior to polish, wood housing availability would be verified. After proper verification, the three key components would be released for processing—wood to NC machining (NC machining of the wood housing was under the support service manager) and the others in matched sets to polish. These would be completed and used in the assembly process within 24 hours. Essentially, the product-line assembly supervisor would specify the models to be built and the component crib personnel would take care of releases.

FIGURE 8.3

Logistical Organization of SportIt's Material Flow

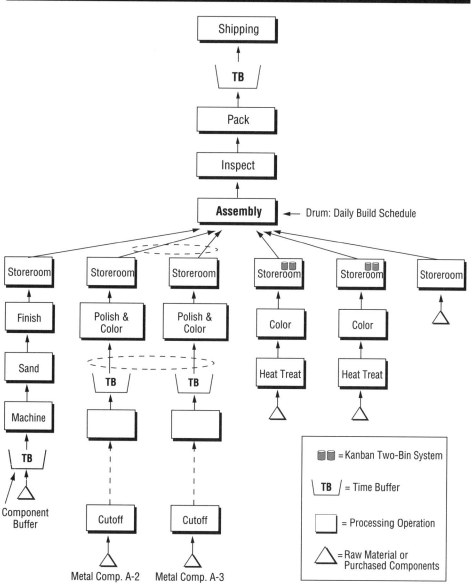

Notes: • Assembly daily build schedule, modified by the availability of wood housings, provides the drumbeat.
       • Dotted rings linking metal components A-2 and A-3 are used to indicate that the components are released from the time buffers and are sent to assembly in matched sets.
       • Most miscellaneous components are managed through the use of a two-bin system.
       • Rope ties are from the assembly daily build schedule to the release of material.

Shared and miscellaneous components would be handled using a bin system. The components would be issued to the assembly area from part specific bins. When parts in a bin were completely used up it would be exchanged for a new full bin. Bin size was determined by usage and space requirements of each part. A number of full bins were to be in the stock room—the exact number being mostly determined by part-specific details such as usage, bin size, and replenishment time. The standard replenishment time for most of these miscellaneous components was three days.

Meaningful performance measures for each area would have to be developed and clearly communicated. Product-line managers were to be treated as business managers responsible for both customer satisfaction and asset productivity. A full set of Synchronous Management measures would be used to evaluate these managers. Each specific production area would be measured on performance to schedule, defined as "the number of items completed on time and in the right amount," ratio of units shipped to total expenses (including salaries, overtime, scrap, etc.), and the level of work-in-process inventory (WIP).

The sales and marketing group was a separate group outside the plant. Both the sales manager and product-line manager would be held accountable for finished-goods inventory.

Support services would be reorganized into responsive units. The polish and color area that supported all product lines would be charged with the responsibility of delivering a steady stream of matched sets to the various assembly departments with a one-shift turn-around time. They would have to accomplish this with minimum material loss. Performance on these two criteria would be the measures for these areas. The supply function for miscellaneous and small components was organized into a single support center serving all products.

The product design function would be reorganized and synchronized to slash new product design time A flow diagram for the design and prototype processes would be constructed to identify opportunities for streamlining and overlapping activities. Shared resources (both within the design activity as well as with regular production work) would be identified and appropriate procedures would be developed to assure proper utilization of shared resources. Once design engineers recognized the disruptive influence of "breaking into" production activities, and once production personnel clearly understood the competitive need for new products, both groups would work as a team. The design function would become a routine and less disruptive part of shop activities.

Step 4 – Implement The New System, Then Return to Step 1

The changes necessary to establish the new system would be implemented in stages. In order to establish and maintain the momentum needed to feed the implementation, each stage would have to generate significant results. This was true at the corporate level, plant management level, and employee level. The activities planned for the next 18 months were organized into three six-month phases:

Phase I: The key objective was to increase throughput by focusing on the constraint and reducing misallocation.

Phase II: The key objective was to streamline the organizational structure and implement a drum-buffer-rope system to synchronize and accelerate material flow.

Phase III: The key objective was to achieve full organizational teamwork with the proper focus on the customer and continuous improvement.

Phase I   Activities undertaken in this phase fell into three broad categories; improve availability and utilization of constraint material; reduce material misallocation by improving control and execution of the production plan; and prepare for Phase II by beginning to address issues that relate to mindset and measures.

Improve Availability and Utilization of Constrained Material   A two-pronged improvement plan was initiated. To achieve better availability of the constraint material, a vendor assistance program was quickly initiated. To better utilize the constraint material, actions were taken to prevent damage to constraint material during handling and processing. The first step in this effort was to communicate the value of the constraint material in terms of lost throughput, not just its scrap value. Awareness sessions were held with everyone from the receiving dock to final packaging on all three shifts. A general plan was presented and suggestions were solicited. A multitude of action items came out of these sessions and were quickly implemented. Some of the more visible items included:

- Be more careful handling the wood component.
- Redesign the trolleys used to transport constraint material to improve product separation and padding.
- Post the number of units damaged and the value of throughput lost due to handling damage each day in each area.
- Reduce rework and scrap at in-house operations through more careful monitoring and posting of scrap related data. (Supervisors were

authorized to purchase cutting tools or other low-cost items that could improve process yields.)

- Determine the causes for scrap and rework that involve the constraint material in each area. Process engineers were assigned to the floor to quickly resolve problems and find ways to eliminate the causes of scrap and rework.

To better utilize constraint material, it was also necessary to reduce constraint material misallocation. This meant that the assembly areas had to exercise discipline and not use the constraint material to assemble products just to meet daily production quotas.

To fully accomplish this would take six months and would require that other procedural and organizational issues be addressed. However, informal discussions were held with the different assembly supervisors and schedulers to impress upon them the importance of proper allocation of the wood component. Two important action items resulted from these discussions:

- Stop building products that were already well in excess of planned stock levels in the warehouse, even if this was all that could be built. This began the process of chipping away at the ingrained practices that contributed to material misallocation.
- Begin clearing out the rework pile. Top priority was given to those items that contained good wood components.

In order to help ensure an increased supply of wood housings, SportIt initiated a vendor assistance program. Until recently the wood component had been produced at SportIt. This vast knowledge and valuable expertise was available at SportIt. Prior to the Synchronous Management implementation, there had been some discussion of ways to help the vendor, but none had been implemented. With the new recognition that the wood component was SportIt's primary constraint, a series of recommendations were carefully developed and implemented:

- SportIt provided the resources to help the vendor identify and manage its bottleneck. This included off loading the sanding and finishing processes for the wood component back to SportIt. This made particular sense since the sanding and finishing operations at the vendor were experiencing significant losses and most of the equipment previously used at SportIt was still in-house.
- SportIt provided needed expertise to help the vendor run his bottleneck process.

Reduce Misallocation by improving Control and Execution of the Production Plan

This was achieved by implementing changes in four specific areas. First, planned lead times were reduced. Second, a mode of working strictly to priorities on the floor was established. Third, unnecessary expediting, particularly from the assembly area, was reduced. Fourth, actions to move from performance measures based on efficiency to measures based on utilization were initiated.

Planning lead times are essentially a self-fulfilling prophecy. For example, if the planning lead time is four weeks, then four weeks of work will be in the system. This automatically means that, without expediting, a new unit introduced into the flow will take four weeks to reach the shipping dock. If the lead time is increased to six weeks, then six weeks worth of material will be in the system, and it will take six weeks to finish any new unit introduced into the system. Likewise, when trying to reduce lead times, the battle is mostly won when the decision is made to do it. At SportIt, after much agonizing and heated debates, about half of the major component managers agreed that they could safely reduce their lead time by about two weeks. This was sufficient to clearly show that lead time reductions could be achieved, and this led to additional lead time reductions.

From a Synchronous Management standpoint, excess material on the floor adds to the confusion of which material to process and increases the opportunity for resource and material misallocation. Reduction in planned lead times and work-in-process inventory makes managing the material flow much easier.

Driven by measures of local efficiency, supervisors and operators had routinely scheduled work to optimize local performance. This resulted in massive priority distortions and was one of the key contributors to mismatched components at SportIt. Under the old system, dispatch lists issued to the floor showed a four-week window, and supervisors were allowed to sequence the orders in whatever way would best achieve high efficiencies. It was decided to reduce the dispatch window to one week, and supervisors were instructed not to process material that was not on the dispatch list. This significantly enhanced material processing in the correct priority sequence. Spot checks were conducted by area managers to ensure that the new rules were being followed.

Expediting at SportIt was rampant and had to be significantly reduced. In the normal sequence of events, assembly would discover a component shortage and scramble to see what alternative models could be built. Of course, this created another shortage list, comprised of parts that were "stolen" to build the alternate products. Then parts from both the original and new shortage lists would be expedited. The result was that most components were being expedited. Since each expedite (especially those from the new shortage list) created disruptions to material flow, a tidal wave of chaos was the inevitable result.

The answer to the expediting problem was obvious. Assembly would be allowed only minimal expedites. With few exceptions, components would be allowed to flow into the component crib and pulled only in the original priority sequence. Most people agreed that if the component areas were disturbed less, delivery of the right components to the assembly process would improve. This meant that assembly would eventually achieve higher production rates. The problem was that it was estimated that it would take up to four weeks before the higher production rates would kick in. In the meantime, total assembly output would be lower than before the change. This proposed action caused the greatest amount of initial resistance in the plant.

In a plant driven by "units packed per day," allowing minimal expedites was extremely disturbing to some individuals. It was analogous to a first-timer jumping out of a plane, knowing that theoretically the parachute should open, but still very nervous about the outcome. Senior management commitment and progressive-minded "pioneer" shop supervisors were both required to implement this action early in the project. Fortunately, both were present at SportIt. The success of this action went a long way to increasing plant-wide acceptance of the logical and common-sense rules of Synchronous Management.

To support the other action items implemented in Phase I, performance measures based on efficiency were changed to measures based on utilization. The reduction of lead times and the execution of tasks to a strict priority sequence meant that a number of work centers would have periods of idle time caused by the non-availability of the right material. It was emphasized to everyone that this was not only okay, it was expected since all of the work centers were non-bottlenecks.

During Phase I, one of the more time-consuming activities was to constantly walk the floor to make sure that the production rules were understood and were being followed. It was counter to supervisors' and operators' long years of experience that a better way to schedule and run the factory was to periodically have operators stand around and do nothing. The fundamental concept of teamwork had to be hammered home. Some grasped this concept quickly. They became floor champions who eventually persuaded the rest of the employees.

The idea of "opportunity time" was also thoroughly discussed with operators and supervisors. But it was not sufficient to make the argument that employees could contribute to the company's goals by doing things other than "cutting chips" when they had idle time. They were provided with ample opportunities to contribute.

As in all change efforts, a significant factor contributing to success at SportIt was making sure valid suggestions were quickly implemented. Few things can derail a change effort faster than good ideas that are seemingly ignored by those driving the change.

Prepare for Phase II by Beginning to Address Mindset and Measures
Considerable time and effort were spent to create awareness about the implementation process and how it would affect daily work activities. More important, people learned how they could contribute to the process.

All first- and second-line supervisors were trained in basic concepts, with key emphasis on the system or team nature of a manufacturing organization in general, and SportIt in particular. The initial training activities began well before the implementation started. It was during these training sessions and early shop implementation activities that the people who would emerge as floor champions surfaced.

A critical factor in successful implementations is the continuous development and implementation of appropriate new performance measures, especially early in the process. Any appropriate set of performance measures cannot simply be developed after implementation. Synchronous Management measures should actually spearhead the process and help cause the needed changes during the implementation.

Thus, at SportIt, traditional measures were downplayed in all management meetings and discussions. Because the tentacles of traditional measures and mindset were pervasive, changing people's opinions about the validity of existing measures and mindset could not be accomplished in a few meetings. But change must start somewhere and management spearheaded this change. A carefully selected cross-functional group began developing a new, balanced set of measures. This group continued to work on this critically important task during the entire implementation period to ensure the full development of the new measurement system.

Key Results From Phase I   At the end of this first six-month phase, significant results had already been achieved. Throughput, the most important measure, increased by 18 percent after two months, 20 percent after four months, and 38 percent after six months! Manufacturing lead time dropped from 20 weeks to 10 weeks in six months. Performance to schedule increased from 79 percent to 82 percent. These improvements are fully illustrated in Figure 8.4.

The drop in performance to schedule in the initial period cries out for an explanation, since adherence to schedule is a key tenet of Synchronous Management. The focus of initial activities was on improving utilization of the wood housing, i.e., making sure that the wood housing was not damaged, scrapped or otherwise misallocated. The conversion of wood receipts into products that could be shipped immediately was a key local measure. This measure actually improved during the first few months and is reflected in the

FIGURE 8.4

Key Results Achieved at the End of Phase I (6 months)

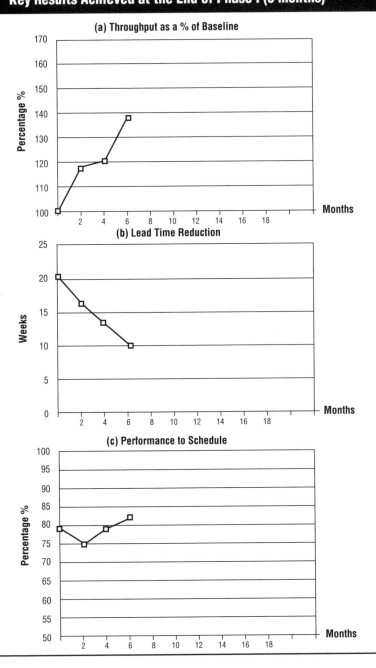

increase in total units produced. However, early in this period the supplier's performance deteriorated significantly, more than erasing the gains made through better utilization of the wood housings. This reinforced the need to provide the supplier with both management and technical assistance.

Despite the significant improvements in company performance, much skepticism remained. But the improvements, combined with the symbolic action of slowing assembly, albeit temporarily, was beginning to have an effect on the organizational mindset. People were willing to acknowledge that this management team was committed to improvements through serious and sustained change. We note that, for Phase I activities, most employees had been either reluctantly following a small set of new rules or sitting on the sidelines. Housekeeping, opportunity time activities, and improvement suggestions provided a suitable mechanism for willing employees to participate in the program.

Phase II   The activities implemented and initiated during this phase fell into four broad categories. One, the company reorganized to simplify and streamline key processes. Two, a drum-buffer-rope system was implemented. Three, support group activities were coordinated. And four, groundwork was laid for Phase III.

Reorganization to Simplify and Streamline Key Processes   During Phase II, SportIt's organizational structure was changed from a part orientation and functional focus to a product-line focus. The previous organizational structure followed the traditional functional orientation, with shop managers organized by resource and part type. A supervisor managed several resources that worked on parts of the same type, and each area served different end products. The new organizational structure created product-line managers who had responsibility for all fabricated components used in their product line. A major issue in all assembly environments is the synchronization of components flowing to the assembly process. This new structure facilitated synchronization by eliminating some dependencies and by providing a common focus for the entire product team. A major change involved the production assignments of the FMS and the manual production lines. Even though the FMS was, by definition, a flexible work center, the previous production assignments given to the FMS had been made on the basis of maximizing FMS output. Using traditional cost methods, this was the only way to justify the huge investment. By clearly perverse logic, the FMS was therefore used to process large volumes of standard parts, while the less flexible manual line was asked to pick up the numerous low-volume parts. The manual line was also used as flex capacity (on weekends) to make up for volume shortfalls at the FMS.

The FMS and manual line assignments were immediately reversed. The manual line assumed the production of high-volume jobs on a fixed five-day basis. The FMS was assigned all other jobs and used weekends to make up any manual line shortfalls.

This action had the same symbolic impact as the fall of the Berlin Wall. People reacted as if they had been slapped into the realization that the ground rules for making decisions had been fundamentally altered at SportIt. They had!

Changing the work assignments also delivered a second powerful message. While everyone agreed (at least in theory) that production for the sake of production was undesirable, the nagging feeling remained that management would not tolerate operators standing around idle. In the case of the FMS, this feeling was very strong since management had battled for continuous manning of the FMS in vigorous labor negotiations. Of course, when component lead times were reduced, a gaping hole soon appeared in the work schedule at both the FMS and the manual line. The agonizing, but necessary, decision was made to shut down the FMS for three full days—while continuing to pay the work force. This action was probably the single most important factor that convinced line supervisors that completing required jobs had replaced keeping people and machines busy as a key driving force!

New operational measures of throughput, inventory, and operating expense were developed for the product lines by a cross-functional, cross-product team. Meaningful definitions of these operational measures were developed for each product line to supplement the performance-to-schedule measure implemented during Phase I. These measures were soon expanded to include local-area performance.

Expediting responsibility was transferred from senior plant staff to first-line supervisors. Expediting, by its very nature, represents local adjustments to accommodate disruptions to the original plan. The more quickly the adjustments can be made, the less should be the disruption and the magnitude of the required adjustment. And waiting for information to flow up the hierarchical chain and the resulting decision to flow back down does not enhance the appropriateness of the decision. Thus, once senior management had established an overall game plan, adjustments to the plan (expediting) were made in daily meetings at the production-floor level by shop supervisors.

The overall game plan (master production schedule or drum beat) must be designed to achieve good overall performance. Thus, a coordinator/master scheduler position, which reported to the plant manager, was created. Since several key resources and components were shared among the product lines, it was clear that each individual product line striving to achieve its own local optimum might not result in the global optimum for SportIt. The role of master scheduler became very important, and this person reported directly to the plant manager, along with the product-line managers. The master scheduler was given responsibility for the long-term production plans, as well as the short-term detailed assembly-build schedules.

The number of cribs was reduced. As described earlier, SportIt had created many levels in the bill of material, and each level had a designated crib. This had been done in the interest of gaining tighter control of material and improving responsiveness through well-stocked cribs. But the result was an increased level of process complexity and cribs jammed with slow moving or defective products. And by adding steps to both the product flow and the planning operation, the overall component production lead times had been significantly increased. The task of reducing the number of cribs was done in stages on a product line by product line basis.

The role of the remaining cribs was changed from an inventory holding area to a schedule control point. Once released from a crib, material would be processed as expeditiously as possible using simple priority rules to the next crib. Material would never be set aside on the production floor due to a change in assembly priorities. Any change in assembly priorities (remember that the frequency of such changes had been significantly reduced) would be reflected in the material released from the cribs.

Implementation of a Drum-Buffer-Rope System   Some elements of the drum-buffer-rope system have already been discussed in the previous sections. The old, highly dysfunctional system for planning and control at SportIt (both the computerized MRP system and actual execution on the factory floor) was systematically transformed to a DBR system in a series of steps. The initial steps were described under Phase I and included identifying the constraint, reducing lead times, working to priorities, and reducing expediting. In Phase I, the first steps toward a full DBR system were undertaken.

By the beginning of Phase II, the primary constraint that determined the drum beat was still the availability of wood housings. However, supply reliability had increased significantly. Thus, the idea of developing a rhythmic and stable production plan was slowly being accepted by everyone, including the master scheduler and the product-line managers. A rolling four-week assembly-build plan, with the first five days frozen, provided the cornerstone for the DBR system.

While time buffers were implicitly present (the component lead times were well in excess of minimum production times) there were no formal buffer locations established or monitored. The only buffer management activity was monitoring the expedite zone in the daily expedite meetings! (The implementation of formal buffer locations and buffer management would not be undertaken until Phase III.)

The rope had been tied, albeit loosely, in Phase I when material release was tightly controlled and the dispatch window reduced to one week. In Phase II, four additional steps were taken to tighten the ropes.

- The transfer batch concept was instituted, particularly in areas that were organized as production cells. Material that previously was processed and moved as a single lot of 500 pieces was now moved through the cell in lots of 100 pieces. Since material usually followed the same sequential routing in a cell, it was possible to do this without losing track of the material.

- Dispatch lists and shop move tickets were eliminated. Instead, materials were processed on a first in, first out (FIFO) basis. It was explained in Chapter 9 of Volume 1 that, as the release of material to the shop floor is tightly regulated to match the rate of consumption, detailed priority rules become unnecessary. Only one batch of the right material is normally available to most work centers, making priority decisions a non-issue. Since SportIt had been through a major MRP implementation effort just a few years earlier, there was considerable resistance to giving up the dispatch list. This was in spite of the fact that most supervisors felt the list was only a starting point for them to make their decisions and that it was full of mistakes. Where, one supervisor wondered, would he make his notes of shop activities?

  As an intermediate step to a strict FIFO system, a color-code system was adopted. Priority was assigned at the time material was released from a crib, and this priority was indicated by a colored dot affixed to the shop paperwork. The priority sequence of the colors was displayed prominently at several points on the factory floor.

- Lead times were further reduced. The lead-time reductions implemented in Phase I, on a select family of components, had not resulted in the disasters that non-believers anticipated. Somewhat reluctantly, the previous non-participants agreed to reduce lead times by two weeks (in some cases, one week now and another week a month later). Meanwhile, the pioneers began to make additional significant reductions in lead time and ultimately would set the model for steadily driving lead times down. In what became an ongoing activity, component lead times were reduced by nearly 50 percent during Phase II.

- A bin system for managing miscellaneous parts was initiated. This simplified the previous planning and control system by moving to a physical rather than a computerized system. Although the planners and system personnel were initially resistant, this move made perfect sense to the operators in both the stock room and the assembly area. The move to a bin system was implemented using a Pareto analysis, with the high-usage parts being addressed first.

Coordination of Support Group Activities   Under the old system, and without a clear recognition of their role in maintaining a smooth product flow, support areas had organized their activities to suit their individual desires and local performance criteria. Failure of the support groups to take timely and appropriate actions meant that disruptions often exceeded the safety cushion provided by buffers, resulting in missed customer shipments. Thus, in Phase II, several support group initiatives were implemented.

Maintenance areas were educated on the critical importance of constraints. This meant that the maintenance group would assign highest priority to work centers involved in machining the constraint wood housings material whether the work center was broken down or the work center capability was simply drifting out of specification. The second highest priority went to a highly shared resource, the color work center.

The responsiveness of all support activities was targeted for improvement. Each support group was charged with achieving turnaround service times consistent with the buffers. Maintenance, for example, was required to repair any piece of equipment within two days. (It was decided to start with a feasible time target and drive it down continuously by making this turn-around time the key performance measure for maintenance.) In this mode, maintenance gave the appropriate priorities to constraint-related requests, but otherwise worked mostly to a FIFO system. Detailed scheduling was done by maintenance with little interference from others. For their part, production areas had to be disciplined not to cry wolf and wait patiently according to their priority. The queue of work at maintenance was carefully reviewed and priorities set. Each request was monitored to ensure that service and turn-around standards were being met.

Large cross-functional team meetings were initiated to continue driving home the idea of the team nature of the business. Twice a week, a "stand-up" meeting (so it would be a short meeting) was held with the extended product-line team that included support area personnel from purchasing, engineering, and maintenance. Overall performance of the product line, performance to schedule and asset productivity, and issues specific to the support groups were discussed first. Support personnel could leave before specific production details were discussed.

Preparation for Phase III   Simplification and coordination were the major themes for Phase II. The driver for local activities was changed from local optimization (or cost control) to effective support of the overall product flow. Finally, widespread support needed for the smooth transition to the remaining phases was established.

Training was provided to all employees concerning the new procedures and what it meant to them on a daily basis. Sessions were timed to coincide with changes being initiated that affected their area. The timing insured that session participants would be more motivated to learn about the changes than if the sessions were removed in time from any noticeable change. This extensive training was necessary to lay the foundation for future implementation initiatives.

Credibility for the new process was established. Each major change in shop procedures was introduced through short awareness sessions to all shop personnel. Those directly involved in the implementation of the Synchronous Management process constantly walked the floor to ensure understanding and to surface both objections and suggestions. As a result, many excellent ideas were suggested. It was partially through the timely implementation of these suggestions that credibility for the process was earned.

Activities designed to shift the focus from internal goals to achieving customer satisfaction became more prominent during Phase II. This change in focus is the main theme for the next phase of activities. The groundwork was laid by increasingly raising customer-related issues during discussions. Key customers were profiled and reasons why they buy from SportIt were discussed. These discussions also served to emphasize the importance of competitive performance.

Key Results From Phase II   At the end of Phase II, additional significant results had been achieved. Throughput increased from 138 percent of baseline after six months to 147 percent of baseline after twelve months. Throughput was essentially constant during much of this phase. This was the result of the lag between operational improvements being achieved and the translation or leveraging of these improvements into new additional sales. Customers as well as sales personnel needed time to recognize improvements as 'real' and change their buying/selling habits. Manufacturing lead time had dropped from 20 weeks to 10 weeks after the first six months. By the end of Phase II, lead time had been further reduced to six weeks. During Phase II, performance to schedule further increased from 82 percent to 90 percent. These improvements are fully illustrated in Figure 8.5.

By the end of Phase II, people had bought into the new way of doing business and were sufficiently buoyed by the results to keep the improvement process moving forward. The old adage "nothing breeds success like success" was

FIGURE 8.5

Key Results Achieved at the End of Phase II (12 months)

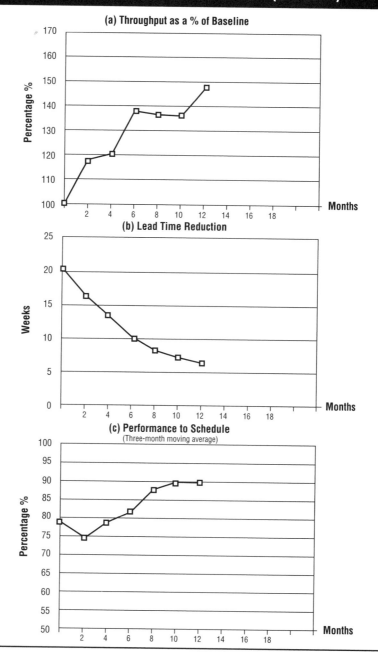

certainly true at SportIt. Particular care had been taken to ensure that significant results were achieved quickly and that the organization clearly associated the results with the Synchronous Management initiatives.

Phase III   In the first two phases, the focus was on implementing constraint management and a workable drum-buffer-rope system. This required a shift from resource management for local optimization to product flow management for system optimization. This was accomplished by implementing a number of very detailed changes in a logical time sequence. The results of the first two phases speak volumes to their success. In Phase III, the objective was to continue the team-oriented improvement process while bringing the organization to internalize the concept that achieving customer satisfaction would be the driving force to ever higher levels of performance and profitability.

Continuing the Improvement Process   Balancing customer satisfaction with asset productivity was promoted by replacing the budget/variance reports for managers at all levels with the ratios T/I and T/OE, and associated analytical information. As with most companies, the budget and variance reports at SportIt provided little useful information or feedback. Huge amounts of time were wasted in developing the reports and trying to explain away the variances. As a result, most employees were glad to see the traditional budget/variance reports replaced. The complete balanced scorecard presented the overall picture and became the basis for decision making.

The logistical organization of material flow continued to improve in Phase III as the DBR system implementation proceeded. Lead times were reduced in incremental steps and were at a maximum of two weeks for fabricated components. Along with tightening the rope, time buffers were formally defined and established in this phase. Responsibility for monitoring and managing the time buffers naturally fell to stock room personnel. They were trained in the concept of time buffers, the different buffer zones, and how they should be managed. More important, they were specifically trained in proper execution of buffer management at SportIt—monitoring material flow into the buffers as well as releasing material to the assembly areas. Note that this changed the stock room personnel from just being clerks to managers. On their own initiative, they arranged the stock room into a well organized, visual buffer. In fact, the stock room became the location for daily meetings to evaluate status and make adjustments to the plan and also to collect data to drive the engineering initiatives to improve products and processes.

Shifting to a Customer Focus   Product-line teams were expanded to first include support areas and later to include all members of the supply chain, vendors as well as customers. A successful vendor partnering initiative was launched. A major factor contributing to the success of this initiative was that SportIt personnel had already learned how to operate as team players. The final step in completing the supply-chain linkage was the inclusion of customers as active participants to help SportIt improve those aspects of service that were individually important to each customer. For example, the detailed logistical methods and techniques that were developed to reduce production lead times were modified and applied to yield significant lead time reductions in the design and development of new products.

The shift from internal team performance to customer satisfaction was achieved by defining performance in increasingly customer-oriented terms, and by gradually tightening requirements for acceptable performance. As an example of this process, consider the performance to schedule measure. Early in Phase III, it was first changed from a weekly measure to a daily measure. Eventually, it became an operational measure and was replaced by daily customer-delivery performance.   Thus, instead of measuring whether the products were built according to plan, actual shipments to customers were measured against their request dates.   This last change generated some initial grumbling about "unreasonable" dates, but the message of trying to give the customer what they want was ultimately widely accepted.   (After all, outside the workplace, SportIt employees were also customers. So they were able to relate to changing customer expectations and increasing choices for the customer.)   This new customer orientation provided the needed foundation to fully achieve the Phase III objectives.

Key Results At The End of Phase III   Adoption of Synchronous Management at SportIt resulted in a vast number of significant changes in day-to-day activities. Moreover, the new way of thinking engendered by Synchronous Management, supported by new performance measures, resulted in numerous operational procedures being modified. Many of the new processes were suggested by operators and supervisors.

From a management standpoint, the challenge is to encourage these changes to occur everywhere without resulting in chaos. Employee involvement and momentum are critical, and few things slow down a change process more than a simple, valid suggestion being ignored. If you want people to think differently and accept the changes in procedures, than you must let, and even encourage, them to actively participate in the process. The challenge is to do so without losing sight of overall priorities and coordination.

FIGURE 8.6

Key Results Achieved at the End of Phase III (18 months)

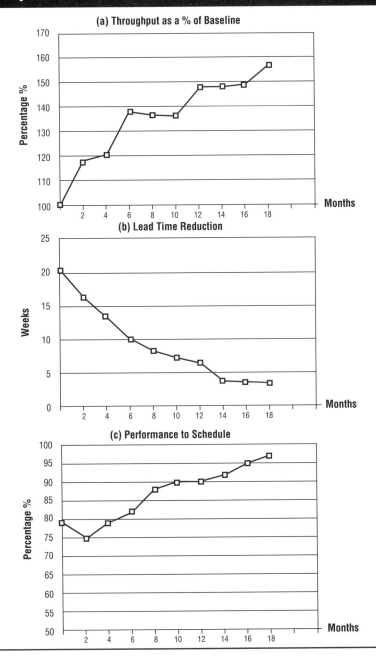

(a) Throughput as a % of Baseline

(b) Lead Time Reduction

(c) Performance to Schedule

SportIt made continuing major progress during Phase III. Changes in throughput, lead times, and performance to schedule are summarized in Figure 8.6. These include an increase in throughput to 158 percent of baseline over 18 months; a reduction in lead time to three weeks from 20 weeks; and an increase in performance to schedule to 97 percent from the original 80 percent.

Additional results, not shown in Figure 8.6, were tabulated for the 18-month implementation period. Productivity increased by 45 percent (labor per unit of product decreased from 3.9 hours to 2.1 hours). Overtime dropped by 33 percent. Work-in-process inventory was reduced by 88 percent, while finished-goods inventory was cut by 50 percent.

To get a complete feel for the magnitude of changes at SportIt, it is useful to view the new company from the vantage point of the key players in the business—customers, employees, and management. To fully appreciate what SportIt accomplished, contrast these player's new perceptions with their old perceptions as presented at the beginning of this case.

The customers' view of SportIt was that it had excellent products with the best delivery in the business. Not only could customers get the right product at the right time, they could get products faster and more reliably than from any other competitor. They felt that SportIt worked hard to understand and satisfy their needs. They also felt that SportIt knew how to work with the customer to reduce costs and then to pass the cost savings back to the customer in the form of lower prices.

The employees saw a sense of order and control. Everyone knew what was expected of them and how their activities related to the performance of the entire team. This resulted in a feeling of involvement, instead of the previous widespread alienation. Employees felt that proposed changes had a well-defined purpose. Furthermore, the connection between the proposed changes, performance, and the eventual business result became increasingly clear as they gained more experience with the new system and new way of thinking.

Company managers were under less stress, even though performance expectations were continually being raised. This was because they understood the causes for their current levels of performance (constraints and the dynamic nature of interactions in their organization) and consistently made good decisions. Fire fighting had been replaced by planning and orderly execution. Finally, the company was in excellent financial condition and had been removed from the "critical review" list of the parent corporation and placed on the "best-practices" list!

Index

A

Activation:
    definition of, 27
    and high-inventory operation, 8
    (*see* also Overactivation, Utilization)
Activity-outcome measures, 189–191
A-plants:
    background information, 138-139
        assembly points, 56-58, 124
        batch size considerations, 58-59
        characteristics, 56-58, 122-125
        competitive elements, 61
        component parts uniqueness, 56
        consequences of traditional management
            practices, 58-60
        conventional performance-improvement
            strategies, 60
        effects of expediting, 142-143
        feast-or-famine situation, 58-59
        fundamental problems, 139, 141
        managerial concerns, 59
        material flow problem, 142-143
        plant description, 55
        problem identification, 58-59
        product flow characteristics, 56-58
        product flow diagram, 57, 140
        quality problems, 142-143
        resource misallocation, 58-59
        shipping problem, 141
        traditional management approach, 141-143
    case study, 138-151
    DBR system implementation in, 125-138,
        143-151
        assembly schedule, 135
        assembly time buffers, 132, 134, 145-147
        batch size, 61, 136-137, 149-150
        buffer locations, 133, 146
        buffer sizes, 132-134
        CCRs, 144-145
        CCRs/setup time arrangements, 135
        component stock buffers, 130-132
        constraint time buffer, 132, 145
        establishing MPS, 134-135, 147-149
        FIFO system, 150
        identifying constraints, 61, 125-129, 143
        key rope system outcomes, 136
        lead times, 136-137, 149-150

material constraints, 126-127, 143-144
monitoring performance/progress,
    137-138, 151
versus MRP system, 149-150
overview of issues, 122-125
performance concerns, 123, 125
product flow concerns, 123-124
product flow diagram, 124
product stock buffers, 130
schedule control points, 135-137, 149-150
setting the buffers, 61, 130-134, 145
shipping time buffer, 132, 147
stock buffers, 145
stock/time buffer location, 132-133
Synchronous Management
    objectives for, 125
time buffers, 132, 134, 145-147
Synchronous Management application to, 61-62
Assembly operations:
    assemble-to-order, 70
    buffer protection of, 132–134
    illustrations of, 26, 32, 41–44
    NBN in, 28 (*see* Non-bottleneck resources)
    resource misallocation and, 58–59
    as schedule control points, 62
Assembly points:
    in A-plants, 56–58, 124
    in combination plants, 71–73
    divergence, 65
    in product flow diagrams, 24, 57
    resource-product interactions at, 58
    T-plant/A-plant comparison of, 63–65
    (*see* also Convergence points)
Assembly time buffer, 132
Asset productivity, 182–184
Asset use, 187

B

Batch size:
    and CCRs, 92–95, 136
    in DBR/MRP comparison, 149–150
    EBQ and, 164
    and inventory levels, 61
    and lead time, 52, 67, 136–137
    and material flow, 58–59
    and misallocations, 36, 59

Q

R

S